THE
BARBECUE
BOOK
Everything you need to know about Barbecues

GAIL DUFF

PRISM PRESS
Sherborne, Dorset · San Leandro, California

Acknowledgements

We greatly appreciate help given by:

Eric Hopper, Black Knight Barbecues, Westlawn, Works, Loose Valley, Loose, Maidstone, Kent.

Notcutts Garden Centre, Bearsted, Maidstone, Kent.

British Alcan Products Ltd., Raans Road, Amersham, Bucks.

The Barbecue Book

© Gail Duff

ISBN 0 907061 69 9 Hardback
ISBN 0 907061 70 2 Paperback

Published in the United Kingdom in 1985 by
PRISM PRESS,
Sherborne, Dorset.
and in the U.S.A. by Prism Press
P.O. Box 778,
San Leandro, CA 94577.

Distributed by:

U.S.A. — Interbook Inc.,
14895 East 14th Street, Suite 370, San Leandro, CA 94577.

AUSTRALIA — Book and Film Services,
P.O. Box Box 226, Artarmon, N.S.W. 2064.

CANADA — Raincoast Book Distribution Ltd.,
15 West 6th Ave., Vancouver, BC V5Y 1K2.

NEW ZEALAND — Roulston Greene Ltd.,
P.O. Box 33-850, Takapuna, Auckland 9.

SOUTH AFRICA — Trade Winds Press (Pty) Ltd.,
P.O. Box 20194, Durban North 4016.

Typeset by Margaret Spooner Typesetting, Dorchester, Dorset
Printed by Purnell and Sons (Book Production) Ltd.,
Paulton, Bristol

CONTENTS

Introduction

Cooking on Open Barbecues

Introduction — First Courses — Fish — Beef — Pork —
Lamb — Poultry and Game — Vegetarian Dishes —
Vegetables — Breads — Desserts

Cooking in Kettle Barbecues

Introduction — First Courses — Fish — Pork — Beef —
Lamb — Poultry and Game — Vegetables — Desserts — Baking

Smoke Cookery

Introduction — Recipes

Barbecue Parties

Brunch Party for Six — Barbecue Picnic or Beach Party —
Anniversary Party — Family Sunday Lunch — Teenage Party —
Eastern Style Barbecue — Special Occasion Barbecue —
Entertaining the In-Laws — Children's Parties

Gas & Electric Barbecues

Introduction — Cooking Times

INTRODUCTION

Every year more and more people are discovering the pleasures of cooking out of doors. Hardware shops, garden centres and chain stores which may have started by selling the odd bag of charcoal and a few of the smallest and simplest types of barbecue, are increasingly adding to their ranges. There are more and more specialist barbecue shops stocking everything from insect repellant candles to the most sophisticated smoker.

What is the attraction? Even though cooking over an open fire started in prehistoric times as a matter of necessity, for us in the twentieth century, with our sophisticated kitchens and home computers, it is something of a challenge. Having a barbecue is a small adventure in our own back garden. We have to light and control a fire instead of turning a switch; we can sit round it for warmth and appreciate the aroma of the smoke; we can forget for a while the ties of the electronic kitchen and enjoy the great outdoors. There is a challenge in getting the food cooked to perfection and a tremendous feeling of satisfaction when you succeed.

Beside this, any barbecue will create an atmosphere of relaxed informality which is ideal whether you are cooking Sunday lunch for your family, or a meal for guests that you wish to impress. Barbecuing breaks down barriers and everyone wants to gather round the fire and become involved in the cooking, fetching and carrying.

You can cook any type of food on a barbecue, from sausages to a large turkey and if you or the guests are vegetarian it is still possible to cook an enjoyable meal. Barbecues can be held at any time of day. If you have time, why not cook a leisurely breakfast or brunch one weekend? You can cook a quick snack for lunch, a party for twelve or a sophisticated meal for six.

Even if you do not have a garden big enough, you can take your barbecue on a camping or caravanning holiday or even out to a picnic site for the day.

Many people confine barbecuing to a few summer days but, provided the weather is not wet or excessively windy, you can cook outdoors all through the year. It may not be warm enough to eat outside but you can always 'cook-out-eat-in'. If you have a covered barbecue you can even use it to cook your Christmas goose or Thanksgiving turkey.

Barbecuing is not difficult. There has been a certain mystique attached to it, but once you have mastered a few basic rules you will find that there is no need for this at all.

Admittedly, if a beginner walks into a barbecue shop for the first time the range of equipment, fuel and accessories can be rather bewildering. This book is intended to help you choose the type of barbecue that is right for you, whether you have a tiny patio or unlimited space; whether you are cooking for two or a crowd; whether you want your barbecue in a fixed position or you want to take it on an expedition; whether you want to cook the odd chop or steak, or intend to use your barbecue frequently for cooking the Sunday joint.

Are all those gleaming accessories necessary? There is a list of the most useful. Which fuel do you use and how do you light it? There is information about that too.

But with all this technical information, we must not forget the most important thing, the food. In the end, nobody minds if you are turning it with specially made barbecue accessories or the kitchen fish slice, but it does have to taste good and be cooked to perfection. This, in fact, is not difficult but it helps to know which cuts of meat are the most suitable, how to prepare them and how best to cook them.

Barbecue food can be absolutely plain and still taste good, but once you can basically grill, try out different marinades and sauces, make kebabs or cook in foil. Instructions are given on how to cook most vegetables on the barbecue, but do not forget that many of the dishes will taste as good, accompanied by a salad. The salads, of course, are outside the scope of this book. The possibilities are endless. Nevertheless, barbecued food is basically simple and healthy, since the fat runs away and there are no heavy sauces.

Once you have started barbecuing it will probably become a way of life and as soon as the weather is dry, you will be running to find the charcoal. Go on, have that back garden adventure — and enjoy it!

Barbecues. Back: Gas; right: Brazier; front right: Small Kettle; front left: Portable Picnic; left: Large Kettle.

Selection of Fuel Lighters.

COOKING ON
OPEN
BARBECUES

The first barbecue that most households own is usually one of the open type. These come from picnic size to those mounted on enormous trolleys. There are round ones, square ones and rectangular ones. When you first decide to buy an open barbecue, the selection can be rather bewildering. To help you decide, first consider a few important points.

How much do you want to spend?

It has often been said that the more you pay for a barbecue, the better its performance and durability, and that there is no point in buying a cheap one. The first statement is certainly true and if you are an experienced and regular outdoor cook, then it would definitely be best to choose a fairly expensive model. However, if you have never cooked on a barbecue before you have got to find out whether, in practice, outdoor cooking will come up to your expectations. There is no point in paying a lot of money for a piece of equipment that will become redundant soon after it has been used for the first time. If you are a beginner, therefore, look at the cheaper, but not the cheapest, end of the market.

If you enjoy barbecuing, you can then go on to buy a more expensive one the following summer, using the first for extra dishes or for keeping things warm. If you don't, then the small amount that you have paid will not matter too much.

How big does the barbecue need to be?

How many people are you going to be cooking for, two, four or six? Will you use your barbecue most often for family meals or for parties and dinner parties? How big is your garden or patio? Will an enormous wagon grill fill it up leaving you no space to move? On the other hand, do you want to take your barbecue with you on holiday or when you camp? If this is the case, you will not be able to fit a larger model in the car.

Height and stability

Barbecues must be comfortable for you to work at and they must be safe. Picnic-type barbecues and hibachis (see below) usually have short, stumpy legs and working at ground level is often the most practical method for the situations in which they are going to be used. Other types of barbecue vary slightly in height. Stand beside them to make sure that you do not have to bend over too much or reach up to an awkward high level.

Make sure that the legs are steady and do not stick out too far and that the barbecue will not fall over if it is tipped only slightly. If the legs are screw-in and/or telescopic, make sure that they will stay in place and at the right height even when the barbecue is full of charcoal and meat is on the spit roaster. If the barbecue is on a separate stand, this should be safe, steady and non-collapsible. Check that there are not too many nuts and bolts in any part of the construction which may fall out and get lost.

Barbecue grill

If the grill is made from thin, lightweight material, it will probably bow towards the heat as soon as any food is placed on it, causing uneven cooking and burning. If the bars are too far apart there is the danger of food falling through on to the fire. Ideally the grill should be made from heavy, chrome or nickel plated steel with the bars fairly close together.

There should be a facility on the barbecue by which you easily raise and lower the height of the grill. This is important as it is the most effective way of altering the cooking temperature. Check that it will work even when there is food on the grill and that the handle, if there is one, will not get hot.

Wheels

Small barbecues can be lifted from place to place. Larger ones must be wheeled, so check that this can be done easily and that the wheels are free-moving.

Finish

Many open barbecues are made from porcelain enamelled steel. Provided you are careful when removing and storing and when laying the fire this should present no problems. Rough handling may chip it. Other types are made from cast aluminium or cast iron and are more durable, but heavier and often more expensive.

TYPES OF OPEN BARBECUE

Picnic barbecue

This is made to be carried easily in a car or rucksack and is therefore very small and light. Most picnic barbecues have very short legs and no stand. Some are circular, some are square and some are rectangular. Some have a small wind shield and some may have a small spit.

Hibachi

Hibachi is the Japanese word for fire-bowl. It is the smallest and cheapest type of barbecue for home use and is therefore the ideal type for the beginner. The best quality hibachis are made from cast iron. Those made from pressed steel are not as durable. All hibachis should have air vents in the fire-bowl. The fire-bowl itself is round or square. It should be at least 3 inches deep and there should be a separate rack below the grill rack on which to place the charcoal.

No hibachi is larger than 45 cm/18 inches square, but double versions, with two fire-bowls hinged together, and also triple versions are available.

Some hibachis have small feet which necessitates their use at ground level, or on a firm brick pillar or metal table. Others are either fixed onto legs or come with an optional stand.

Brasero

This is a ceramic version of the hibachi which is popular in the United States and which came originally from Mexico.

Brazier

Brazier barbecues consist basically of a fire-box and a grill rack mounted on a stand to give a convenient working height. Round and rectangular versions are available, varying in size from about 45 cm/18 inches diameter.

In some models, the charcoal is put directly into the fire-box. In others, a charcoal rack is provided. For successful barbecuing, this is an essential feature. It provides a free flow of air round the fire and enables ash to drop away from the burning charcoal.

Many braziers have a small windshield. This is made of thin metal, about 25-30 cm/10-12 inches deep and fits half-way round the edge of the fire-box. It is often capable of taking a spit mechanism and slots are cut in it for the barbecue grill. The grill is raised or lowered by putting it into another slot.

If there is no wind shield, the grill may fit on to a central pedestal, which can be raised or lowered with a crank mechanism. Some means of altering the grill height is essential.

For easy moving, many brazier barbecues have wheels. Some are fitted with hangers for cooking implements and some with a small work shelf.

Modular barbecue

This is a version of a brazier which enables you to buy a small, reasonably priced barbecue and to improve upon it if you decide to make barbecuing a regular method of cooking. You start with a small fire-bowl shaped like a third of a circle which can be used for picnics or on a table top in a similar way to a hibachi. The next addition is a further third of a circle plus a sturdy wheeled stand. Then a third section completes the circle. Spit roasting attachments, extra grills and also a cover for converting the basic kit to a kettle barbecue are available.

Hooded barbecue

This is basically a brazier barbecue fitted with a semi-circular hood. The hood acts as a wind shield and must be placed towards the wind, as if you cook with your back to the wind the smoke will swirl back into your face. This facility is useful where prevailing winds tend to be high, but is not normally necessary.

The hood also provides fittings for a spit attachment, and provides a convenient warm surface for plates and cooked food.

Euro-style barbecue

This again is basically a brazier style barbecue. It is rectangular in shape and the grill can either be used in a conventional manner, or it can be placed upright with the charcoal behind it. A spit is placed in front with the drip tray underneath it. This ensures that poultry and large cuts of meat can be cooked at a steady, even temperature. One disadvantage is that if the drip tray is placed too near the charcoal, the ash may spill down into it preventing you from using the drippings in the tray for basting the meat.

Wagon barbecue

Wagon barbecues are usually rectangular in shape. The fire-box may have one or more vents in the side to aid airflow. The grill and charcoal rack are the same as those on an ordinary brazier.

The main feature of the wagon barbecue is that it is mounted on a wheeled trolley with built-in work surfaces and shelves. In the more elaborate models there may be a warming oven. A hood may also be fitted, in which case it may be used like a kettle barbecue.

Brick-built barbecues

Metal barbecues are efficient but they do have disadvantages. If they are not stored properly during the winter, or even if they are left out in heavy rain several times, they will eventually start to corrode. Although the designs are perfectly functional, they may not be particularly attractive, looking incongruous on a brick- or stone-built patio.

Brick-built barbecues solve these problems. With a permanent structure you will not have to find large amounts of storage space when the barbecue is not in use. All you have to take under cover is the grill, charcoal racks and a flat ash-tray. A barbecue built into a patio wall against the side of the house fits in well with its surroundings and can be an attractive feature. You can make your brick structure permanent, building with cement like an ordinary wall, or you can make the bricks free-standing, building it in overlapping layers to make a stable construction which can be dismantled, if wished, at the end of the summer.

When deciding where to build your barbecue, find a sheltered spot, preferably near the house so that fetching and carrying will not be a problem. The site must be level and there must be plenty of room for the cook to work properly and for guests to stand around. Any protection from the rain, such as a house or garage wall or a bank of trees, is useful but make sure that there is some wind as charcoal needs a good airflow in order to burn well. The barbecue should not be too near trees or shrubbery for obvious fire-prevention reasons.

Before you start to build, obtain your grill and charcoal racks. It would be most frustrating to build a large and elaborate barbecue only to find that there are no racks anywhere which will fit it. You need a grill rack, a rack on which to put the charcoal and a metal plate to go underneath the charcoal rack to catch the ash. Racks from old refrigerators and ovens can be used or those from a metal barbecue which you no longer use.

To save you searching scrap yards or begging from neighbours, barbecue kits are now available, providing you with all you need plus easy instructions for building. The racks are usually rectangular, of varying sizes, but there are also triangular racks which will fit across the corner of a garden wall, and semi-circular racks for free-standing constructions.

The construction of a permanent barbecue can be as simple or elaborate as you wish. Basically you need three sides of a square or rectangle, the inside measurements being the same as those of your grill or slightly larger. To make the grill supports, place the centre three or four bricks in three alternate rows at right angles to the others. On the top set put the grill rack, on the middle set the charcoal rack and on the bottom one a flat metal plate. If you have room, you can build a small warming oven next to the barbecue or shelves beside it to use as a work surface.

If you have not built the barbecue on an existing patio, it is best to pave the area immediately around it. This will protect the barbecue and also provide a safe surface for standing and working on.

Barbecue accessories

Cooking Foil. This is the outdoor cook's best friend. Food can be wrapped in it for cooking. A sheet of foil can be laid on the barbecue grill for cooking foods which are too soft or crumbly to remain on top of the grill bars. If other food is too fatty, lay a sheet of perforated foil on the grill rack and cook the food until all the excess fat has drained away. This method will prevent flare-ups from ruining your meat, but by finishing off directly on the grill the food will still have that authentic barbecue flavour. When spit-roasting, if you do not have a ready made drip-tray, you can make your own with foil.

If possible always use heavy duty foil when barbecuing. If this is not available, use a double thickness of standard weight foil.

Long-handled Tools. To save burning your hands, use tools such as forks, fish slices, palette knives and basting brushes with extra long rods and preferably wooden handles. A selection is usually available at most barbecue shops. The most convenient place to keep tools is on a small rack which can be fitted to the side of the barbecue.

Heat-proof Gloves. Make sure these are long. Non-flammable types can be bought from barbecue shops.

Kebab Skewers. Various types are available. Thick and flattened or square are the best as the food will not rotate on them when they are turned. Make sure they are long enough to take sufficient food for one serving, and that they have easily manageable handles. Handles made by turning the top of the skewer into a large loop should be big enough to be picked up while you are wearing heat-proof gloves. Wooden handled skewers are also available. If you use these, make sure that the wooden part does not come directly over the charcoal.

Kebab units consist of six or eight kebab skewers fitted on a frame or stand. Some must be turned manually; others are turned by a system similar to a spit roaster.

Hinged Grills (Broilers). These are made from two pieces of wire mesh, similar to that used for cake cooling racks, hinged together. Food is enclosed between the two for easy turning. They are ideal for keeping together foods such as burgers or fish which may fall apart if placed directly over the barbecue grill. The smaller ones are square, others circular, rectangular or fish-shaped to take whole fish.

Work Surface. Some models of barbecue have a small work surface that can be fitted to the side; others come with a lid that can also be used as a small side-table. If one is not supplied, make sure that you place a convenient work surface somewhere near the barbecue. You will need it for bowls of sauces and bastes, for laying down utensils and for keeping the plates handy.

The fire

Fuel. Charcoal should be used on all types of open barbecue. There are two types, lumpwood and briquettes.

Lumpwood charcoal is made by charring wood, usually softwood, in a kiln. It is a dark, shiny black colour and comes in irregular shaped pieces. It ignites quickly and burns very fast, giving off a very high heat for a short time (30-40 minutes). If you want to cook steaks or chops on your barbecue without any first course, vegetables or dessert, then lumpwood charcoal is ideal. If, however, you wish to cook the whole meal on the barbecue, you will find that with lumpwood charcoal you will have to make up the fire more than once.

Charcoal briquettes are made by crushing charcoal and re-forming it with a bonding agent, usually cornstarch. The mixture is then compressed into egg shaped briquettes. The briquettes are twice as dense as lumpwood charcoal. They therefore take a longer time to light and to reach cooking temperature. However, once glowing they burn steadily for longer. They are best for food that takes a long time to cook and also for spit-roasting.

A good idea is to start the fire with lumpwood charcoal and add briquettes, several at a time, as the lumpwood burn away. You will then have the advantages of both quick lighting and long cooking.

Fire Lighters. Whichever fire lighter that you choose, make sure that it is one that has been manufactured especially for barbecue use. Never use petrol, lighter fuel, naphtha, paraffin, or kerosene. These are highly volatile and may well cause the fire to get out of hand. Even if they do not, they will give an unpleasant taste to the food. This also applies to the white, petrol-based domestic fire-lighters. These are safe but taint the food.

Solid, odourless fire-lighters made especially for the barbecue are now available. They come in short, oblong sticks of compressed board which has been impregnated with a liquid fire-lighter. To use them, break one into two or three pieces and put them into the centre of a pyramid of charcoal. Light the pieces at either end.

Liquid fire-lighters are efficient but must be used carefully. Pour or spray them very carefully on the pyramid of charcoal, being careful not to let any collect in the bottom of the fire bowl. Wait for a few minutes for the liquid to impregnate the charcoal before lighting with a long match or a taper. The advantage of a liquid fire-lighter is that it is the charcoal itself that you are actually lighting rather than something which in turn has to catch it alight.

Jellied fire-lighters work in the same way as liquid. They are slightly easier to use since there is no fear of the jelly running into the base of the fire-bowl. Put several teaspoons of the jelly between the charcoal in the base of the pyramid. Wait for a few minutes and then ignite the jelly with a long match or taper.

Self-igniting charcoal briquettes are efficient but expensive. They come in a block similar in shape to egg trays. This is placed near the bottom of your pyramid of charcoal and ignited.

Continually buying fire-lighters can be inconvenient and, in the long run, expensive, therefore, if you are going to be barbecuing frequently, it is worth thinking of mechanical fire-lighters. These are expensive at first but will last a long time.

The fire-lighting hood or chimney is made from a tall can, tapered at one end and with a grill in the centre. Charcoal is put into the top, narrower part and paper underneath. Ignite the paper and wait for it to catch the charcoal alight. Pour the charcoal carefully out on to the barbecue grill and place more charcoal on top.

Electric fire-lighters are clean, efficient and safe. They consist of a small round element that is placed near the base of the pyramid of charcoal, turned on and left for 5-10 minutes. These are the most expensive type of fire-lighter, but well worth it. You must, however, make sure that you have a power point near the barbecue, or that you can fit an extension lead that will reach the nearest point in the house or garage.

Domestic electric fire-lighters which blow hot air can also be used. You may well have to stand and hold these until the charcoal is alight.

Lighting the Fire. When using lumpwood charcoal, the fire should be lit 15-20 minutes before you intend to start cooking. Charcoal briquettes take 30-40 minutes to become fully alight.

Before arranging the charcoal, line the fire-bowl of hibachi, picnic and brazier type barbecues with heavy duty foil or a double thickness of standard weight foil. This will preserve the life of the barbecue and will also make it easier to remove the ash.

Position the charcoal grill. Put a pyramid of charcoal in the centre of the grill. Ignite it by the method chosen. When the fire is ready, spread the charcoal out to cover the grill.

If the fire needs to be made up during cooking, before the first charcoal has burned away position more round the outside of the fire. Move it into the centre when it has caught alight.

Temperature. No barbecue temperature is absolutely accurate. The coals will be ready for cooking when a dusting of grey ash has developed on the surface. As a rough guide to temperature hold your hand 10-15 cm/4-6 inches over the coals. If you can stand it for only 2 seconds, the fire is hot and will easily sear foods. If your hand can stay for 4 seconds, the fire is medium hot; if you can leave it for 4-6 seconds, the fire is low.

To increase temperature open all grill vents (if your barbecue is of a type that has them), push all the coals to the centre, tap off excess ashes then lower the barbecue grill.

To decrease heat partially close all grill vents, spread the coals out, make a circular well in the centre of the coals then raise the height of the grill.

Putting out the Fire. You can simply let your barbecue burn out, or you can save unburned briquettes for later use. Scatter sand or gravel on the fire to put it out and carefully lift out unburned charcoal with long-handled tongs and put into a metal bucket.

Basic brazier cooking

1. Prepare meat as in the following pages.
2. Lightly grease the barbecue grill using fat trimmed from the meat or a good quality vegetable oil.
3. To give the meat a slight herb flavour, scatter dried herbs or fresh herb sprigs on the charcoal.
4. If the meat has not been marinated, baste it with oil and season with freshly ground black pepper, or use one of the recommended basting sauces. The marinade mixtures can also be used as a baste. If you are using a baste which contains sugar, honey or sweet chutney, it is best to brush with oil first and use the baste only for the final 5 minutes of cooking time.
5. Sear the meat and cook as directed. Once meat is on the barbecue it is wise not to leave it since flare-ups seem to occur as soon as your back is turned. Flare-ups are caused by excess fat dripping down on to the charcoal and igniting. As soon as this happens, move the meat to a different spot, not necessarily a cooler one. With constant attention, you can prevent the meat from charring. After about 5 minutes most of the fat will have gone but it will still pay you to watch carefully.
6. To keep meat warm while other meat is cooking, place it right on the edge of the barbecue grill, away from all coals. It can safely stay there for 5-10 minutes.

Spit-roasting

Spit-roasting attachments are available for most Euro-style barbecues, brazier-type and brick-built barbecues and some picnic barbecues. These basically consist of a spit rod with holding forks and a turning mechanism.

If possible choose a square spit rod. This will hold the meat more firmly and will also enable the forks to be tightened securely without the use of pliers. The forks should be double-pronged and preferably made from flat metal rather than from narrow rods.

The turning mechanism can be wind-up, electric or battery driven. If it is a wind-up one, remember to rewind it frequently. If you choose an electric one you should be able to reach a power-point easily (with an extension lead if necessary). Batteries should be checked frequently.

Meat for spit-roasting should be even-shaped or rolled and tied securely. Before rolling it can be brushed with oil and sprinkled with herbs and/or chopped garlic so that it will be flavoured from the inside.

Put one holding fork on one end of the spit, prongs pointing inwards. Push the other end of the spit through the centre of the meat. Push the meat towards the fork. Put on the other fork, prongs pointing towards the meat. Push it into the meat. Tighten the forks securely.

To check that the meat is well balanced, hold the spit rod in the open palms of your hand and slowly rotate it. If the meat causes it to roll quickly, re-position the spit if possible, otherwise uneven cooking may occur. Baste the outside of the meat.

Insert a meat thermometer into the thickest part of the meat, not touching the spit rod or any bone. This is the best way of telling whether or not the meat is cooked.

For irregular shaped pieces of meat that are difficult to skewer, cylindrical wire baskets are available. The meat is placed inside and is tumbled round as the spit rotates. Separate chops or spare ribs can be put inside the basket as well as larger cuts.

Spit-roasting on a brazier is carried out over indirect heat. Once the spit has been positioned, place a drip tray directly under the meat. Put charcoal either all at one side of the tray, or on both sides, depending on the positioning of the spit on the barbecue.

The drip tray can be used simply to catch the fat, or you can put quartered onions and herbs into it and, once the fat from the meat has started to drip into them, use these as a baste. Whether using liquid from the tray or a separate mixture, baste the meat about every 15 minutes throughout the cooking time.

Always add extra charcoal to the fire before it has completely died down. Add a little at frequent intervals to maintain an even heat.

Maintenance

To clean the barbecue grill, wait until you use it the next time, heat it over hot coals and brush it with a stiff wire brush.

Always empty the ash after use.

After the barbecue has cooled completely store it, if possible under cover.

At the end of a long summer season clean the barbecue inside and out, and also the grill, with oven cleaner or a kitchen degreaser. Store movable barbecues under cover. Take the grills and racks of brick-built barbecues inside.

Safety first

Always keep a first aid kit which includes a burn spray handy.

If insects are a problem, insect spray and insect repellant candles are available from barbecue shops.

FIRST COURSES

So that you will not have to spend too long standing over the barbecue, keep first courses uncomplicated and quick cooking.

If the main course is also a quick cooking one, cook the first course completely before starting the main course. If the main course takes longer, the first course can be cooked alongside it and eaten and cleared away before it is ready.

Serve first courses, if wished, with any of the hot, flavoured breads and rolls on page 70.

MINTED GRAPEFRUIT

METRIC/IMPERIAL	*AMERICAN*
2 large grapefruit	2 large grapefruit
4 tablespoons pear and apple spread	¼ cup pear and apple spread
4 tablespoons chopped mint *or* 4 teaspoons dried	¼ cup chopped mint *or* 4 teaspoons dried
freshly ground black pepper	freshly ground black pepper
oil for greasing	oil for greasing

Cut the grapefruit in half crossways. Divide the segments and cut away any tough skin. Put 1 tablespoon apple and pear spread on top of each grapefruit half. Sprinkle with the mint. Season lightly with pepper.

Wrap each half in heavy duty foil or a double thickness of standard weight foil. Place on the barbecue grill, cut side up, 10-15 cm/4-6 inches over medium coals for 15 minutes.

To serve, undo the foil and fold it back leaving the grapefruit halves in a foil cup. Place each one in an individual dish.

SWEETCORN

One cob per person

SWEETCORN IN THE HUSK Carefully pull back the husks and remove the silk. Fold the husks back into place, tying them at the top with string. Soak the cobs in iced water for 30 minutes. Drain them but do not dry.

Cook 10-15 cm/4-6 inches over hot coals for 15-20 minutes, turning several times.

Serve with butter and freshly ground black pepper.

SWEETCORN IN FOIL Strip both husk and silk from the cobs. Spread each cob with softened butter or flavoured butter. Wrap in heavy duty foil or a double thickness of standard weight foil.

Cook 10-15 cm/4-6 inches over hot coals for 15-20 minutes, turning several times.

Flavourings for Butter. Tomato paste; paprika; cayenne pepper; finely diced chillies or red or green peppers; chopped parsley with a dash of Worcestershire sauce; other chopped herbs such as thyme or marjoram; celery salt; crushed garlic or garlic salt.

MUSHROOM KEBABS

METRIC/IMPERIAL	*AMERICAN*
450 g/1 lb button mushrooms	1 lb button mushrooms
150 ml/¼ pint natural yoghurt	5 fl oz unflavored yoghurt
2 tablespoons oil	2 tablespoons oil
1 tablespoon tomato paste	1 tablespoon tomato paste
grated rind and juice ½ lemon	grated rind and juice ½ lemon
2 tablespoons chopped parsley	2 tablespoons chopped parsley
1 tablespoon chopped thyme	1 tablespoon chopped thyme
1 garlic clove, crushed	1 garlic clove, crushed
freshly ground black pepper	freshly ground black pepper

Trim the stalks of the mushrooms to about 1 cm/½ inch long. In a bowl large enough to take all the mushrooms, mix the remaining ingredients together well. Turn the mushrooms in the mixture and leave for 2 hours at room temperature, turning several times.

Thread the mushrooms on to four kebab skewers, reserving the marinade. Cook 10-15 cm/4-6 inches over hot coals for 10 minutes, turning several times and basting with the marinade.

AVOCADO AND SALAMI KEBABS

METRIC/IMPERIAL

2 avocados, ripe but firm
4 tablespoons olive oil
juice ½ lemon
2 tablespoons chopped parsley
1 garlic clove, crushed
freshly ground black pepper
50g/2oz thinly sliced salami

AMERICAN

2 avocados, ripe but firm
¼ cup olive oil
juice ½ lemon
2 tablespoons chopped parsley
1 garlic clove, crushed
freshly ground black pepper
2oz thinly sliced salami

Cut the avocados into 2.5 cm/1 inch squares. Beat together the oil, lemon juice, parsley, garlic and pepper. Coat the avocados in the mixture. Quarter the salami slices.

Place alternate pieces of avocado and salami on to kebab skewers, starting and ending with salami.

Cook 10-15 cm/4-6 inches over hot coals for 5 minutes, or until heated through, turning several times.

BANANA AND BACON KEBABS

METRIC/IMPERIAL

4 small firm bananas
4 rashers streaky bacon
3 tablespoons oil
1 tablespoon cider vinegar
¼ teaspoon ground cinnamon
2 sage leaves, chopped

AMERICAN

4 small firm bananas
4 slices streaky bacon
3 tablespoons oil
1 tablespoon cider vinegar
¼ teaspoon ground cinnamon
2 sage leaves, chopped

Cut each banana into four crossways pieces. Cut each bacon rasher (slice) into five pieces. Place alternate pieces of bacon and banana on to four skewers. Beat together the oil, vinegar, cinnamon and sage. Brush the mixture over the bacon and bananas.

Cook 10-15 cm/4-6 inches over hot coals for 5-7 minutes, turning several times.

MARINATED SKEWERED PRAWNS (SHRIMP)

METRIC/IMPERIAL	AMERICAN
225g/8oz prawns in shell	½lb shrimp in shell
4 tablespoons oil	¼ cup oil
2 tablespoons soy, shoyu or tamari sauce	2 tablespoons soy, shoyu or tamari sauce
15g/½oz fresh ginger root, peeled and grated	2 teaspoons fresh ginger root, peeled and grated
1 garlic clove, crushed	1 garlic clove, crushed

In a large bowl mix together the oil, soy sauce, ginger root and garlic. Turn the prawns (shrimp) in the marinade and leave for at least 2 hours at room temperature.

Put the prawns (shrimp), still in their shells, on to fine skewers. Cook 10-15 cm/4-6 inches over hot coals for 2 minutes each side or until heated through.

DEVILLED CRAB

METRIC/IMPERIAL	AMERICAN
2 small crabs, dressed, shells reserved	2 small crabs, dressed, shells reserved
25g/1oz butter	2 tablespoons butter
2 teaspoons tomato paste	2 teaspoons tomato paste
juice ½ lemon	juice ½ lemon
¼ teaspoon Tabasco sauce	¼ teaspoon Tabasco sauce
1 teaspoon paprika	1 teaspoon paprika
4 tablespoons chopped parsley	¼ cup chopped parsley

Put the crab meat in a bowl. Melt the butter in a small pan on a low heat. Stir in the tomato paste, lemon juice, Tabasco sauce and paprika. Add the mixture to the crab with the parsley. Mix well.

Put the crab into the shells. Wrap each shell in buttered heavy duty foil or a double thickness of standard weight foil.

Put the parcels on the barbecue grill, shell side down, 10-15 cm/4-6 inches over hot coals and cook for 15 minutes.

FISH

Whether fish is large or small, whole or filleted, it cooks to a delicious flakiness over an open barbecue. In order to keep it moist, marinate it before cooking and turn and baste it several times while it is on the grill. The juices can also be preserved by wrapping the fish in lettuce or vine leaves or in a parcel of foil.

Preparation

Clean whole fish thoroughly, scraping away any blood that has collected by the back bone. Scale if necessary. Remove any large bones from fillets. Thick cutlets can be skinned and boned if they are to be cooked in a hinged wire grill. The skin on large whole fish acts as a protection during cooking and is best removed just before serving.

Brush fish with oil or melted butter. If possible, marinate for at least 1 hour before cooking.

Basic cooking methods

If possible use a hinged wire grill, either square or oblong for cutlets, small fish and fillets, or fish-shaped for whole large fish. Oil it well. If a hinged grill is not available, oil the grill rack well.

Always use medium size coals. Turn small fish, cutlets and fillets three times during the total cooking time to prevent drying. Larger fish should be turned every 10 minutes.

Wrapping in leaves

Vine leaves give a slightly sharp flavour to whole fish, lettuce one that is light and fresh. Marinate the fish first. Wrap it in three layers of leaves. Cook it directly on the barbecue grill. The leaves will dry and char slightly. Peel them away before serving. The skin should come away with them leaving moist, subtly flavoured flesh.

Single portion sized fish weighing 225-300g/8-10oz are the most suitable for this method.

Wrapping in foil

Whole fish, large or small, cutlets, fillets and small portions can all be wrapped in lightly greased foil. This keeps the fish moist and also gives more scope for adding flavouring ingredients such as chopped tomato, cucumber, red or green peppers or mixtures of chopped fresh herbs.

Use heavy duty foil or a double thickness of standard weight foil. If possible seal it at the sides so the fish can be turned easily and cooked evenly. Wrap whole fish, cutlets and fillets separately. Diced fish or fish cut into small squares can be wrapped in portions.

Fish kebabs

Use only firm fleshed fish for kebabs. Cut it into 2.5 cm/1 inch cubes and marinate before putting on to the skewers. If possible use flat or square skewers.

Spit-roasting

Use large, round-shaped, firm fleshed fish. Eviscerate it through the gills and fill the body cavity with herbs. Make diagonal slits on either side of the body and marinate the fish for at least 1 hour. Secure the fish on the spit. Tie it round with fine string or wrap it with clean chicken wire. Cook for 12 minutes per pound. If the tail end looks as though it may burn, wrap it in foil.

When the fish is done, the flesh should look opaque and flake when tested with a fork.

Skewered small fish

Fish that weigh 125 g/4 oz or less can be skewered head to tail, between two skewers. If they are first salted, they will become firm and easy to handle.

Cooking Times

FILLETS

2 cm/¾ inch thick: 10-14 minutes total time

CUTLETS

2.5 cm/1 inch thick: 12-16 minutes total time
5 cm/2 inches thick: 20-24 minutes total time

WHOLE FISH

Small fish: 12-15 minutes total time
Large fish: 8-10 minutes per 450 g/1 lb
Foil-wrapped fish: add approximately 20% to the total cooking time

SHELLFISH

Prawns (shrimp), unshelled: 2 minutes each side
Lobster, raw: 15 minutes, shell side down plus 5 minutes cut side down
Crab, dressed, in shell, foil wrapped: 15 minutes, shell down

MARINADES FOR FISH

75 g/3 oz/¾ cup butter, melted, grated rind and juice 1 lemon, freshly ground black pepper, 1 tablespoon each chopped parsley, thyme and marjoram (best for white fish) *or*

4 tablespoons oil, juice 1 lemon, 3 tablespoons grated horse-radish, 4 tablespoons chopped parsley (best for oily fish) *or*

4 tablespoons oil, 2 tablespoons white wine vinegar, 1 teaspoon ground ginger, 1 teaspoon ground cinnamon, 2 tablespoons chopped parsley *or*

Right: Creole Fish; bottom: Parcels of Fish and Mushrooms; top: Flat Fish with Sorrel Sauce.

Top right: Gingered Skirt (Flank); bottom: Fillet (Tenderloin) Steaks with Mozarella; left: Spiced Super Burger.

4 tablespoons oil, grated rind and juice 1 lime, ¼ teaspoon cayenne pepper, 3 tablespoons each chopped parsley (for oily fish add 1 tablespoon chopped mint) *or*

4 tablespoons oil, juice ½ lemon, 1 teaspoon mustard powder, 4 tablespoons chopped chervil *or*

4 tablespoons olive oil, 4 tablespoons dry white wine, 2 tablespoons chopped dill weed or 1 teaspoon dill seeds, pinch cayenne pepper *or*

4 tablespoons each oil, dry white wine and tomato juice, plus 1 crushed garlic clove and ¼ teaspoon Tabasco sauce *or*

4 tablespoons oil, 4 tablespoons Chinese rice wine or dry sherry, 2 tablespoons soy, tamari or shoyu sauce, 15 g/½ oz peeled and grated ginger root, 2 chopped spring onions (scallions) *or*

4 tablespoons oil, juice 1 lemon, 4 tablespoons natural (unflavored) yoghurt, ¼ teaspoon each paprika, ground cumin and ground coriander, 1 teaspoon curry powder, 1 green chilli, cored, seeded and chopped, if available *or*

4 tablespoons oil, 4 tablespoons dry white wine, juice ½ lemon, 1 very finely chopped shallot or small onion, 4 tablespoons chopped fennel.

SMALL SALTED FISH WITH MUSTARD SAUCE

METRIC/IMPERIAL	AMERICAN
900 g/2 lb small oily fish 10-15 cm/4-6 inches long	2 lb small oily fish 4-6 inches long
225 g/8 oz coarse sea salt	¾ cup coarse sea salt
sauce	*sauce*
175 g/6 oz low fat soft cheese	6 oz low fat soft cheese
4 tablespoons soured cream	¼ cup dairy sour cream
2 teaspoons made English mustard	2 teaspoons made English mustard
1 tablespoon spiced granular mustard	1 tablespoon spice granular mustard

Wash and dry the fish. Leave them whole and do not clean. Spread half the salt in the bottom of a large, flat dish. Lay the fish on top. Cover with the remaining salt. Put into the refrigerator for 2 hours. Take them out and brush away all the salt.

To make the sauce, beat the cheese until it is soft. Gradually beat in the soured cream and then the two types of mustard.

Skewer the fish, about six at a time, between two fine skewers, placing them head to tail. Brush with oil.

Oil the barbecue grill. Cook 10-15 cm/4-6 inches over medium coals or 15-20 cm/6-8 inches over hot coals for 5 minutes on each side, basting them with more oil before turning. Serve the sauce separately.

MINTED FISH IN LETTUCE LEAVES

METRIC/IMPERIAL	AMERICAN
4 small fish, 225g-275g/8-10oz each	4 small fish, 8-10oz each
6 tablespoons olive oil	6 tablespoons olive oil
1 tablespoon white wine vinegar	1 tablespoon white wine vinegar
4 tablespoons chopped mint	¼ cup chopped mint
freshly ground black pepper	freshly ground black pepper
2 large round lettuces	2 large round lettuces

Clean the fish. The heads can be left on or removed according to preference. Make two diagonal slashes on each side, running backwards from head to tail. Mix together the oil, vinegar and mint, and season with the pepper. Brush the fish inside and out with the mint mixture, including into the slits. Put into a flat dish and leave for 2 hours at room temperature.

Take the largest leaves from each lettuce. Wash and dry them well. Wrap each fish completely in lettuce leaves.

Oil the grill rack. Cook 10-15cm/4-6 inches over medium coals or 15-20cm/6-8 inches over hot coals for a total of 15 minutes, turning three times.

Serve the fish in the lettuce leaves. Before eating, however, the leaves should be peeled away, taking the skin with them.

FISH WITH STEEPED PARSLEY

METRIC/IMPERIAL	AMERICAN
4 oily fish 225-275g/8-10oz each	4 oily fish, 8-10oz each
3 tablespoons olive oil	3 tablespoons olive oil
pinch ground ginger	pinch ground ginger
freshly ground black pepper	freshly ground black pepper
50g/2oz coarse oatmeal	2oz coarse oatmeal
50g/2oz parsley, chopped	2oz chopped parsley
1 teaspoon ground ginger	1 teaspoon ground ginger
1 teaspoon ground cinnamon	1 teaspoon ground cinnamon
4 tablespoons olive oil	¼ cup olive oil
2 tablespoons white wine vinegar	2 tablespoons white wine vinegar

Clean the fish. Leave the heads on. Cut the tails into even V-shapes. Mix together the oil, pinch of ginger and pepper. Brush the mixture over the inside and outside of the fish. Leave for 1 hour at room temperature.

Put the parsley into a bowl and mix in the remaining ginger, cinnamon, oil and vinegar. Leave for 1 hour.

Coat the fish in the oatmeal. Place in a hinged grill. Cook 10-15cm/4-6 inches over medium coals or 15-20cm/6-8 inches over hot coals for 15 minutes, turning three times.

Serve the fish plainly, with the parsley in a separate dish.

FLAT FISH WITH SORREL SAUCE

METRIC/IMPERIAL	AMERICAN
4 small flat fish, heads removed, skinned, left on bone	4 small flat fish, heads removed, skinned, left on bone
40g/1½oz butter	3 tablespoons butter
juice 1 lemon	juice 1 lemon
2 tablespoons chopped lemon thyme	2 tablespoons chopped lemon thyme
2 tablespoons chopped parsley	2 tablespoons chopped parsley
freshly ground black pepper	freshly ground black pepper
sauce	*sauce*
125g/4oz sorrel leaves	¼lb sorrel leaves
15g/½oz butter	1 tablespoon butter
6 tablespoons dry red wine	6 tablespoons dry red wine

Put the butter and lemon juice into a small pan. Set on a low heat for the butter to melt. Pour into a large flat dish. Cool slightly. Add the herbs and season well with the pepper. Turn the fish in the marinade and leave for at least 2 hours at room temperature.

To make the sauce, remove the stems from the sorrel and chop the leaves finely. Melt the butter in a frying pan on a high heat. Add the sorrel and stir until it softens and darkens in colour. Pour in the wine and bring to the boil. Simmer for 2 minutes.

Cook 10-15cm/4-6 inches over medium coals or 15-20cm/6-8 inches over hot coals for a total of 15 minutes, turning three times, keeping the sauce warm on the side of the grill. Serve the sauce separately.

PARCELS OF FISH AND MUSHROOMS

METRIC/IMPERIAL	AMERICAN
four 225-275g/8-10oz fish	four 8-10oz fish
225g/8oz button mushrooms	½lb button mushrooms
150ml/¼ pint single cream	5fl oz light cream
juice ½ lemon	juice ½ lemon
4 tablespoons chopped parsley	¼ cup chopped parsley
freshly ground black pepper	freshly ground black pepper
butter for greasing	butter for greasing

Clean the fish and cut off the fins and heads. Slice the mushrooms thinly. Put into a bowl and mix in the cream, lemon and parsley. Season with the pepper.

Lay each fish on a sheet of buttered foil. Spoon the mushroom mixture over the top. Seal the packets of foil on one side and secure the ends tightly.

Cook 10-15cm/4-6 inches over hot coals for 30 minutes, turning three times. Unwrap the parcels onto individual plates.

WHITE FISH KEBABS WITH LEMON

METRIC/IMPERIAL	AMERICAN
675g/1½lb firm white fish	1½lb firm white fish
juice 2 lemons	juice 2 lemons
6 tablespoons olive oil	6 tablespoons olive oil
2 teaspoons ground cumin	2 teaspoons ground cumin
4 bay leaves, torn into small pieces	4 bay leaves, torn into small pieces
freshly ground black pepper	freshly ground black pepper
4 small onions	4 small onions
1 green pepper	1 sweet green pepper
225g/8oz tomatoes	½lb tomatoes
50g/2oz parsley, chopped	1 cup chopped parsley
1 lemon, cut into wedges	1 lemon, cut into wedges

Cut the fish into 2.5cm/1 inch cubes. Mix together the lemon juice, oil, cumin, bay leaves and pepper. Turn the fish in the mixture and leave for 30 minutes at room temperature.

Peel the onions, drop into boiling water, simmer for 5 minutes and drain. Pour boiling water over the pepper. Leave it for 5 minutes and drain. Core and seed the pepper and cut into 2.5cm/1 inch squares.

Thread the fish cubes, pepper and pieces of bay leaf on to four kebab skewers. Top each with an onion. Cook over medium coals, or sparsely-spaced hot coals for 6-7 minutes, turning several times.

Serve on a bed of parsley, garnished with tomato and lemon wedges.

CREOLE FISH

METRIC/IMPERIAL	AMERICAN
4 white fish steaks, 2.5cm/1 inch thick	4 white fish steaks, 1 inch thick
450g/1lb tomatoes, ripe	1lb tomatoes, ripe
1 green pepper	1 sweet green pepper
1 large celery stick	1 large celery stick
1 medium onion	1 medium onion
3 tablespoons oil	3 tablespoons oil
1 garlic clove, finely chopped	1 garlic clove, finely chopped
¼ teaspoon chilli powder	¼ teaspoon chili powder
1 teaspoon paprika	1 teaspoon paprika
2 tablespoons white wine vinegar	2 tablespoons white wine vinegar
1 teaspoon Barbados sugar	1 teaspoon Barbados sugar

Scald, skin and chop the tomatoes. Chop the pepper, celery stick and onion finely. Heat the oil in a saucepan on a low heat. Add the pepper, celery, onion and garlic and cook them, stirring occasionally, until they begin to brown. Add the tomatoes, chilli powder, paprika, vinegar and sugar. Cover and cook very gently, for 20 minutes or until you have a thick sauce. Cool completely.

Pour the sauce into a large flat dish. Turn the fish steaks in it and leave for 30 minutes at room temperature.

Put the sauce into a small pan and reheat it on the side of the barbecue grill. Put the fish steaks into an oiled, hinged grill. Cook 15-20 cm/6-8 inches over hot coals for 12 minutes, turning three times. Serve the sauce separately.

BEEF

Think of a barbecue and you will most probably think of a juicy steak, cooked to perfection and flavoured very slightly with herbs. A charcoal fire will sear the outside beautifully, keeping the inside moist and full of flavour whether rare, medium or well done.

Beef for the barbecue

Choose the best quality meat that you can afford. It must be lean, firm and bright red with a brownish tinge. The more expensive cuts from the hindquarter are most able to withstand a high heat without becoming tough. Choose rump, sirloin, fillet (tenderloin), T-bone, entrecote, porterhouse and rib steaks. Skirt (flank) can also be cooked over an open barbecue provided that it is marinated first and only cooked until it is rare. Burgers are always popular barbecue fare.

Preparing beef

Trim any border fat to a thickness of 6 mm/¼ inch. This will give enough to keep the meat moist but will avoid too much fat dripping down on to the coals and causing flare-ups. Slash the remaining fat at 2.5 cm/1 inch intervals to prevent curling during cooking.

Never cook beef from refrigerator temperature. It should be brought to room temperature and left for at least 1 hour before cooking. Brush with oil, season with pepper and rub with a cut garlic clove, before placing on the grill.

All steaks benefit from being steeped in a marinade which both tenderises and flavours. Marinate for 1 hour or longer. The longer the beef is in the marinade, the stronger the added flavours after cooking.

Do not add salt to steaks before cooking as this draws out the natural juices.

Making burgers

Allow 125 g/4 oz lean minced (ground) beef per burger. Season with freshly ground black pepper, plus chopped herbs and/or a little grated onion if wished. If possible, use a burger press for making to achieve an even size and thickness.

When the burgers are made, refrigerate for 30 minutes to set them into shape and then leave at room temperature for a further 30 minutes. Since burgers contain a certain percentage of fat, they do not need to be oiled before cooking. They are best cooked in a hinged wire grill that has been lightly oiled.

Beef kebabs

Use any of the steaks, or top rump, silverside, topside or aitchbone.

Cooking steaks

All steaks are cooked directly on the barbecue grill, and whether you want them rare, medium or well done, they should all first be seared for 1-2 minutes on each side directly over the hottest parts of the fire. The first side has been properly seared when droplets of red appear on the top. Raise the grill rack 2.5-5 cm/1-2 inches and continue cooking on that side for the required amount of time. Return the grill rack to its original position, turn the steak and cook the other side in the same way. More juices will be preserved by only turning the steak once.

To test for "doneness", press the back of a fork lightly against the steak. If it feels soft it is rare, if it feels springy it is medium, and a well-done steak should feel stiff.

Serving steaks

Serve all steaks as soon as possible in order to preserve juices and flavour. Extra thick steaks such as cuts from the sirloin or skirt (flank) are best cut into thin diagonal slices and served on bread with a sauce.

Spit-roasting beef

Suitable cuts for spit-roasting include rolled rib and brisket, topside, silverside, top rump (round rump), aitchbone, whole sirloin and chuck. Tie them round tightly with fine string to keep them firmly in an even shape.

Large beef joints can be marinated for up to 24 hours if wished. They must all be well basted during cooking.

A meat thermometer is a great help in assessing whether the meat is done or not.

Many prepared beef joints are of an even thickness. Increasing the weight will therefore increase the length rather than thickness and so cooking times will not be changed.

Cooking Times

STEAKS, BURGERS AND KEBABS

Always cook over hot charcoal

Cut	Thickness	Minutes per side		
		Rare	Medium	Well done
Steak	2.5 cm/1 inch	5-6	7-8	10-12
Steak	4 cm/1½ inches	6-7	9-10	12-15
Skirt (flank)	whole	5-6	—	—
Kebab		4-5	6-8	10-12
Burger	2.5 cm/1 inch	3-4	5-6	7-10

SPIT-ROASTED BEEF

Cut	Weight	Approximate hours cooking time		
		Rare (65°C/150°F)	Medium (70°C/160°F)	Well done (80°C/180°F)
Rolled rib, Brisket	1.8-2.7 kg/4-6 lb	2-2½	2¼-3	3¼-4-4½
Sirloin, Topside, Silverside, Chuck	1.35-2.7 kg/3-6 lb	1½-2	2¼-3	3-4
Rump, Aitchbone	1.35-2.25 kg/3-5 lb	1½-2	2¼-3	3-4

MARINADES FOR BEEF

150 ml/¼ pint/5 fl oz dry red wine, 2 tablespoons olive oil, 1 tablespoon chopped marjoram, 1 crushed garlic clove, freshly ground black pepper, 6 black olives, stoned (pitted) and crushed *or*

150 ml/¼ pint/5 fl oz dry red wine, 2 tablespoons olive oil, 2 tablespoons chopped parsley, 1 tablespoon each chopped thyme and marjoram, 2 teaspoons Dijon mustard, 1 small onion, grated *or*

4 tablespoons olive oil, 4 anchovy fillets, pounded to a paste, 1 crushed garlic clove, 2 tablespoons chopped thyme, freshly ground black pepper. (Brush over the surface of the steak rather than dipping the steak into the mixture.) *or*

6 tablespoons olive oil, juice 1 lime, ¼ teaspoon cayenne pepper, 1 crushed garlic clove, 4 tablespoons chopped parsley *or*

4 tablespoons dry red wine, 2 tablespoons olive oil, 2 tablespoons Worcestershire sauce, 2 crushed garlic cloves, freshly ground black pepper, 2 tablespoons chopped parsley, 1 tablespoon chopped thyme *or*

4 tablespoons sesame oil, 4 tablespoons tamari, shoyu or soy sauce, 2 tablespoons hot Chinese black bean paste, 1 crushed garlic clove, 1 spring onion (scallion), finely chopped *or*

4 tablespoons oil, 4 tablespoons Chinese rice wine or dry sherry, 15 g/½ oz peeled and grated fresh ginger root, 1 crushed garlic clove, 2 spring onions (scallions), finely chopped *or*

4 tablespoons oil, 4 tablespoons dry white wine, 2 tablespoons tomato paste, 2 tablespoons mushroom ketchup, 1 very finely chopped shallot or small onion, 4 tablespoons chopped parsley *or*

4 tablespoons oil, 4 tablespoons tomato juice, 1 teaspoon

paprika, 1 small onion, very finely chopped, ½ small green pepper, very finely chopped *or*

4 tablespoons olive oil, juice ½ lemon, 1 tablespoon Worcestershire sauce, 1 tablespoon tomato paste, 2 teaspoons mustard powder, 1 tablespoon grated horse-radish.

BLACK BEAN AND CHILLI BASTING SAUCE

METRIC/IMPERIAL	AMERICAN
1 green or red chilli	1 green or red chili
4 tablespoons oil	¼ cup oil
1 small onion, finely chopped	1 small onion, finely chopped
1 garlic clove, finely chopped	1 garlic clove, finely chopped
15g/½oz ginger root, peeled and grated	½oz ginger root, peeled and grated
3 tablespoons Chinese black bean paste	3 tablespoons Chinese black bean paste
1 tablespoon white wine vinegar	1 tablespoon white wine vinegar

Core, seed and chop the chilli finely. Heat the oil in a small pan on a low heat. Add the onion, garlic and ginger and cook until the onion is soft. Take the pan from the heat and tip the contents into a bowl. Mix in the chilli, black bean paste and vinegar. Leave until completely cool.

Brush steaks with the mixture before putting on the grill and baste when turning and just before cooking finishes.

RED WINE AND HERB BASTING SAUCE

METRIC/IMPERIAL	AMERICAN
50g/2oz butter	¼ cup butter
1 garlic clove, crushed	1 garlic clove, crushed
4 tablespoons dry red wine	¼ cup dry red wine
2 tablespoons chopped parsley	2 tablespoons chopped parsley
1 tablespoon chopped thyme	1 tablespoon chopped thyme
1 tablespoon chopped marjoram	1 tablespoon chopped marjoram
2 sage leaves, chopped	2 sage leaves, chopped
freshly ground black pepper	freshly ground black pepper

Melt the butter in a small pan on a low heat. Stir in the remaining ingredients. Cool.

Brush steaks with the mixture before placing on the grill. Brush again when turning and once just before removing them.

WHITE WINE AND TOMATO BASTING SAUCE

METRIC/IMPERIAL	AMERICAN
50g/2oz butter	¼ cup butter
1 garlic clove, crushed	1 garlic clove, crushed
4 tablespoons dry white wine	¼ cup dry white wine
2 tablespoons chopped parsley	2 tablespoons chopped parsley
1 tablespoon chopped thyme	1 tablespoon chopped thyme
1 tablespoon tomato paste	1 tablespoon tomato paste
freshly ground black pepper	freshly ground black pepper

Melt the butter in a small pan on a low heat. Stir in the remaining ingredients. Cool.

Brush steaks with the mixture before placing on the grill. Brush again when turning and once just before removing them.

HORSERADISH BURGERS

METRIC/IMPERIAL	AMERICAN
900g/2lb minced beef	1lb ground beef
2 tablespoons grated horseradish	2 tablespoons grated horseradish
1 teaspoon made English mustard	1 teaspoon made English mustard
1 small onion	1 small onion
6 tablespoons chopped parsley	6 tablespoons chopped parsley

Put the beef into a bowl. Add the horse-radish and mustard. Grate in the onion. Add the parsley and mix well.

Form the mixture into four burger shapes and chill for 30 minutes. Take into room temperature for 30 minutes.

Place the burgers in a hinged wire grill. Cook 10-15cm/4-6 inches over hot coals for 8-20 minutes, turning once.

FILLET (TENDERLOIN) STEAKS WITH MOZARELLA

METRIC/IMPERIAL	AMERICAN
8 slices fillet steak 2.5cm/1 inch thick	8 slices tenderloin steak, 1 inch thick
125ml/4floz dry red wine	½ cup dry red wine
4 tablespoons olive oil	¼ cup olive oil
2 tablespoons chopped thyme	2 tablespoons chopped thyme
1 garlic clove, crushed	1 garlic clove, crushed
freshly ground black pepper	freshly ground black pepper
125g/4oz Mozarella cheese	¼lb Mozarella cheese
8 black olives	8 black olives

Cut a crossways slit through the side of each piece of steak, approximately three-quarters of the way through. In a large, flat dish mix together the wine, oil, thyme, garlic and pepper. Turn the pieces of steak in the mixture making sure that it reaches inside the slits. Leave for at least 30 minutes at room temperature.

Cut eight small, thin slices of mozarella. Halve and stone (pit) the olives. Push a piece of mozarella and two olive halves into each piece of steak.

Cook 10-15 cm/4-6 inches over hot coals for 5-8 minutes on each side, or to your liking.

BEEF SATAY

Although some store cupboard ingredients are used for this recipe, it still maintains an authentic Indonesian flavour.

METRIC/IMPERIAL	AMERICAN
675 g/1½ lb top rump of beef	1½ lb round rump of beef
marinade	*marinade*
2 cm/¾ inch cube tamarind	¾ inch cube tamarind
2 tablespoons boiling water	2 tablespoons boiling water
1 small onion, grated	1 small onion, grated
juice ½ lemon	juice ½ lemon
2 tablespoons soy, tamari or shoyu sauce	2 tablespoons soy, tamari or shoyu sauce
1 garlic clove, crushed with pinch sea salt	1 garlic clove, crushed with pinch sea salt
sauce	*sauce*
125 g/4 oz crunchy peanut butter (preferably health shop variety)	½ cup crunchy peanut butter (preferably health store variety)
225 ml/8 fl oz thick coconut milk (can be bought in tins from delicatessen)	1 cup thick coconut milk (can be bought in cans from delicatessen)
juice ½ lemon	juice ½ lemon
1 teaspoon chilli powder	1 teaspoon chili powder
lemon or lime for garnish	lemon or lime for garnish

Cut the beef into 2.5 cm/1 inch cubes. Put the tamarind into a bowl, pour on the boiling water and leave for 10 minutes. Rub the tamarind plus the water through a sieve into a large bowl. Add the remaining marinade ingredients and mix well.

Mix in the beef. Cover and leave at room temperature for at least 2 hours. Put the peanut butter into a bowl and gradually mix in the coconut milk to make a smooth, thick sauce. Alternatively use a blender or food processor. Mix in the lemon juice and chilli powder. Put the sauce into a small, heavy-based saucepan.

Divide the beef between four skewers. Cook 10-15 cm/4-6 inches over hot coals for 20 minutes, turning once, or until tender and cooked through. While the kebabs are cooking, put the pan of sauce on the side of the grill to heat through.

Serve the sauce separately as a dip with wedges of lemon or lime to use as required.

SPICED SUPER BURGER

METRIC/IMPERIAL	AMERICAN
575g/1¼lb minced beef	1¼lb ground beef
½ small onion	½ small onion
1 garlic clove, crushed	1 garlic clove, crushed
2 tablespoons tomato paste	2 tablespoons tomato paste
2 tablespoons natural yoghurt	2 tablespoons unflavored yoghurt
1 tablespoon chopped thyme	1 tablespoon chopped thyme
3 sage leaves, chopped	3 sage leaves, chopped
1 teaspoon ground cinnamon	1 teaspoon ground cinnamon
sauce	*sauce*
150ml/¼ pint natural yoghurt	5floz unflavored yoghurt
2 tablespoons tomato paste	2 tablespoons tomato paste
1 garlic clove, crushed	1 garlic clove, crushed
½ teaspoon ground cinnamon	½ teaspoon ground cinnamon

one 20cm/8 inch round loaf, or make the spiced loaf below.

Put the beef into a bowl. Grate the onion into it. Add the remaining ingredients and mix well. Press the mixture into an 18cm/7 inch diameter cake tin and put in the refrigerator for 2 hours to set into shape. Take into room temperature for 30 minutes.

For the sauce, mix together the yoghurt, tomato paste, garlic and cinnamon. Place the burger in a hinged grill (broiler). Cook 10-15cm/4-6 inches over hot coals for 8 minutes on each side.

Split the loaf horizontally. Place the burger in the loaf with the sauce on top. Cut into four wedges for serving.

SPICED LOAF

METRIC/IMPERIAL	AMERICAN
15g/½oz fresh yeast or 2 teaspoons dried	1 tablespoon fresh yeast or 2 teaspoons dried
150ml/¼ pint warm water	5floz warm water
1 teaspoon honey, if using dried yeast	1 teaspoon honey, if using dried yeast
225g/8oz wholewheat flour	2 cups wholewheat flour
1 teaspoon sea salt	1 teaspoon sea salt
1 teaspoon cumin seeds	1 teaspoon cumin seeds
¼ teaspoon ground coriander	¼ teaspoon ground coriander
4 tablespoons olive oil	¼ cup olive oil

If you are using fresh yeast crumble it into the warm water; if using dried yeast dissolve the honey in the water and scatter in the yeast. Leave in a warm place to froth.

Put the flour into a bowl with the salt and spices. Make a well in the centre. Pour in the yeast and oil. Mix everything to a dough and knead it on a floured board until smooth. Return the dough to the bowl, cover with a clean cloth and leave in a warm place for 1 hour or until doubled in size.

Heat the oven to 200°C/400°F/gas mark 6. Knead the dough again. Roll out to a 20 cm/8 inch round and place in an oiled cake tin. Leave in a warm place to prove for 10 minutes.

Bake for 25 minutes or until it sounds hollow when tapped. Turn it on to a wire rack to cool completely.

GINGERED SKIRT (FLANK)

METRIC/IMPERIAL	AMERICAN
675g/1½lbs skirt of beef	1½ flank steak
marinade	*marinade*
1 teaspoon ground ginger	1 teaspoon ground ginger
juice 1 lemon	juice 1 lemon
4 tablespoons oil	¼ cup oil
2 tablespoons Worcestershire sauce	2 tablespoons Worcestershire sauce
1 tablespoon tomato paste	1 tablespoon tomato paste
4 tablespoons chopped parsley	¼ cup chopped parsley
sauce	*sauce*
2 tablespoons oil	2 tablespoons oil
1 medium onion, finely chopped	1 medium onion, finely chopped
1 garlic clove, finely chopped	1 garlic clove, finely chopped
1 tablespoon wholewheat flour	1 tablespoon wholewheat flour
1 tablespoon tomato paste	1 tablespoon tomato paste
275ml/½ pint stock	1¼ cups stock
2 tablespoons Worcestershire sauce	2 tablespoons Worcestershire sauce
2 tablespoons tamari, shoyu or soy sauce	2 tablespoons tamari, shoyu or soy sauce
for serving	*for serving*
1 wholewheat french loaf	1 wholewheat french loaf

Keep the meat in one piece. Pull away any pieces of tissue or fat from the outside. In a large, flat dish mix together the marinade ingredients. Turn the beef in the mixture, cover and leave for at least 4 hours at room temperature, turning several times.

To make the sauce, heat the oil in a saucepan on a low heat. Add the onion and garlic and cook until they are just turning golden. Stir in the flour and tomato paste. Stir in the stock and bring to the boil. Add the Worcestershire and tamari sauces. Simmer uncovered and stirring occasionally, for 15 minutes.

Cut the loaf into four equal pieces. Split them almost in half crossways and scoop out some of the soft crumb.

Cook the steak for 5 minutes on each side 10-15 cm/4-6 inches over hot coals. It must be rare. Take it off the grill and cut into very thin, diagonal slices. Put the slices into the prepared bread and top with sauce.

HORSERADISH-BASTED BEEF

METRIC/IMPERIAL	AMERICAN
1.35-1.57kg/3-3½lb beef topside or top rump, in one piece	3-3½lb topside or round rump, in one piece
basting sauce	*basting sauce*
75g/3oz grated horseradish	3 oz grated horseradish
2 teaspoons mustard powder	2 teaspoons mustard powder
6 tablespoons olive oil	6 tablespoons olive oil
125ml/4floz dry red wine	½ cup dry red wine

Secure the beef on a spit and if possible insert a meat thermometer. Mix together the ingredients for the basting sauce.

Set the spit over a roasting pan in the centre of, or beside, hot coals. Baste well.

Cook for 1½-2½ hours or until the required temperature is reached, basting frequently.

VEAL KEBABS

METRIC/IMPERIAL	AMERICAN
675g/1½lb veal escalopes	1½lb veal cutlets
1 large onion	1 large onion
125ml/4floz olive oil	½ cup olive oil
juice 2 lemons	juice 2 lemons
4 tablespoons chopped parsley	¼ cup chopped parsley
1 tablespoons chopped thyme	1 tablespoon chopped thyme
¼ teaspoon ground mace	¼ teaspoon ground mace
¼ nutmeg, grated	¼ nutmeg, grated

Cut the escalopes into 2.5cm/1 inch squares and the onion into 2.5cm/1 inch pieces. In a large bowl beat together the remaining ingredients. Fold in the veal and onion. Leave for at least 4 hours at room temperature.

Place alternate pieces of veal and onion on four kebab skewers.

Cook 10-15cm/4-6 inches over hot coals for a total of 20 minutes, turning and basting with the marinade several times.

PORK

Pork is a rich meat but tends to be slightly tougher than beef or lamb. It therefore benefits considerably by being marinated before cooking over medium coals to the well-done stage.

Pork for the barbecue

Loin chops, spare rib chops, leg steaks, 6mm/¼ inch thick belly rashers (slices), spare ribs and tenderloin are all suitable for barbecueing.

Thick cut slices of gammon or ham steaks make a delicious change.

Preparing pork

Cut off all but a 6mm/¼ inch layer of fat from the outside of chops. Slash the remaining fat at 2.5cm/1 inch intervals. Marinate for up to 6 hours. Marinate spare ribs for the same amount of time.

Remove the thin layers of fat and skin from the outside of tenderloin. Marinate tenderloin well and cook in 10-15cm/4-6 inch lengths.

Cut the rind and all but a 6mm/¼ inch layer of fat from gammon. Slash the remaining fat at 2.5cm/1 inch intervals.

Cut liver into thin slices. Halve and core kidneys. Marinate for up to 4 hours.

Prick sausages to prevent them bursting. If they are fat, they can be slashed two or thee times on each side. For easy handling, and to prevent curling, skewer them lengthways two to a skewer.

Spit-roasting pork

Choose boned and rolled loin, rolled shoulder, a spare-rib joint, the shank end of the leg, or cooked or uncooked ham.

Rub the joints with crushed herbs, garlic and spices such as crushed juniper, allspice and black peppercorns. Baste well with oil.

Cooking small cuts of pork

Always cook pork 10-15cm/4-6 inches over medium coals, turning most cuts once only. Tenderloin should be turned several times to ensure even cooking. Spare ribs, which require longer cooking, should also be turned several times.

Cooking Times

CHOPS AND STEAKS

Chops, 2-2.5cm/¾-1 inch: 15-20 minutes per side
Leg steaks: 15-20 minutes per side
Tenderloin: 40 minutes total time
Belly Rashers: 15-20 minutes per side
Spare Ribs: 1 hour total time (low-medium coals)

HAM

Gammon, 1.5cm/½ inch thick: 10-15 minutes per side
Ham Steaks: 8-10 minutes per side

KEBABS

Use hand and spring or leg, cut into 2.5cm/1 inch cubes, or belly rashers (slices) cut into 2.5cm/1 inch squares. Marinate before putting on to kebab skewers. Cook over medium coals for a total of 30-40 minutes.

LIVER AND KIDNEYS

Cook liver over hot coals for 4-5 minutes on each side. Cook kidneys over medium coals for 15-20 minutes on each side.

SAUSAGES

Cook over medium coals for a total of 20-25 minutes, moving them as soon as dripping fat causes a flare-up.

SPIT-ROASTED PORK

Pork must always be well done, 85°C/190°F.
Loin, Shoulder or Leg: 2-3 hours
Spare ribs: 1¼-1¾ hours
Uncooked ham: 25 minutes per 450g/1lb
Cooked ham: 12 minutes per 450g/1lb

MARINADES FOR PORK

Spread chops, rashers, ribs or tenderloin with a spiced granular mustard *or*

Mix to a paste: 2 tablespoons mustard powder, 125ml/4floz/½ cup dry cider, pinch sea salt, 8 chopped sage leaves, 2 teaspoons chopped rosemary, 2 tablespoons chopped thyme. Spread over the meat *or*

6 tablespoons concentrated apple juice, 6 tablespoons cider vinegar, 1 teaspoon mustard powder, 1 crushed garlic clove, 4 chopped sage leaves *or*

275ml/½ pint/1¼ cups dry cider, 2 teaspoons ground ginger, 4 tablespoons chopped parsley, 1 teaspoon honey *or*

150ml/¼ pint/5floz natural (unflavored) yoghurt, 1 teaspoon mustard powder, 1 tablespoon cider vinegar, 4 chopped sage leaves, 1 tablespoon chopped marjoram *or*

150ml/¼ pint/5floz dry white wine, 1 tablespoon chopped thyme, 6 chopped sage leaves, 1 crushed garlic clove, freshly ground black pepper *or*

125ml/4floz/½ cup orange juice, 125ml/4floz/½ cup pineapple juice, 2 tablespoons tomato paste, pinch cayenne pepper, 1 crushed garlic clove, 1 teaspoon chopped rosemary *or*

125ml/4floz/½ cup cider vinegar, 12 coarsely crushed black peppercorns, 8 coarsely crushed allspice berries, 1 chopped or crushed garlic clove, 4 chopped sage leaves *or*

150 ml/¼ pint/5 fl oz dry white wine, 2 teaspoons spiced granular mustard, 1 teaspoon honey, 6 chopped sage leaves, 2 teaspoons chopped rosemary, 1 tablespoon chopped thyme *or*

4 tablespoons oil, 4 tablespoons hoisin sauce, 2 tablespoons Chinese oyster sauce, 4 tablespoons Chinese rice wine or dry sherry, 2 tablespoons tamari, shoyu or soy sauce, ½ teaspoon five-spice powder, 2 spring onions (scallions), finely chopped.

PINEAPPLE AND TOMATO BASTING SAUCE

METRIC/IMPERIAL	AMERICAN
450 g/1 lb ripe tomatoes	1 lb ripe tomatoes
6 tablespoons pineapple juice	6 tablespoons pineapple juice
½ teaspoon paprika	½ teaspoon paprika
1 tablespoon white wine vinegar	1 tablespoon white wine vinegar
1 tablespoon tamari, soy or shoyu sauce	1 tablespoon tamari, soy or shoyu sauce
1 tablespoon Worcestershire sauce	1 tablespoon Worcestershire sauce
2 tablespoons oil	2 tablespoons oil
1 garlic clove, crushed	1 garlic clove, crushed

Scald, skin and chop the tomatoes. Put into a saucepan with the rest of the ingredients. Set the pan on a low heat and cook gently until the tomatoes have been reduced to a thick, pulpy sauce. Cool.

Dip pork in the mixture before placing it on the grill. Baste again just before removing it.

Serve any remaining sauce, heated, as an accompaniment.

SPICED CIDER BASTING SAUCE

METRIC/IMPERIAL	AMERICAN
4 tablespoons oil	¼ cup oil
1 small onion, finely chopped	1 small onion, finely chopped
2 teaspoons mustard powder	2 teaspoons mustard powder
125 ml/4 fl oz dry cider	½ cup dry cider
6 allspice berries, coarsely crushed	6 allspice berries, coarsely crushed

Heat the oil in a small pan on a low heat. Add the onion and soften it. Stir in the mustard powder. Pour in the cider and bring to the boil, stirring. Add the allspice berries and simmer for 1 minute. Cool.

Brush the pork with the mixture before placing on the grill, once again when turning and once just before removing it.

Pork Rashers with Peaches; Ham & Apple Kebabs; Pumpkin Kebabs; Grilled Aubergine (Eggplant) Slices.

Top: Mongolian Barbecued Lamb; bottom left: Moulded Lamb with Avocado Sauce; right: Mushroom Stuffed Lamb Chops.

PORK AND ROSEMARY BURGERS

METRIC/IMPERIAL	AMERICAN
675g/1½lb lean pork	1½lb lean pork
1 tablespoon Dijon mustard	1 tablespoon Dijon mustard
2 teaspoons chopped rosemary	2 teaspoons chopped rosemary
25g/1oz seasoned wholewheat flour	3 tablespoons seasoned wholewheat flour
6 tablespoons oil	6 tablespoons oil

Finely mince (grind) the pork. Put it into a bowl. Beat in the mustard and rosemary. Form the mixture into eight round, flat burgers. Coat in seasoned flour and leave on flat plates for 30 minutes in the refrigerator to set into shape. Bring into room temperature for 30 minutes.

To cook, brush the burgers with oil. Place them, four at a time, in a hinged wire grill. Cook 10-15cm/4-6 inches over hot coals for 6-7 minutes on each side or until cooked through.

Serve with apple sauce.

SKEWERED PORK TENDERLOIN

METRIC/IMPERIAL	AMERICAN
675-900g/1½-2lb pork tenderloin	1½-2lb pork tenderloin
275ml/½ pint dry cider	1¼ cups dry cider
4 sage leaves, chopped	4 sage leaves, chopped
10 black peppercorns	10 black peppercorns
4 juniper berries	4 juniper berries
¼ teaspoon sea salt	¼ teaspoon sea salt
4 long rashers streaky bacon	4 long slices streaky bacon

Cut the tenderloin into four even-sized pieces. Pour the cider into a large, flat dish. Scatter in the sage leaves. Crush the peppercorns, juniper berries and salt together and mix into the cider. Put the pieces of tenderloin into the dish. Leave for 8-10 hours, turning several times.

When you are ready to cook, dry the pork with kitchen paper and wrap a rasher (slice) of bacon in a spiral round each piece. Push a kebab skewer through one end of the bacon and down the centre of the piece of tenderloin, skewering the other end of the bacon as it comes through.

Oil the barbecue grill and place it 10-15cm/4-6 inches over hot coals. Cook for 30-40 minutes, turning several times. The bacon should be crisp and the juices run clear when the tenderloin is pierced with a skewer.

MIXED PORK GRILL

METRIC/IMPERIAL	AMERICAN
4 pork spare rib chops	4 pork spare rib chops
350g/12oz pig's liver	¾lb pig's liver
8 sage leaves, chopped	8 sage leaves, chopped
6 tablespoons chopped chives	6 tablespoons chopped chives
2 tablespoons mustard powder	2 tablespoons mustard powder
4 tablespoons milk	¼ cup milk

Cut the liver into 1 cm/⅜ inch thick slices. Trim any excess fat from the chops if necessary.

Mix together the herbs, mustard powder and milk. Spread the chops and liver with the mixture on both sides.

Oil the barbecue grill and place it 15-20 cm/6-8 inches over hot coals. Lay the chops on the grill and cook for about 7 minutes or until the under-side is brown. Turn them over. Lay the liver on the grill. Cook for a further 7 minutes, turning the liver once, so that both chops and liver are cooked through.

PORK RASHERS (SLICES) WITH PEACHES

METRIC/IMPERIAL	AMERICAN
900g/2lb belly pork rashers cut 6mm/¼ inch thick	2lb belly pork slices cut ¼ inch thick
4 tablespoons dry white wine	¼ cup dry white wine
2 tablespoons white wine vinegar	2 tablespoons white wine vinegar
1 teaspoon Tabasco sauce	1 teaspoon Tabasco sauce
1 teaspoon paprika	1 teaspoon paprika
2 teaspoons honey	2 teaspoons honey
1 teaspoon chopped rosemary	1 teaspoon chopped rosemary
1 garlic clove, crushed with pinch sea salt	1 garlic clove, crushed with pinch sea salt
3 peaches	3 peaches

Cut the rind and any bones from the pork. Cut the rashers in half and lay the pieces in a flat dish. Mix together all the remaining ingredients apart from the peaches. Pour over the pork. Leave for 4 hours at room temperature, turning several times.

Take the pork from the marinade. Cut the peaches into thin slices and place in the marinade to coat them. Cook the pork 10-15 cm/4-6 inches over hot coals for 6 minutes on each side until well browned or cooked through. If you have a hinged wire grill, put the peach slices into that and cook over the coals for 3 minutes each side to heat through. If you do not have a hinged grill, carefully cook them on the barbecue grill.

Serve the pork garnished with the peaches.

SPIT ROASTED PORK RIBS WITH MUSHROOM SAUCE

METRIC/IMPERIAL

one 1.125 kg/2½ lb joint pork spare ribs
marinade
125 ml/4 fl oz oil
125 ml/4 fl oz mushroom ketchup
4 tablespoons Worcestershire sauce
4 tablespoons tomato paste
sauce
25 g/1 oz butter
2 medium onions, thinly sliced
1 garlic clove, finely chopped
125 g/4 oz mushrooms, finely chopped
450 g/1 lb tomatoes, scalded, skinned and chopped
4 tablespoons stock or water
2 teaspoons mushroom ketchup
1 teaspoon Worcestershire sauce
1 teaspoon made English mustard
1 teaspoon Barbados sugar

AMERICAN

one 2½ lb joint pork spare ribs
marinade
½ cup oil
½ cup mushroom ketchup
¼ cup Worcestershire sauce
¼ cup tomato paste
sauce
2 tablespoons butter
2 medium onions, thinly sliced
1 garlic clove, finely chopped
¼ lb mushrooms, finely chopped
1 lb tomatoes, scalded, skinned and chopped
¼ cup stock or water
2 teaspoons mushroom ketchup
1 teaspoon Worcestershire sauce
1 teaspoon made English mustard
1 teaspoon Barbados sugar

Lay the joint, meaty side up, and trim away as much fat and skin as possible. Turn it over and pull away any skin.

Mix together the marinade ingedients. Put into a large, flat dish. Brush over the pork. Leave for at least 4 hours at room temperature.

To secure on the spit, place the pork on a work surface, bony side up. Starting at the smaller end, push the spit through the meat between the first and second ribs. Weave it in and out through the ribs, if possible going over and then under two ribs at a time. If this is difficult, do it three ribs at a time. Push the holding forks well into the meat and tighten them as much as possible.

Place the spit in position so that one flat surface of the meat faces the heat. Leave the spit still for 10-15 minutes for the meat to brown. Turn the other side to the heat and brown it. Baste well with the marinade. Set the spit turning and cook for 1 hour, basting several times, so it is cooked through.

HAM AND APPLE KEBABS

METRIC/IMPERIAL	AMERICAN
450g/1lb cooked lean ham	1lb cooked lean ham
2 small cooking apples	2 small cooking apples
1 large onion	1 large onion
6 tablespoons oil	6 tablespoons oil
2 tablespoons cider vinegar	2 tablespoons cider vinegar
1 teaspoon honey	1 teaspoon honey
1 teaspoon spiced granular mustard	1 teaspoon spiced granular mustard
3 sage leaves, finely chopped	3 sage leaves, finely chopped

Cut the ham into 2.5cm/1 inch cubes. Peel and core the apples and cut into 2.5cm/1 inch cubes. Cut the onion into 2.5cm/1 inch squares.

In a large bowl, mix together the remaining ingredients. Add the ham, apples and onion and turn to coat well. Place alternate pieces of onion, ham and apple on to each of four kebab skewers.

Cook 10-15cm/4-6 inches over hot coals for 10 minutes, turning twice, or until they are heated through and beginning to brown.

LAMB

Lamb is a rich meat that needs little basting or marinating in order to be full of juices and flavour. A light brushing of oil, a rub with a cut garlic clove, a sprinkling of herbs and the flavour of the charcoal are all that is needed to produce a really superb meal.

However, lamb does combine extraordinarily well with many different flavours, from hot spicy curries to gentle herbs and wines, so using these in marinades and basting mixtures will give you a wide variety of barbecue lamb meals.

Lamb for the barbecue

Loin and chump chops are the best for barbecuing. If possible, ask your butcher to leave the aprons or tails on the loin chops so that these can be wrapped round to keep the meat moist.

Best end neck chops tend to be a little tougher and need longer cooking. This cut is best boned and rolled and cut into rounds or noisettes.

Steaks cut from the leg can be cooked in a similar way to chops.

Breast of lamb, if cut into fingers and well marinated can also be cooked over an open barbecue.

Preparing chops

Cut off all but a 6 mm/¼ inch layer of fat from the outside. Cut away the wedge of fat where the main part of the chop meets the apron. Wrap the apron round the main part and secure with cocktail sticks (wooden picks) that have been soaked in cold water for 10 minutes.

Brush the chops lightly with oil. Rub with a cut garlic clove. Season with pepper only and sprinkle lightly with thyme, mint, marjoram, oregano or rosemary.

Alternatively marinate for up to 6 hours if wished.

Cooking Times

CHOPS

Whether the chops are to be rare, medium or well done, each side should be seared 10-15 cm/4-6 inches over the hottest part of the fire for 1-2 minutes.

Lay the chops over the coals. Cook until red beads of liquid come to the surface. Raise the grill 2.5-5 cm/1-2 inches and continue cooking on that side for the required amount of time. Lower the grill again and cook the second side in the same way.

For 2.5 cm/1 inch thick chops allow 5-6 minutes each side for rare, 7-8 minutes for medium, 10-12 minutes for well done.

BREAST

Sear pieces of breast and then cook over medium coals for about 45 minutes, turning several times.

Cut liver into thin slices. Halve and core the kidneys. Both are better marinated. Cook liver for 4-5 minutes on each side 10-15 cm/4-6 inches over hot coals. Cook kidney halves for 5-6 minutes on each side, moving to medium coals if necessary.

LAMB KEBABS

Use leg of lamb or the lean meat from the shoulder, cut into 2.5 cm/1 inch cubes. Marinate before threading on to lightly oiled skewers.
Sear kebabs 10-15 cm/4-6 inches over hot coals for 4 minutes, turning several times. Raise the grill and continue cooking for the required amount of time.
Total cooking time for rare is 10-12 minutes, for medium 14-16 minutes and for well done 20 minutes.

SPIT ROASTING LAMB

Choose leg of lamb or boned and rolled shoulder. Prepare the leg of lamb as in the recipe below. Shoulder of lamb can be sprinkled with herbs and/or garlic slivers and brushed with a basting mixture before rolling and tying securely.

	Rare (65°C/150°F)	*Medium* (70°C/160°F)	*Well done* (80°C/180°F)
Leg	1¼-1½ hours	1½-2 hours	2-3¼ hours
Shoulders	1½-1¾ hours	1¾-2¼ hours	2½-3¼ hours

MARINADES FOR LAMB

125 ml/4 fl oz/½ cup tarragon vinegar, 2 tablespoons chopped mint, 2 tablespoons chopped tarragon, 2 tablespoons oil, pinch cayenne pepper *or*

150 ml/¼ pint/5 fl oz dry white wine, grated rind and juice 1 lemon, 4 crushed anchovy fillets, 2 tablespoons chopped tarragon or marjoram, 1 crushed garlic clove *or*

4 tablespoons/¼ cup olive oil, grated rind and juice 1 lemon, 1 teaspoon ground cumin, 1 teaspoon ground coriander, 1 crushed garlic clove, freshly ground black pepper *or*

150 ml/¼ pint/5 fl oz natural (unflavored) yoghurt, 2 teaspoons cumin seeds, 2 teaspoons ground coriander, 1 teaspoon ground turmeric, ½ teaspoon cayenne pepper *or*

6 tablespoons oil, 4 tablespoons/¼ cup dry red wine, 2 tablespoons each chopped thyme, marjoram and parsley, 1 crushed garlic clove *or*

4 tablespoons/¼ cup olive oil, 4 tablespoons/¼ cup dry sherry, 2 teaspoons chopped rosemary *or*

150 ml/¼ pint dry cider, 1 finely chopped small onion, 1 teaspoon ground cinnamon, ¼ nutmeg, freshly grated *or*

4 tablespoons/¼ cup dry red wine, 4 tablespoons/¼ cup olive oil, 1 teaspoon Dijon mustard, 4 stoned (pitted) and crushed green olives, 1 tablespoon chopped thyme *or*

4 tablespoons/¼ cup olive oil, juice 1 lemon, 4 tablespoons chopped parsley, 1 tablespoon chopped oregano, 1 tablespoon chopped thyme, 1 bay leaf, halved, 1 crushed garlic clove *or*

4 tablespoons/¼ cup oil, 2 tablespoons tamari, shoyu or soy sauce, 2 tablespoons Chinese rice wine or dry sherry, 15g/½oz peeled and grated fresh ginger root, 1 chopped garlic clove, 2 chopped spring onions (scallions). 2 tablespoons yellow bean paste can be added to this if wished.

MINT AND CITRUS BASTING SAUCE

METRIC/IMPERIAL	AMERICAN
50g/2oz butter	¼ cup butter
grated rind and juice ½ medium orange	grated rind and juice ½ medium orange
grated rind and juice 1 lemon	grated rind and juice 1 lemon
4 tablespoons chopped mint	¼ cup chopped mint

Melt the butter in a small pan on a low heat. Stir in the remaining ingredients. Cool without letting the butter set.

Brush the lamb before putting it on the barbecue grill, once when turning and once towards the end of cooking time.

SWEET CURRY BASTING SAUCE

METRIC/IMPERIAL	AMERICAN
4 tablespoons oil	¼ cup oil
1 small onion, finely chopped	1 small onion, finely chopped
1 garlic clove, finely chopped	1 garlic clove, finely chopped
1 teaspoon ground turmeric	1 teaspoon ground turmeric
1 teaspoon ground cumin	1 teaspoon ground cumin
1 teaspoon ground coriander	1 teaspoon ground coriander
¼ teaspoon chilli powder	¼ teaspoon chili powder
4 tablespoons mango chutney	4 tablespoons mango chutney

Heat the oil in a saucepan on a low heat. Add the onion, garlic and spices and cook gently until the onion is soft. Take the pan from the heat and stir in the chutney.

Brush the lamb with oil and cook as directed. Baste with the curry mixture for the final 5 minutes of cooking time.

MARSALA LAMB GRILL

METRIC/IMPERIAL	AMERICAN
4 small lamb chops	4 small lamb chops
350g/12oz lamb's liver	¾lb lamb's liver
marinade	*marinade*
150ml/¼ pint marsala	¼ pint marsala
grated rind and juice 1 lemon	grated rind and juice 1 lemon
2 tablespoons chopped thyme	2 tablespoons chopped thyme
¼ teaspoon cayenne pepper	¼ teaspoon cayenne pepper
butter	*butter*
75g/3oz unsalted butter	6 tablespoons unsalted butter
¼ teaspoon cayenne pepper	¼ teaspoon cayenne pepper
grated rind ½ lemon	grated rind ½ lemon
2 tablespoons chopped thyme	2 tablespoons chopped thyme
1 tablespoon marsala	1 tablespoon marsala

Trim all but a thin layer of fat from the chops. Cut the liver into 1 cm/⅜ inch slices. In a large, flat dish mix together the ingredients for the marinade. Put in the chops and liver. Turn them and leave for 4 hours at room temperature, turning several times.

To make the butter, beat it until soft. Beat in the cayenne pepper, lemon rind and thyme. Add the marsala drop by drop. Form the butter into a roll, wrap in greaseproof paper and chill.

Cook the chops 10-15 cm/4-6 inches over hot coals for 8 minutes each side, cook the liver for 4-5 minutes each side.

Cut the butter roll into round pats and serve separately.

MUSHROOM-STUFFED LAMB CHOPS

METRIC/IMPERIAL	AMERICAN
8 loin lamb chops each with a boned and untrimmed apron or tail, about 2.5cm/1 inch thick	8 loin lamb chops with each with a boned and untrimmed apron or tail, about 1 inch thick
8 large open mushrooms	8 large open mushrooms
marinade	*marinade*
6 tablespoons olive oil	6 tablespoons olive oil
6 tablespoons dry white wine	6 tablespoons dry white wine
2 tablespoons tomato paste	2 tablespoons tomato paste
1 garlic clove, chopped	1 garlic clove, chopped
freshly ground black pepper	freshly ground black pepper
2 teaspoons rosemary leaves	2 teaspoons rosemary leaves

Cut the outer layer of the main part of the chops and the aprons to a thickness of 6 mm/¼ inch. Cut away the wedge of fat where the apron meets the chop. Quarter the mushrooms.

In a small saucepan, gently heat the marinade ingredients, stirring until well mixed. Do not let them boil. Pour the marinade into a flat dish and cool. Put in the chops and mushrooms. Turn them and leave for at least 4 hours at room temperature.

When you are ready to cook, soak eight cocktail sticks (wooden picks) in water for 10 minutes. Wrap the aprons round the chops, putting four pieces of mushroom inside. Secure with the cocktail sticks (wooden picks), pushing them through the apron, mushrooms and chop.

Sear the chops 1-15 cm/4-6 inches over hot coals for 2 minutes on each side. Move them to the side of the grill or raise the grill slightly and continue cooking for 8 minutes or until done to your liking, turning once.

MONGOLIAN BARBECUED LAMB

METRIC/IMPERIAL	AMERICAN
900 g/2 lb lean, boneless lamb from fillet or leg	2 lb lean, boneless lamb from fillet or leg
8 wholemeal rolls	8 wholemeal rolls
sauce	*sauce*
2 tablespoons black bean paste	2 tablespoons black bean paste
2 tablespoons tamari, shoyu or soy sauce	2 tablespoons tamari, shoyu or soy sauce
1 tablespoon Barbados sugar	1 tablespoon Barbados sugar
1 tablespoon sesame oil	1 tablespoon sesame oil
1 teaspoon salt	1 teaspoon salt
½ teaspoon freshly ground black pepper	½ teaspoon freshly ground black pepper
125 ml/4 fl oz white wine vinegar	½ cup white wine vinegar
15 g/½ oz fresh ginger root	½ oz fresh ginger root
½ green pepper	½ sweet green pepper
1 red chilli	1 red chili
4 spring onions	4 scallions
1 garlic clove	1 garlic clove

Cut the lamb into small, very thin slices. Divide it between four small bowls.

To make the sauce mix together the bean paste, tamari sauce, sugar, sesame oil, salt and pepper. Peel and grate the ginger root. Chop the pepper finely. Core and seed and chop the chilli finely. Chop the spring onions (scallions) and crush the garlic. Mix with the other ingredients. Divide the sauce between four small bowls.

Split the bread rolls across, not quite all the way through. Remove some of the soft crumb.

Lay a fine wire mesh, baking sheet or griddle over the barbecue grill 10-15 cm/4-6 inches above hot coals. Oil it lightly and get it hot.

Give each person a bowl of lamb and another of sauce and either chopsticks or a fork. Everyone takes a small portion of lamb, dips it in the sauce and lays it on the heated grill. Cook for about 5 minutes. Dip in the sauce again and put it in a bread roll. More sauce can be spooned over the top if required. Eat the roll like a hamburger.

LAMB AND ORANGE KEBABS

METRIC/IMPERIAL

675g/1½lb lean lamb, from shoulder or
leg
marinade
grated rind and juice 1 large orange
4 tablespoons olive oil
1 tablespoon chopped lemon thyme
1 tablespoon chopped marjoram
1 teaspoon tomato paste
1 garlic clove, crushed
kebabs
2 small oranges
1 large green pepper

AMERICAN

1½lb lean lamb, from shoulder or leg
marinade
grated rind and juice 1 large orange
¼ cup olive oil
1 tablespoon chopped lemon thyme
1 tablespoon chopped marjoram
1 teaspoon tomato paste
1 garlic clove, crushed
kebabs
2 small oranges
1 large sweet green pepper

Cut the lamb into 2.5 cm/1 inch cubes. In a bowl mix the marinade ingredients together. Add the lamb. Cover and leave for at least 4 hours at room temperature.

Slice the small oranges thinly without peeling them. Core and seed the pepper and cut into 2.5 cm/1 inch squares. Thread the pieces of lamb, orange and pepper on to kebab skewers.

Cook 10-15 cm/4-6 inches over medium coals for 15-20 minutes, turning twice and basting with any remaining marinade.

APRICOT SOSATIES

METRIC/IMPERIAL

900g/2lb boned leg of lamb
1 large onion
125 ml/4 fl oz white wine vinegar
2 tablespoons sugar-free apricot jam
1 tablespoon curry powder
1 teaspoon ground coriander
1 teaspoon ground cinnamon
1 garlic clove, crushed
2 bay leaves, crumbled
16 dried whole apricots
250 ml/8 fl oz orange juice

AMERICAN

2lb boned leg of lamb
1 large onion
½ cup white wine vinegar
2 tablespoons sugar-free apricot jelly
1 tablespoon curry powder
1 teaspoon ground coriander
1 teaspoon ground cinnamon
1 garlic clove, crushed
2 bay leaves, crumbled
16 dried whole apricots
1 cup orange juice

Cut the lamb into 2.5 cm/1 inch cubes and the onion into 2.5 cm/1 inch pieces. Put the vinegar, jam (jelly), curry powder, spices, garlic and bay leaves into a saucepan. Stir on a low heat until the jam (jelly) has melted. Take from the heat, pour into a bowl and cool. Add the lamb and onions. Leave for at least 12 hours at room temperature.

Put the apricots into a saucepan with the orange juice. Bring to the boil and remove from the heat. Leave to soak for the same time as the lamb is marinated.

Just before cooking, place alternate pieces of lamb, onion and apricot on kebab skewers. Cook as directed for lamb kebabs, basting with any remaining marinade while they are cooking.

SPIT ROASTED LEG OF LAMB WITH HERBS

METRIC/IMPERIAL	*AMERICAN*
1.8-2g/4-4½lb leg of lamb	4-4½lb leg of lamb
1 sprig each thyme, marjoram and mint	1 sprig each thyme, marjoram and mint
basting mixture	*basting mixture*
125ml/4floz olive oil	½ cup olive oil
grated rind and juice 2 lemons	grated rind and juice 2 lemons
2 teaspoons paprika	2 teaspoons paprika
2 tablespoons chopped thyme	2 tablespoons chopped thyme
2 tablespoons chopped marjoram	2 tablespoons chopped marjoram
2 tablespoons chopped mint	2 tablespoons chopped mint
freshly ground black pepper	freshly ground black pepper
1 garlic clove, crushed	1 garlic clove, crushed

Remove and discard the pelvic bone from the fillet end of the leg (or ask your butcher to do it for you). This should leave a free flap of meat at the fillet end. Pull off the outer skin from the leg. Trim any remaining fat to a thickness of 6mm/¼inch.

Push the spit rod into the leg at the shank end and let it follow the bone until emerging at the fillet end. Mix the basting ingredients together. Brush the mixture all over the outer surface of the leg and over all cut surfaces at the fillet end. Put the herb sprigs inside the flap of meat at the fillet end. Fold over the flap. Either secure it with the spit rod, or, if it comes through the meat at the wrong angle for this, with cocktail sticks (wooden picks) that have been soaked for 10 minutes in cold water. Secure and tighten the spit forks. Insert a meat thermometer.

Place the lamb on the barbecue either beside or above hot coals. Cook for 1½-2 hours or until the required temperature is reached, basting frequently. Remove from the spit and leave to stand for 20 minutes before carving.

MOULDED LAMB WITH AVOCADO SAUCE

METRIC/IMPERIAL	AMERICAN
675 g/1½lb boned shoulder of lamb, about one-eighth fat	1½lb boned shoulder of lamb, about one-eighth fat
1 small onion	1 small onion
1 green pepper	1 sweet green pepper
1 garlic clove, finely chopped	1 garlic clove, finely chopped
2 tablespoons tomato paste	2 tablespoons tomato paste
2 teaspoons paprika	2 teaspoons paprika
1 teaspoon ground cumin	1 teaspoon ground cumin
¼ teaspoon chilli powder	¼ teaspoon chili powder
oil for greasing	oil for greasing
sauce	*sauce*
1 ripe avocado	1 ripe avocado
150 ml/¼ pint natural yoghurt	5 fl oz unflavored yoghurt
2 green or red chillies	2 green or red chilies
1 garlic clove, crushed	1 garlic clove, crushed

Mince (grind) the lamb, using a fine blade. Quarter the onion; core, seed and dice the pepper. Mince (grind) the lamb again with the onion, pepper and garlic. Add the tomato paste and spices and knead well with your fingers so the spices become well incorporated. Chill the mixture for 1 hour.

To make the sauce, peel, stone (pit) and mash the avocado. Gradually mix in the yoghurt. Core, seed and chop the chillies finely. Mix them into the avocado with the garlic.

Form the lamb into eight long sausage shapes. Oil four flat or square skewers. Push them through the centre of the sausages. Gently squeeze the sausages with your fingers to make sure they are firmly wrapped round the skewers.

Lay the skewers on an oiled barbecue grill 10-15 cm 4-6 inches over hot coals. Cook them for 20 minutes, or until they are lightly browned all over and feel firm to the touch, turning them several times.

Serve the sauce separately.

POULTRY AND GAME

Barbecue cooking keeps poultry and game moist and full of flavour. All types readily acquire the varied and subtle flavours of marinades and basting mixtures.

Preparing for the barbecue

A large, whole bird will not cook on an open barbecue unless it is jointed or split.

To split a chicken first turn it over on its breast. Using sharp kitchen scissors or poultry shears cut down on either side of the backbone to remove it completely. Turn the chicken over and press down hard to flatten it. Alternatively, cut through the skin only down the centre of the backbone. Using a sharp knife, loosen the skin and flesh from the rib cage. Remove the rib cage in one piece.

Cut small turkeys and capons into joints and cut the joints into smaller pieces. Cut ducks into four pieces as for chicken.

To joint smaller birds such as pheasant or guinea-fowl, remove the rib cage as above. Cut the two wing pieces off together, joined by a piece of the breast. Cut the remaining piece into two, each consisting of a leg and piece of breast.

Split pigeons, partridge and grouse by cutting out the back bone as for chicken.

Cut rabbit or hare into joints. Cook the joints singly or skewered in pairs.

All poultry and game are better marinated.

Cooking

Cook all poultry and game over a medium heat, joints and split birds skin side down first, turning and basting with the marinade throughout cooking.

Spit-roasting

All birds can be spit-roasted. Turkeys and capons must be of low weight. Small birds can be put on the spit together.

For smaller birds push the spit rod through the neck and out just above the tail. Larger birds will be better balanced if the spit rod goes diagonally through the neck flap just below the breast bone and out just above the tail.

In order to release excess fat, prick the skin of ducks all over with a fork and rub it lightly with salt.

Baste all birds frequently as they cook to keep them moist and to give added flavour.

Fill the body cavity of a rabbit with a herb and breadcrumb stuffing and sew it up. Push the spit through the centre of the rabbit through the neck end, pushing the holding forks through the shoulders and the tops of the legs. Truss the back legs and front legs securely. If wished, a rabbit can be larded with 6 mm/¼ inch thick strips or pork fat. Baste frequently while it is cooking.

All poultry should be cooked to 85°C/185°F. Insert a meat thermometer through the thickest part of the thigh.

Cooking Times

CHICKEN

Joints or split: 35-40 minutes total time
Spit-roasted: 1.125-1.35 kg/2½-3 lb, 1-1¼ hours
1.35-2 kg/3-4½ lb, 1¼-1¾ hours
Poussins, spit-roasted: 1 hour

DUCK

Joints: 40-50 minutes total time
Spit-roasted: 1.8 kg/4 lb: 1½-2 hours

TURKEY

Breast, sliced 10-12 minutes each side
Drumsticks 50-60 minutes total time
Spit-roasted: 2.7-3.2 kg/6-8 lb, 2½-3½ hours

CAPON

Spit-roasted: 2.25-2.7 kg/5-6 lb, 2-2½ hours

PHEASANT

45-50 minutes total time
Spit-roasted: 1-1¼ hours

GUINEA-FOWL

Joints or split 35-40 minutes total time
Spit-roasted: 1-1¼ hours

PIGEONS

Split 35-45 minutes total time
Spit-roasted: 1 hour

RABBIT

Jointed 25-30 minutes total time
Spit-roasted: 1-1¼ hours

HARE

Jointed 30-40 minutes total time

MARINADES FOR CHICKEN AND TURKEY

4 tablespoons/¼ cup olive oil, grated rind and juice 1 lemon, 1 teaspoon paprika, pinch cayenne pepper, 4 tablespoons chopped parsley. 1 tablespoon tomato paste can be added if wished *or*

150 ml/¼ pint natural (unflavored) yoghurt, 2 tablespoons chopped parsley, 1 tablespoon chopped thyme, 1 tablespoon chopped marjoram, freshly ground black pepper *or*

4 tablespoons/¼ cup oil, 4 tablespoons/¼ cup dry white wine, 4 tablespoons/¼ cup chopped fennel leaves, freshly ground black pepper *or*

6 tablespoons dry cider, 4 tablespoons/¼ cup oil, 4 chopped sage leaves, 1 teaspoon mustard powder or spiced granular mustard *or*

4 tablespoons/¼ cup oil, 2 tablespoons tamari, shoyu or soy sauce, 1 tablespoon Worcestershire sauce, 1 tablespoon tomato paste, ½ teaspoon mustard powder, 2 chopped spring onions (scallions) *or*

4 tablespoons/¼ cup oil, 6 tablespoons medium sherry, 1 chopped garlic clove, 1 tablespoon chopped oregano, 2 tablespoons chopped parsley *or*

150 ml/¼ pint natural (unflavored) yoghurt, 1 teaspoon each cumin and coriander seeds, coarsely crushed together, 1 crushed clove garlic, 25 g/1 oz peeled and grated fresh ginger root (or 1 teaspoon ground ginger and juice ½ lemon), 2 tablespoons chopped fresh coriander *or*

50 g/2 oz butter, melted and simmered for 2 minutes with 2 teaspoons each ground cumin, coriander and turmeric and 2 tablespoons mango chutney *or*

4 tablespoons/¼ cup olive oil, 4 tablespoons Chinese rice wine or dry sherry, 2 tablespoons tamari, shoyu or soy sauce, 15 g/½ oz peeled and grated fresh ginger root, 2 chopped spring onions (scallions), ½ teaspoon five-spice powder (optional) *or*

4 tablespoons/¼ cup oil, 4 tablespoons/¼ cup dry white wine, 2 tablespoons tarragon vinegar, 4 tablespoons chopped tarragon, 1 very finely chopped shallot or small onion, freshly ground black pepper.

CHORIZO BASTING SAUCE FOR CHICKEN

METRIC/IMPERIAL	*AMERICAN*
125 g/4 oz Spanish Chorizo sausage	¼ lb Spanish Chorizo sausage
450 g/1 lb tomatoes	1 lb tomatoes
1 tablespoon oil	1 tablespoon oil
1 teaspoon paprika	1 teaspoon paprika
¼ teaspoon cayenne pepper	¼ teaspoon cayenne pepper
1 garlic clove, crushed	1 garlic clove, crushed
2 tablespoons chopped parsley	2 tablespoons chopped parsley

Slice the sausage thinly. Scald, skin and chop the tomatoes. Heat the oil in a saucepan on a low heat. Add the pieces of sausage and cook gently until the red fat begins to run. Stir in the tomatoes, paprika, cayenne pepper and parsley. Cook gently, uncovered, until the tomatoes are reduced to a purée.

Remove the pieces of Chorizo. Dip the chicken into the tomato sauce before placing it on the grill. Baste twice during cooking.

Return the Chorizo pieces to the sauce. Reheat the sauce and serve separately.

The sauce can also be used for guinea-fowl or pheasant.

GREEN PEPPERCORN BASTING SAUCE FOR CHICKEN

METRIC/IMPERIAL	*AMERICAN*
75 g/3 oz butter	3 tablespoons butter
2 teaspoons green peppercorns, crushed	2 teaspoons green peppercorns, crushed
2 tablespoons chopped parsley	2 tablespoons chopped parsley
2 tablespoons dry red wine	2 tablespoons dry red wine

Melt the butter in a small pan on a low heat. Stir in the remaining ingredients. Take the pan from the heat and cool the mixture without letting the butter solidify.

Baste the chicken all over with the mixture before putting it on the barbecue grill. Baste a further three times during cooking.

This is also suitable for duck.

MARINADES FOR DUCK

Grated rind and juice 1 large orange, 6 tablespoons dry red wine, 2 tablespoons oil, 2 chopped sage leaves, 2 tablespoons chopped thyme *or*

6 tablespoons dry red wine, 2 tablespoons red wine vinegar, 2 tablespoons oil, 6 crushed juniper berries, 6 crushed allspice berries, freshly ground black pepper *or*

6 tablespoons Chinese rice wine or dry sherry, 2 tablespoons oil, 4 tablespoons tamari, shoyu or soy sauce, 15 g/½ oz peeled and grated fresh ginger root or 1 teaspoon ground ginger, 1 chopped garlic clove, 2 finely chopped spring onions (scallions), 1 teaspoon honey *or*

6 tablespoons dry cider, 2 tablespoons oil, 4 chopped sage leaves, 4 tablespoons/¼ cup chopped parsley, 1 tablespoon chopped thyme, 1 teaspoon coarsely crushed black peppercorns.

Top: Provençal Chicken Parcels; bottom: Pineapple Chicken with Rice; right: Oat Coated Drumsticks.

Spit Roasted Peking Duck.

MARINADES FOR GAME

125 ml/4 fl. oz/½ cup dry red wine, 4 tablespoons/¼ cup oil, 1 crushed garlic clove, 2 tablespoons each chopped parsley and thyme, ¼ teaspoon cayenne pepper *or*

4 tablespoons/¼ cup oil, grated rind and juice 1 lemon, grated rind and juice 1 medium orange, ½ teaspoon cayenne pepper, 2 tablespoons chopped thyme, 4 teaspoons chopped rosemary *or*

150 ml/¼ pint/5 fl. oz beer, 4 tablespoons oil, 4 chopped sage leaves, 1 tablespoon each chopped parsley and thyme, 1 very finely chopped small onion *or*

125 ml/4 fl. oz/½ cup dry white wine, 4 tablespoons/¼ cup oil, ¼ teaspoon ground mace, ¼ freshly grated nutmeg, 4 tablespoons chopped parsley, 1 tablespoon each chopped thyme and marjoram.

OAT-COATED DRUMSTICKS

METRIC/IMPERIAL	AMERICAN
12 chicken drumsticks	12 chicken drumsticks
marinade	*marinade*
6 tablespoons tomato juice	6 tablespoons tomato juice
1 tablespoon Worcestershire sauce	1 tablespoon Worcestershire sauce
4 tablespoons oil	¼ cup oil
1 teaspoon made English mustard	1 teaspoon made English mustard
coating	*coating*
125 g/4 oz porridge oats	4 oz porridge oats
1 teaspoon mustard powder	1 teaspoon mustard powder
1 teaspoon paprika	1 teaspoon paprika

Mix the ingredients for the marinade together. Turn the drumsticks in the marinade and leave for at least 4 hours at room temperature. Mix together the oats, mustard powder and paprika. Roll the drumsticks in the mixture to coat.

Cook 10-15 cm/4-6 inches over medium coals for 30 minutes, carefully turning several times. When done, the juices should run clear when the meat is pierced with a skewer.

ROSEMARY CHICKEN

1.575 kg/3½ lb roasting chicken
marinade
6 tablespoons olive oil
juice 1 lemon
4 tablespoons dry white wine
½ tablespoon chopped rosemary
2 tablespoons chopped parsley
1 medium onion, finely chopped
¼ teaspoon ground ginger
freshly ground black pepper
sauce
2 garlic cloves, crushed
2 tablespoons olive oil
2 rosemary sprigs, bruised not chopped
2 tablespoons tomato paste
225 ml/8 fl oz dry white wine

3½ lb roasting chicken
marinade
6 tablespoons olive oil
juice 1 lemon
4 tablespoons dry white wine
½ tablespoon chopped rosemary
2 tablespoons chopped parsley
1 medium onion, finely chopped
¼ teaspoon ground ginger
freshly ground black pepper
sauce
2 garlic cloves, crushed
2 tablespoons olive oil
2 rosemary sprigs, bruised, not chopped
2 tablespoons tomato paste
1 cup dry white wine

Joint the chicken. In a large, flat dish mix together the marinade ingredients. Turn the chicken joints in the marinade, cover and leave for 4 hours at room temperature, turning several times.

To make the sauce, heat the oil in a saucepan on a medium heat. Add the crushed garlic and leave until it begins to sizzle. Add the rosemary sprigs, tomato paste and wine. Stir well. Simmer for 2 minutes and keep warm.

Place the joints, skin side down, on an oiled grill 10-16 cm/4-6 inches over medium to hot coals. Cook for 5 minutes and then turn. Continue cooking for 25 minutes, turning every 5 minutes and basting with the marinade. When done, the juices should run clear when the thickest part of the flesh is pierced with a fork.

Serve the hot sauce separately.

PINEAPPLE CHICKEN WITH RICE

METRIC/IMPERIAL

1.575 kg/3½ lb roasting chicken
4 rings fresh pineapple, cored
marinade
225 ml/8 fl oz pineapple juice
4 tablespoons oil
2 tablespoons peach chutney
2 teaspoons curry powder
¼ teaspoon chilli powder
1 red pepper, cored, seeded and finely
chopped
1 garlic clove, crushed
rice
1 red pepper
1 green pepper
575 ml/1 pint stock
225 g/8 oz long grain brown rice
sea salt and finely ground black pepper
2 rings fresh pineapple

AMERICAN

3½ lb roasting chicken
4 rings fresh pineapple, cored
marinade
1 cup pineapple juice
¼ cup oil
2 tablespoons peach chutney
2 teaspoons curry powder
¼ teaspoon chili powder
1 sweet red pepper, cored, seeded and
finely chopped
1 garlic clove, crushed
rice
1 sweet red pepper
1 sweet green pepper
2½ cups stock
1¼ cups long grain brown rice
sea salt and freshly ground black pepper
2 rings fresh pineapple

Joint the chicken. In a large, flat dish mix together the marinade ingredients. Turn the chicken pieces in the marinade. Cover and leave for at least 2 hours at room temperature, turning several times.

Start cooking the rice so that it is ready at the same time as the chicken. Core, seed and chop the peppers finely. Put the stock and rice into a saucepan and bring to the boil. Add the peppers and season. Cover and cook gently for 45 minutes or until the rice is tender and all the stock absorbed. Chop the pineapple rings finely. Fork them into the rice. Cover and keep warm.

Take the chicken pieces from the marinade. Place skin side down on an oiled grill, 10-15 cm/4-6 inches over medium to hot coals. Cook for 5 minutes. Turn and continue cooking for 25 minutes, turning every 5 minutes and basting with the marinade. When done the juices should run clear when the thickest part of the flesh is pierced with a fork.

Just before the chicken is cooked, lay the pineapple slices on the grill and cook for 2 minutes each side to heat through.

Serve the chicken pieces each with a pineapple slice on top. Serve the rice separately.

SPLIT STUFFED CHICKEN

METRIC/IMPERIAL	AMERICAN
1.575 kg/3½ lb roasting chicken	3½ lb roasting chicken
350 g/12 oz back bacon rashers	8 lb Canadian bacon slices
175 g/6 oz mushrooms	6 oz mushrooms
2 tablespoons chopped thyme	2 tablespoons chopped thyme
freshly ground black pepper	freshly ground black pepper
6 tablespoons olive oil	6 tablespoons olive oil

Lay the chicken breast down. With sharp kitchen scissors or poultry shears, cut down on either side of the breast bone to remove it completely. Turn the chicken breast side up and press down to flatten it. Carefully loosen the skin at the neck end. Slide your hand under the skin and loosen the skin from the breast and leg areas.

Chop the bacon and mushrooms very finely. Mix together and add the thyme. Put an even layer of the mixture between the chicken skin and meat. Oil the chicken well.

Lay the chicken skin side down 10-15 cm/4-6 inches over hot coals. Leave for 5 minutes to sear. Turn over and sear the other side. Raise the grill rack. Continue cooking for a further 30 minutes, turning several times, until the juices run clear when the flesh is pierced with a fork.

PROVENÇAL CHICKEN PIECES

METRIC/IMPERIAL	AMERICAN
1.575 kg/3½ lb roasting chicken	3½ lb roasting chicken
450 g/1 lb tomatoes	1 lb tomatoes
1 green pepper	1 sweet green pepper
1 garlic clove, finely chopped	1 garlic clove, finely chopped
4 tablespoons olive oil	¼ cup olive oil
4 tablespoons medium sherry	¼ cup medium sherry
1 tablespoon chopped marjoram	1 tablespoon chopped marjoram
1 tablespoon chopped thyme	1 tablespoon chopped thyme
freshly ground black pepper	freshly ground black pepper

Cut the chicken into four joints. Chop the tomatoes finely. Core, seed and chop the pepper finely. Mix them in a bowl with the oil, sherry, herbs and pepper.

Put one chicken piece just off the centre of a square piece of foil. Spoon over half the tomato mixture. Bring the largest side of the foil over the top and seal the edges together at one side. Seal the ends and roll them upwards. Repeat with the other pieces of chicken.

Cook the parcels 10-15 cm/4-6 inches over hot coals for 50-60 minutes, turning several times.

To serve, unwrap the parcels onto individual plates.

BREADCRUMBED SPITTED CHICKEN

METRIC/IMPERIAL

1.35 kg/3 lb roasting chicken
25 g/1 oz seasoned wholewheat flour
1 egg, beaten
75 g/3 oz fresh, fine wholewheat
  breadcrumbs
sauce
75 g/3 oz butter
1 tablespoon wholewheat flour
½ tablespoon mustard powder
275 ml/½ pint chicken stock
juice 1 lemon
1 teaspoon paprika
½ teaspoon chilli powder
1 garlic clove, crushed
¼ teaspoon Tabasco sauce
1 teaspoon Worcestershire sauce

AMERICAN

3 lb roasting chicken
3 tablespoons seasoned wholewheat flour
1 egg, beaten
1½ cups fresh, fine wholewheat
  breadcrumbs
sauce
6 tablespoons butter
1 tablespoon wholewheat flour
½ teaspoon mustard powder
1¼ cups chicken stock
juice 1 lemon
1 teaspoon paprika
½ teaspoon chili powder
1 garlic clove, crushed
¼ teaspoon Tabasco sauce
1 teaspoon Worcestershire sauce

To make the sauce, melt 25 g/1 oz/2 tablespoons butter in a saucepan on a medium heat. Stir in the flour, mustard powder and stock. Bring to the boil. Add the lemon juice, spices, garlic and sauces. Simmer for 5 minutes, stirring occasionally. Take the pan from the heat and beat in the remaining butter in small pieces.

Truss the chicken and secure it firmly on a spit. Coat with seasoned flour and brush with the beaten egg. Press the breadcrumbs firmly into the egg.

Baste the chicken well with the sauce.

Secure the spit in place. Cook for about 1½ hours, basting frequently with the sauce. When done the juices should run clear when the flesh is pierced with a fork and the internal temperature is 88°C/190°F.

TURKEY AND LEMON KEBABS

METRIC/IMPERIAL

one 900 g/2 lb turkey breast
50 g/2 oz butter
125 ml/4 fl oz dry white wine
grated rind 1 lemon
2 tablespoons chopped tarragon
2 tablespoons chopped parsley
freshly ground black pepper
1 large lemon

AMERICAN

one 2 lb turkey breast
¼ cup butter
½ cup dry white wine
grated rind 1 lemon
2 tablespoons chopped tarragon
2 tablespoons chopped parsley
freshly ground black pepper
1 large lemon

Cut the turkey breast into 2.5 cm/1 inch square pieces. Put the butter into a small pan and melt on a low heat. Stir in the lemon rind, wine, tarragon, parsley and season with the pepper. Take the pan from the heat and pour the mixture into a large, flat dish.

Turn the turkey pieces in the mixture and leave for 1-2 hours at room temperature. Cut the whole lemon into 3 mm/⅛ inch slices. Quarter them.

Put a piece of lemon on to a kebab skewer, two pieces of turkey and one more piece of lemon. Continue in this way with all the pieces of turkey, dividing it between four skewers. End each one with a piece of lemon.

Cook 10-15 cm/4-6 inches over medium coals for 20 minutes, turning twice.

DUCK WITH ORANGE AND OLIVES

METRIC/IMPERIAL	AMERICAN
4 duck joints	4 duck joints
juice 2 medium oranges	juice 2 medium oranges
6 tablespoons dry white wine	6 tablespoons dry white wine
3 tablespoons olive oil	3 tablespoons olice oil
8 green olives	8 green olives
2 teaspoons Dijon mustard	2 teaspoons Dijon mustard
1 medium orange	1 medium orange

Mix together the orange juice, wine and 2 tablespoons oil. Stone (pit), chop and crush the olives and add them to the mixture with the mustard. Mix well.

Put the mixture into a large, flat dish. Turn the duck portions in it and leave for at least 4 hours at room temperature.

Lay the duck joints on a grill rack 10-15 cm/4-6 inches over hot coals and sear for 4 minutes on each side. Move the joints to one side over a medium heat and cook for a further 30 minutes, turning several times and moving them away from any flare-ups that their dripping fat may cause.

Just before they are done, cut the remaining orange into four thick slices. Brush with the remaining oil. Grill for 1 minute on each side over hot coals.

To serve, lay the orange slices on the duck portions.

SPIT-ROASTED PEKING DUCK

METRIC/IMPERIAL	AMERICAN
1.8 kg/4 lb duck	4 lb duck
5 tablespoons honey	5 tablespoons honey
15 g/½ oz fresh ginger root, peeled and chopped	½ oz fresh ginger root, peeled and chopped
2 spring onions, chopped	2 scallions, chopped
2 tablespoons soy, tamari or shoyu sauce	2 tablespoons soy, tamari or shoyu sauce
2 tablespoons Chinese rice wine or dry sherry	2 tablespoons Chinese rice wine or dry sherry
½ teaspoon fine sea salt	½ teaspoon fine sea salt
sauce 1	*sauce 1*
125 ml/4 fl oz hoisin sauce	½ cup hoisin sauce
3 tablespoons soy, tamari or shoyu sauce	3 tablespoons soy, tamari or shoyu sauce
2 tablespoons sesame oil	2 tablespoons sesame oil
sauce 2	*sauce 2*
2 tablespoons tahini (sesame paste)	2 tablespoons tahini (sesame paste)
4 tablespoons soy, tamari or shoyu sauce	¼ cup soy, tamari or shoyu sauce
4 tablespoons sesame oil	¼ cup sesame oil
2 tablespoons white wine vinegar	2 tablespoons white wine vinegar
wholewheat mandarin pancakes	*wholewheat mandarin pancakes*
225 g/8 oz wholewheat flour	2 cups wholewheat flour
150 ml/¼ pint boiling water	¼ pint boiling water
3 tablespoons sesame oil	3 tablespoons sesame oil
for serving	*for serving*
1 cucumber	1 cucumber
4 celery sticks	4 celery sticks
6 spring onions	6 scallions

Put enough water to cover the duck into a large saucepan. Add 3 tablespoons honey, the ginger root and spring onions (scallions). Bring the water to the boil. Put in the duck and cook for 1 minute. Take it out and drain. Hang up by the legs in a cool, airy place to dry overnight. Two hours before cooking, mix together the remaining honey, soy sauce, wine or sherry and salt. Brush the mixture over the duck and hang it up again to dry.

Make the sauces by mixing their respective ingredients together.

To make the pancakes, put the flour into a bowl and make a well in the centre. Mix the water with ½ tablespoon oil and gradually stir into the flour. Divide the dough in half. Roll each piece into a sausage shape about 5 cm/2 inches in diameter. Cut each roll in to six pieces. Roll out the pieces to make thin, flat pancakes about 18 cm/7 inches in diamter.

Brush one side of half the pancakes with the sesame oil. Sandwich them together with the remaining pancakes.

Set a heavy frying pan on a high heat without any fat. When the pan is hot, reduce the heat to moderate. Fry one pancake sandwich at a time, turning when it starts to rise and bubble and when small brown spots appear on the underside. When both sides are done, gently peel the two pancakes apart and fold them in half, oiled side inwards.

Wrap the pancakes in a clean linen towel and keep warm in a low oven.

Truss the duck and prick the skin with a fork or skewer. Secure firmly on the spit. Place a drip tray underneath the spit. Cook either beside or in front of hot coals for 1½-2 hours or until the skin is dark and crisp and the juices run clear when the flesh is pierced with a fork.

While the duck is cooking, cut the cucumber and celery into 5 cm/2 inch lengths. Cut the spring onions (scallions) into 7.5 cm/3 inch lengths and make several cuts in either end. Soak them in iced water for 30 minutes so the ends curl. Chop the remaining spring onions (scallions) finely.

When the duck is cooked, remove the breast and wings and slice the meat. Remove the legs and cut each one into two. Arrange the meat and pieces of leg on a serving plate.

To eat, take a spring onion (scallion) and use it to brush a little of a chosen sauce over a pancake. Put a piece of duck, cucumber, celery and some chopped spring onion (scallion) on to the pancake. Roll or fold the pancake and eat with your fingers.

CURRIED GUINEA-FOWL

METRIC/IMPERIAL	AMERICAN
2 guinea-fowl	2 guinea fowl
4 tablespoons olive oil	¼ cup olive oil
2 tablespoons mango chutney	2 tablespoons mango chutney
1 garlic clove, crushed with pinch sea salt	1 garlic clove, crushed with pinch sea salt
1 teaspoon ground turmeric	1 teaspoon ground turmeric
2 teaspoons hot Madras curry powder	2 teaspoons hot Madras curry powder
1 teaspoon ground coriander	1 teaspoon ground coriander
1 teaspoon cumin seeds	1 teaspoon cumin seeds

Split the guinea-fowl down the back and remove the rib cage, leaving the leg and wing bones in place.

In a large, flat dish mix the remaining ingredients together. Turn the guinea-fowl in the mixture. Leave in the marinade, one on top of the other if necessary, for 4 hours at room temperature.

Cook on an oiled grill 10-15 cm/4-6 inches over medium coals for 5 minutes, skin side down. Turn over and continue cooking for a further 30 minutes, turning several times. The juices should run clear when the flesh is pierced with a fork.

To serve, cut the two wings off together with a piece of breast joining them in the centre. Then cut the remaining piece in half to give two legs, each with a small portion of breast attached.

Serves 4-6.

PHEASANT MARINATED IN LEMON JUICE

METRIC/IMPERIAL	AMERICAN
1 brace pheasants	2 pheasants
grated rind and juice 2 lemons	grated rind and juice 2 lemons
125 ml/4 fl oz olive oil	½ cup olive oil
1 small onion, finely chopped	1 small onion, finely chopped
1 garlic clove, crushed	1 garlic clove, crushed
1 teaspoon paprika	1 teaspoon paprika
2 tablespoons chopped thyme	2 tablespoons chopped thyme

Split the skin of each pheasant down the backbone. Keeping the knife close to the bones, remove the rib cage. Open the pheasants out flat. Cut each one into three pieces by cutting across to remove the two wings together. Then separate the two legs.

In a large, flat dish mix together the remaining ingredients. Turn the pieces of pheasant in the marinade and leave in the refrigerator for 24 hours.

Cook skin side down on an oiled grill 10-15 cm/4-6 inches over medium coals for 5 minutes. Turn and cook for a further 45 minutes, turning and basting frequently with any remaining marinade. The juices should run clear when the flesh is pierced with a fork.
Serves 4-6.

RABBIT MARINATED WITH YOGHURT AND SWEET HERBS

METRIC/IMPERIAL	AMERICAN
one large or two small rabbits	one large or two small rabbits
150 ml/¼ pint natural yoghurt	5 fl oz unflavored yoghurt
2 tablespoons chopped parsley	2 tablespoons chopped parsley
1 tablespoon chopped thyme	1 tablespoon chopped thyme
1 tablespoon chopped marjoram	1 tablespoon chopped marjoram
½ teaspoon mustard powder	½ teaspoon mustard powder

Cut the rabbit into joints. In a flat dish mix together the remaining ingredients. Turn the rabbit pieces in the mixture. Leave for at least 6 hours at room temperature.

Lay the rabbit joints on an oiled grill 10-15 cm/4-6 inches over medium coals and cook for 30 minutes, turning several times, or until the flesh feels very tender when pierced with a fork.

VEGETARIAN DISHES

It is certainly possible to be a vegetarian or to entertain vegetarian guests and still be able to enjoy barbecued meals.

Barbecued vegetables can be served with a variety of different cheeses and ready-cooked dishes of pulses. They can also be combined with cheese, eggs or nuts as in the recipes below. Nut cutlets can be cooked in a hinged wire grill, and so too can burgers made from beans and lentils.

Many different types of cheese can be grilled and topped with herbs or spices, while others can be given coatings of nuts or breadcrumbs, or cooked on skewers.

Eggs can be baked inside bread rolls, inside shells of green pepper or in scooped-out baked potatoes.

GRILLED CHEESE SLICES

Suitable cheeses: Cheddar, smoked Cheddar, Double Gloucester, Double Gloucester with chives, Lancashire, Edam, Gouda, Gruyère, Emmenthal, Jarlsberg, Fontina, Provolone.

Cut the cheese into 1.5 cm/⅝ inch thick slices. Three slices about 5 cm/2 inches square will be ample for each person.

Before cooking, dust the cheese with one of the following (if you are using a mixture of cheeses, use a different flavouring for each cheese): freshly grated nutmeg, ground mace, paprika, curry powder, or spread a little tomato paste or mild mustard over each side.

Place the slices directly on an oiled grill 20-25 cm/8-10 inches over hot coals, for only 1 minute each side or until the cheese begins to soften. As soon as the cheese has been turned place walnut halves, tomato slices or halved olives on top, or sprinkle with chopped parsley.

Serve as soon as possible since cold grilled cheese tends to become hard.

NUT COATED GOATS' CHEESE

METRIC/IMPERIAL	AMERICAN
four 2 cm/¾ inch slices from a 6-8 cm/2½-3½ inch diameter 'log' of goats' cheese, either plain or herb flavoured	four ¾ inch slices from a 2½-3½ inch diameter 'log' of goats' cheese, either plain or herb flavored
50 g/2 oz shelled hazelnuts	½ cup shelled hazelnuts
50 g/2 oz shelled walnuts	½ cup shelled walnuts
1 teaspoon paprika	1 teaspoon paprika
1 teaspoon dried mixed herbs (for plain cheese only)	1 teaspoon dried mixed herbs (for plain cheese only)

Grind the nuts finely. Mix them together and season with the paprika and herbs if using. Coat the slices of cheese in the nut mixture.

Put the cheese slices into a hinged grill. Cook 15-20 cm/6-8 inches over medium coals for 2 minutes on each side or until they feel soft. Serve as soon as possible with crispbreads.

NUT-COATED BEL PAESE Make as above using eight around 25 g/1 oz portions of Bel Paese. Cook for 2 minutes on each side.

ROULÉ IN VINE LEAVES

METRIC/IMPERIAL	AMERICAN
three 2 cm/¾ inch thick slices from a herb flavoured roulé cheese	three ¾ inch thick slices from a log-shaped herb flavored soft cheese
24 vine leaves, fresh or brined	24 vine leaves, fresh or brined

Cut each slice of cheese into quarters. Lay the vine leaves with the veined side uppermost. Lay a piece of cheese on one vine leaf at the stalk end. Fold over the stalk, then the two sides and roll up. Repeat, using a second vine leaf. Wrap the remaining pieces of cheese in the same way.

Place the parcels in a hinged grill. Cook 15-20 cm/6-8 inches over medium coals for 3 minutes on each side or until the cheese feels soft.

Serve as soon as possible. The charred outer coating of vine leaves should be discarded. The inner one, which will have remained moist, can be eaten.

Other cheeses suitable for cooking in vine leaves are:
Brie, Camembert, Bel Paese, firm goats' cheese, Lancashire, Double Gloucester, Emmenthal, Gruyère. The firmer, harder cheeses may need up to 5 minutes cooking on each side.

MOZARELLA KEBABS

METRIC/IMPERIAL	AMERICAN
twenty-four 2.5 cm/1 inch cubes Mozarella cheese	twenty-four 1 inch cubes Mozarella cheese
thirty-two 2.5 cm/1 inch cubes wholewheat bread	thirty-two 1 inch cubes wholewheat bread
24 tomato wedges	24 tomato wedges
parsley butter	*parsley butter*
75 g/3 oz butter	6 tablespoons butter
4 tablespoons chopped parsley	¼ cup chopped parsley
2 tablespoons tomato paste	2 tablespoons tomato paste

Alternate pieces of bread, cheese and tomato on to eight kebab skewers, starting and ending with bread.

To make the parsley butter, put the butter into a small pan and melt gently on the grill. Mix in the parsley and tomato paste. Put to one side of the grill to keep warm.

Cook the kebabs 10-15 cm/4-6 inches over hot coals for about 2 minutes, or until the cheese is soft but not runny, turning several times.

Brush the kebabs with the parsley butter and serve as soon as possible.

TOMATO AND MOZARELLA TOASTS

METRIC/IMPERIAL	AMERICAN
16 large slices wholewheat bread	16 large slices wholewheat bread
125 g/4 oz butter, softened	½ cup butter, softened
2 tablespoons tomato paste	2 tablespoons tomato paste
2 tablespoons chopped thyme	2 tablespoons chopped thyme
8 medium sized tomatoes	8 medium sized tomatoes
225 g/8 oz Mozarella cheese	½ lb Mozarella cheese
16 black olives	16 black olives

Beat the butter with the tomato paste and thyme. Spread over one side of each slice of bread. Cut each tomato into four slices. Lay four tomato slices on each of the eight slices of bread. Slice the cheese thinly and lay it on top of the tomatoes. Halve and stone (pit) the olives and put them on top of the cheese. Top with the remaining bread slices.

Grill the sandwiches 15-20 cm/6-8 inches over hot coals for 2 minutes on each side, or until browned and crisp, turning very carefully.

TOMATO AND EMMENTHAL TOASTS Make as above, using Emmenthal cheese instead of Mozarella. Omit the olives and spread the cheese thinly with a spiced mild mustard.

CHEESE FILLED AUBERGINES (EGGPLANTS)

METRIC/IMPERIAL	AMERICAN
4 medium aubergines, about 225g/8oz each	4 medium eggplants, about ½lb each
6 tablespoons oil	6 tablespoons oil
juice 1 lemon	juice 1 lemon
1 tablespoon tomato paste	1 tablespoon tomato paste
1 garlic clove, crushed	1 garlic clove, crushed
freshly ground black pepper	freshly ground black pepper
175g/6oz Gruyère cheese, finely grated	1¼ cups finely grated Gruyère cheese

Cut each aubergine (eggplants) in half lengthways. make a slit in the side of each half, about three-quarters of the way through, making them into pockets. Sprinkle with salt and leave for 20 minutes in a colander to drain. Rinse with cold water and dry with kitchen paper.

Beat together the oil, lemon juice, tomato paste, garlic and pepper. Brush the aubergines (eggplants), inside and out, with the mixture and leave for 20 minutes. Fill the pockets with the cheese, packing it in firmly.

Grill skin side down first, 10-15cm/4-6inches over hot coals, for 5-7 minutes on each side, or until soft.

HERB OMELETTES IN PEPPERS

METRIC/IMPERIAL	AMERICAN
4 large, even-sized green peppers	4 large, even-sized sweet green peppers
8 eggs	8 eggs
2 tablespoons mixed chopped fresh herbs or 2 teaspoons dried	2 tablespoons mixed chopped fresh herbs or 2 teaspoons dried
8 tomato rings	8 tomato rings

Core the peppers. Cut them carefully in half lengthways and remove the seeds. If any of the pepper halves do not stand completely flat, support them with twists of cooking foil.

Beat the eggs with herbs. Pour the mixture into the pepper halves. Lay sheets of foil on the grill 10-15cm/4-6inches over medium coals, each one large enough to enclose two pepper halves. Lay two pepper halves on each piece of foil, supporting them with more twists of foil so they stand upright. Bring the sides of the foil sheets up and over the peppers. Cook for about 30 minutes or until the eggs are set. Just before they are completely set, lay a tomato ring on each.

EGG BASKETS

METRIC/IMPERIAL	AMERICAN
8 wholewheat bread rolls	8 wholewheat bread rolls
75g/3oz Cheddar cheese, finely grated	¾ cup finely grated Cheddar cheese
8 eggs	8 eggs

Cut 6mm/¼inch slices from the tops of the rolls and reserve them. Hollow out the crumb from the rolls leaving shells about 6mm/¼inch thick. Put about 2 teaspoons grated cheese in the base of each roll. Carefully break in an egg. Scatter 2 teaspoons cheese over the top. Put back the tops of the rolls. Wrap each roll separately in foil.

Cook 10-15cm/4-6inches over low to medium coals for 30 minutes without turning. The eggs should be just set.

CHICK PEA PATTIES WITH SPICED LEMON SAUCE

METRIC/IMPERIAL	AMERICAN
275g/10oz chick peas, soaked and cooked	1¼ cups Garbanzo beans, soaked and cooked
juice ½ lemon	juice ½ lemon
4 tablespoons natural yoghurt	¼ cup unflavored yoghurt
4 tablespoons tahini	¼ cup tahini
4 tablespoons chopped parsley	¼ cup chopped parsley
25g/1oz wholewheat flour	3 tablespoons wholewheat flour
oil	oil
sauce	*sauce*
3 tablespoons oil	3 tablespoons oil
1 teaspoon ground coriander	1 teaspoon ground coriander
1 teaspoon ground cumin	1 teaspoon ground cumin
1½ tablespoons wholewheat flour	1½ tablespoons wholewheat flour
275ml/½ pint stock	1¼ cups stock
grated rind and juice 1 lemon	grated rind and juice 1 lemon
4 tablespoons chopped parlsey	¼ cup chopped parsley

Mash the chick peas (Garbanzo beans) well. Mix in the lemon juice, yoghurt, tahini and parsley. Form the mixture in to eight round flat patties. Place on a flat plate or board and put into the refrigerator for at least 30 minutes to set into shape. Coat in flour and brush lightly with oil.

To make the sauce, heat the oil in a saucepan on a low heat. Stir in the spices and cook gently for 5 minutes taking care not to let them burn. Stir in the flour and stock. Bring the sauce to the boil, stirring. Add the lemon rind and juice and parsley. Simmer, uncovered, for 5 minutes, stirring occasionally.

To cook the patties, place them in an oiled hinged grill. Cook them 10-15 cm/4-6 inches over hot coals for about 4 minutes on each side or until they are heated through and browned.
Serve the sauce separately.

NUT FILLED COURGETTES (ZUCCHINI)

METRIC/IMPERIAL	*AMERICAN*
6 courgettes 15-18 cm/6-7 inches long	6 zucchini, 6-7 inches long
50 g/2 oz shelled walnuts, ground	½ cup shelled walnuts, ground
50 g/2 oz cashew nuts, ground	½ cup cashew nuts, ground
3 tablespoons oil	3 tablespoons oil
1 medium onion, finely chopped	1 medium onion, finely chopped
1 garlic clove, finely chopped	1 garlic clove, finely chopped
150 g/5 oz fresh wholewheat breadcrumbs	1½ cups fresh wholewheat breadcrumbs
1 tablespoon tomato paste	1 tablespoon tomato paste
125 ml/4 fl oz stock	½ cup stock
3 sage leaves, chopped	3 sage leaves, chopped
1 tablespoon chopped thyme	1 tablespoon chopped thyme
sauce	*sauce*
2 tablespoons oil	2 tablespoons oil
1 tablespoon wholewheat flour	1 tablespoon wholewheat flour
1 tablespoon tomato paste	1 tablespoon tomato paste
275 ml/½ pint stock	1¼ cups stock
2 sage leaves, chopped	2 sage leaves, chopped
2 teaspoons chopped thyme	2 teaspoons chopped thyme

Cut the courgettes (zucchini) in half lengthways. Scoop out all the seeds, leaving shells about 3 mm/⅛ inch thick.

Heat the oil in a frying pan on a low heat. Add the onion and garlic and cook until soft and golden. Take the pan from the heat. Mix in all the remaining ingredients. Fill the courgettes (zucchini) with the mixture.

To make the sauce, heat the oil in a saucepan on a low heat. Stir in the flour and tomato paste. Add the stock and bring to the boil, stirring. Add the herbs. Simmer, uncovered, for 5 minutes.

Lay a sheet of oiled foil on the grill 10-15 cm/4-6 inches over hot coals. Lay the courgettes (zucchini) on the foil, stuffed side down, and cook for 5 minutes. Just before they are done brush the undersides with oil. Carefully turn the courgettes (zucchini) over and continue to cook for about 10 minutes or until heated through and beginning to soften.
Serve the sauce separately.

VEGETABLES

Most vegetables can be cooked on an open barbecue, some directly on the grill and others wrapped in foil.

It is usually quite easy to cook both vegetables and meat together on the barbecue so that they will be ready at the same time. Foil parcels can be placed round the edge of the grill so the vegetables cook slowly in their own juices. Meat cooking in the centre of the grill can be put to one side when it is nearly cooked, to enable unwrapped vegetables to be cooked quickly over the high heat.

In order to prevent splits and a leakage of moisture, use heavy duty foil or a double thickness of standard foil. Butter or oil it well.

For easy turning and even cooking, seal foil packets at the sides rather than on top.

ARTICHOKES, GLOBE: Remove the stems and trim away the top third of the leaves. Place each one on a separate sheet of lightly buttered or oiled foil. Pour in 1 tablespoon water and add either a small piece of butter or 1 tablespoon oil. The water can be replaced with red or white wine or lemon juice. Seal tightly. Cook 10-15 cm/4-6 inches over medium coals, turning every 10 minutes, for 1 hour or until the base is tender.

ARTICHOKES, JERUSALEM: Peel and slice. Dip into acidulated water. Wrap in 225 g/8 oz packets. Add 2 tablespoons water or stock and dot with butter. Season with pepper and a sprinkling of mustard powder. Add chopped parsley or sage. Cook for 45 minutes 10-15 cm/4-6 inches over medium coals, turning twice.

AUBERGINES(Eggplant): Cut into 1.5 cm/½ inch thick slices either crossways or lengthways. Put into a colander, sprinkle with sea salt and leave to drain for 20 minutes. Rinse with cold water and dry with kitchen paper. Brush with oil and season. Grill 10-15 cm/4-6 inches over hot coals for 6-8 minutes, turning once, or until lightly browned and soft. The oil can be mixed with lemon juice and/or natural (unflavored) yoghurt, tomato paste, spices such as cinnamon, cumin, coriander, and crushed garlic.

For aubergine (eggplant) kebabs cut into 2.5 cm/1 inch cubes. Salt as above. Brush with oil mixture or marinate. Thread on to kebab skewers either alone or with pieces of courgette (zucchini), sweet red or green peppers, pieces of onion, small mushrooms and tomatoes.

ASPARAGUS: Trim away the tough ends. Scrape away any tough fibrous pieces from the outside. Wrap 225 g/8 oz at a time. Dot with butter or pour in 2 tablespoons oil. A squeeze of lemon juice can be added. Season lightly with cayenne pepper. Sprinkle with chopped parsley and/or grated Cheddar or Parmesan cheese. Cook 10-15 cm/4-6 inches over medium coals for 20 minutes, or until tender, turning several times.

Vegetarian Dishes. Top: Herb Omelettes in Peppers; right: Nut Coated Goat's Cheese; bottom right: Nut Filled Courgettes (Zucchini); left: Egg Baskets.

Top: Blackberry & Apple Parcels; Strawberry Kebabs with Carob Fondue; Peach & Nectarine Kebabs with Apricot Fondue.

BROAD BEANS (Lima): Wrap 225g/8oz shelled beans at a time. Add 2 tablespoons water, dry cider or stock. Dot with butter or add 2 tablespoons oil. Add 2 tablespoons chopped parsley and/or 1 tablespoon chopped summer savory if wished, or 25g/1oz finely chopped lean bacon per packet. Cook 10-15cm/4-6inches over medium coals for 20 minutes, turning several times.

BEANS, FRENCH (Green, French style): Top and tail. Leave whole or break into short lengths. Wrap 225g/8oz at a time. Add 2 tablespoons water or wine. Dot with butter or add 2 tablespoons oil. Flavour with chopped parsley, thyme or marjoram and/or a little freshly grated nutmeg. 25g/1oz finely chopped lean bacon can be added if wished. Cook for about 20 minutes 10-15cm/4-6inches over medium coals, turning several times.

BEANS, RUNNER (Green): Trim tops and edges and slice. Wrap 225g/8oz at a time. Add 1 tablespoon water and 1 tablespoon oil. Flavour with 1 tablespoon either thyme, marjoram or summer savory. 25g/1oz finely chopped bacon can be added if wished. Cook 10-15cm/4-6inches over medium coals for 15-20 minutes, turning several times.

BEETROOT (Beets): Choose small beetroot. Leave 1.5cm/½ inch stalk and do not peel or trim ends. Wrap in well-oiled foil. Bake directly over medium coals for 40 minutes or until tender. Peel before serving.

CABBAGE: Shred finely. Wrap 225g/8oz at a time. Add 2 tablespoons water, cider or stock plus 1 tablespoon oil or 15g/½oz butter. Season well with pepper. Add if wished, ½ teaspoon caraway or dill seeds, 2 chopped sage leaves, ¼ teaspoon crushed juniper or allspice berries, 2 tablespoons chopped parsley or fennel. Cook 10-15cm/4-6inches over low coals, or right on the edge of the barbecue for 30 minutes, turning frequently.

CARROTS: Leave tiny carrots whole. Slice larger ones or cut them into matchstick pieces. Wrap 225g/8oz at a time in buttered or oiled foil. Add 2 tablespoons water or stock plus 15g/½oz butter or 1 tablespoon oil. Flavour with chopped parsley, chervil or marjoram and/or freshly grated nutmeg. Cook 10-15cm/4-6inches over hot coals for 25-30 minutes, turning several times.

CELERY: Cut into 2.5-5cm/1-2inch pieces or into matchstick pieces. Wrap 225g/8oz per packet. Add 1 tablespoon water, stock or cider plus 1 tablespoon oil or 15g/½oz butter. Sprinkle with freshly grated nutmeg and/or chopped parsley or sage. Cook 10-15cm/4-6inches over medium coals for 15-20 minutes, turning several times.

COURGETTES (Zucchini): If small, halve lengthways only. If large cut into 1.5cm/½inch slices. For kebabs, cut small ones into 2.5cm/1inch lengths or large ones into 2.5cm/1inch dice. Brush with oil or melted butter. Season with freshly ground black pepper, cayenne pepper or paprika, 1 tablespoon tomato paste or lemon juice, or 2 tablespoons red or white wine can be mixed with 4 tablepoons oil for a basting mixture or marinade. 1 tablespoon chopped thyme or marjoram, or 2 tablespoons chopped parsley can be added. Cook 10-15 cm/4-6 inches over medium coals for 15-20 minutes, turning several times. On kebabs mix courgettes with aubergines (eggplant), sweet red or green peppers, pieces of onion, and/or small mushrooms or tomatoes.

MARINADE FOR COURGETTES (ZUCCHINI)

METRIC/IMPERIAL	*AMERICAN*
4 tablespoons olive oil	¼ cup olive oil
juice ½ lemon	juice ½ lemon
2 tablespoons soured cream	2 tablespoons dairy sour cream
1 teaspoon Dijon mustard	1 teaspoon Dijon mustard
2 tablespoons chopped thyme	2 tablespoons chopped thyme

Mix all the ingredients together. Leave the courgettes in the marinade for 30 minutes.

CUCUMBER: Cut lengthways into quarters. Peel and remove the seeds. Cut the quarters into 2.5 cm/1 inch lengths. Wrap half a large cucumber in each packet. Use oiled foil and add 1 tablespoon oil to the cucumber. Add 1 tablespoon chopped dill or ½ teaspoon dill seeds, 1 tablespoon chopped fennel or 2 tablespoons chopped parsley. Season with freshly ground black pepper or cayenne pepper. Cook 10-15 cm/4-6 inch over medium coals for 10-15 minutes, turning several times.

FLORENCE FENNEL: Halve the bulb. Cut the halves into 1.5 cm/½ inch thick slices. Wrap the halves separately. Add 2 tablespoons oil plus 1 tablespoon freshly squeezed orange juice and 1 tablespoon chopped parsley. Cook 10-15 cm/4-6 inches over medium coals for 20 minutes, turning several times.

MUSHROOMS: For large mushrooms remove or trim the stalks. Brush the caps with oil or melted butter to which can be added Dijon, spiced granular, or German mustard, tomato paste or spices such as curry powder or paprika. Crushed garlic and/or chopped herbs such as parsley or thyme may also be added. Grill the caps for about 4 minutes each side 10-15 cm/4-6 inches over hot coals, stalk side down first. After turning, the caps may be sprinkled with a little grated Cheddar, Gruyère or Edam cheese. Small and button mushrooms can be brushed with the same mixtures and threaded on to kebab skewers either alone or with small tomatoes, pieces of sweet pepper, onion, cubes of aubergine (eggplant) or courgette (zucchini).

ONIONS: Use medium-sized onions for cooking whole. Leave them in their skins and brush with oil. Cook 10-15 cm/4-6 inches above medium coals for 45-50 minutes or until they feel soft when gently squeezed. For serving cut a cross in the top of each one, insert a piece of butter and sprinkle with parsley. A flavoured butter such as those used for French bread (page 70) can also be used.

Alternatively the onions can be peeled and wrapped in foil. Make a cross in the top and put a small piece of butter or flavoured butter on top. Cook 10-15 cm/4-6 inches over medium coals for 45-50 minutes.

Grilled Onion Slices: Cut medium to large onions into 1 cm/⅜ inch thick round slices. Brush with melted butter or oil and put into a hinged wire grill. Cook 10-15 cm/4-6 inches over hot coals for 4-5 minutes each side or until browned and beginning to soften. Sprinkle with chopped parsley or a small amount of chopped thyme just before they are cooked.

Small onions can be blanched in boiling water for 5 minutes, drained, threaded on kebab skewers and brushed with oil or melted butter. Cook 10-15 cm/4-6 inches over hot coals for about 10 minutes or until browned and beginning to soften, turning several times.

PEAS: Wrap 225 g/8 oz shelled peas in foil. Add 2 tablespoons water or stock plus 1 tablespoon oil or 15 g/½ oz butter. 2 tablespoons chopped parsley, 1 tablespoon chopped mint or ½ small firm lettuce, shredded, or 3 chopped spring onions (scallions) may also be added. Instead of water and butter, 4 tablespoons double (heavy) cream can be used.

PEPPERS, SWEET RED AND GREEN: Core, seed and cut into 2.5 cm/1 inch squares and thread on to kebab skewers with other vegetables such as mushrooms, small tomatoes, courgettes (zucchini) and aubergines (eggplant). Brush with oil or melted butter. Peppers can be cooked from raw on skewers or they can be blanched in boiling water for 1 minute and drained. This will prevent their splitting on the skewers.

Grilled Whole Peppers: Oil the peppers and cook 10-15 cm/4-6 inches over hot coals, turning frequently, until the skins are charred. Peel off the skins as soon as they are cool enough to handle. Cut into lengthways quarters and place in a dish. Pour an oil and vinegar dressing over them. These are best cooked before the meat so that you can skin them while the meat is cooking. A mixture of red and green peppers is effective if arranged attractively.

POTATOES: *Jacket:* Scrub even-sized potatoes and brush with oil. Prick on both sides with a fork. Either lay directly on the grill or secure on a potato spike. Cook 10-15 cm/4-6 inches over hot coals for about 30 minutes, turning several times. The outsides will char but will still taste good. The insides will be white and fluffy.

Potato Kebabs: Parboil small new potatoes in their skins for 10 minutes. Drain and skin as soon as they are cool enough to handle. Thread on skewers, pieces of onion can be put between if wished. Brush with melted butter or oil to which can be added chopped parsley and/or a little mustard powder if wished. Grill 10-15 cm/4-6 inches over medium coals for 20 minutes or until browned and tender, turning several times.

Alternatively, wrap the oiled potatoes in foil. The cooking time will be the same and the skins will remain softer.

Grilled Potato Slices: Cut the potatoes lengthways in to 6 mm/¼ inch thick slices. Brush with melted butter or oil and season with freshly ground black pepper. Place on the grill 10-15 cm/4-6 inches over medium coals. Cook for about 30 minutes, or until they are browned and soft, turning several times.

POTATO, SWEET: Bake in foil as for ordinary potatoes, or cook as grilled potato slices, sprinkling with paprika and a little Barbados sugar about 5 minutes before the end of cooking time.

PUMPKIN: Cut the flesh into 2.5 cm/1 inch chunks. Wrap single portions in foil, adding 1 tablespoon oil. Season well. If wished, 1 teaspoon tomato paste or tamari sauce can be added to the oil. Cook 10-15 cm/4-6 inches over medium coals for 30 minutes or until soft.

Pumpkin Kebabs: Use only ripe pumpkin. If it is still slightly green it will be too hard. Cut the flesh into 2.5 cm/1 inch cubes. Brush with melted butter or oil and cook 10-15 cm/4-6 inches over hot coals for 20 minutes, or until soft, turning several times. Sprinkle with chopped fresh herbs, if wished, before serving.

SQUASH: Halve small squash and remove seeds. Fill centres with chopped onion and sprinkle with Barbados sugar. Dot with a small amount of butter or sprinkle with oil. Alternatively, add a little chopped bacon to the onion. Wrap in oiled foil, securing the foil at the side. Cook 10-15 cm/4-6 inches over medium coals for about 45 minutes, or until soft, turning several times.

SWEETCORN: See under first courses (page 12).

TOMATOES: Halve lengthways or crossways. Brush very lightly with oil and season with freshly ground black pepper. Cook 10-15 cm/4-6 inches over hot coals, cut side down first for 1 minute and the 1-2 minutes on the skin side, or until soft but still firm enough to handle. After turning the tomatoes can be flavoured by sprinkling with chopped herbs (basil, thyme, marjoram, oregano), grated Parmesan cheese, celery or garlic salt; or topped with chopped anchovy fillets, halved olives or tiny pieces of salami.

Grilled Tomato Slices: Cut tomatoes into 1 cm/⅜ inch slices. Brush lightly with oil, season with pepper and sprinkle with herbs if wished. Place in a hinged wire grill and cook 10-15 cm/4-6 inches over hot coals for 1 minute each side or until heated through but still firm.

Tomato Kebabs: If possible use very small tomatoes. Scald them quickly and remove the skins. Brush with oil, season with freshly ground black pepper and put on to kebab skewers. Cook 10-15 cm/4-6 inches over medium coals for 10-15 minutes, turning several times. Tomato wedges, unskinned, can be cooked in the same way.

VEGETABLE MARROW: Do not peel. Cut into rings 2.5 cm/1 inch thick. Brush with oil and season with freshly ground black pepper, or use any of the basting mixtures or marinades for courgettes (zucchini). Cook 10-15 cm/4-6 inches over hot coals for 10-15 minutes, turning several times. The outside should be lightly browned and the inside soft.

SPICED MIXED VEGETABLES

If the meat is cooking over indirect heat, put this at the side, directly over the coals.

METRIC/IMPERIAL	AMERICAN
1 medium aubergine	1 medium eggplant
2 teaspoons fine sea salt	2 teaspoons fine sea salt
1 red pepper	1 sweet red pepper
1 green pepper	1 sweet green pepper
2 small courgettes	2 small zucchini
225 g/8 oz tomatoes	½ lb tomatoes
1 medium onion	1 medium onion
1 garlic clove, finely chopped	1 garlic clove, finely chopped
½ teaspoon ground cumin	½ teaspoon ground cumin
½ teaspoon ground coriander	½ teaspoon ground coriander

Cut the aubergine (eggplant) into 1.5 cm/½ inch dice. Put into a colander. Sprinkle with salt and leave to drain for 20 minutes. Rinse with cold water and dry with kitchen paper.

Core and seed the peppers and cut into 2.5 cm/1 inch strips. Slice the courgettes (zucchini) thinly. Chop the tomatoes. Slice the onion thinly.

Put all the vegetables, plus the garlic and spices into a foil tray. Mix well and cover tightly with foil. Cook 10-15 cm/4-6 inches over hot coals for 45 minutes, stirring once. You should have softened vegetables in a small amount of rich, thick sauce.

BREADS

Hot crispy bread, moist on the inside with butter, and flavoured with herbs or other ingredients is so much better than plain sliced bread or rolls and takes very little trouble to make. Foil-wrapped, it can be heating on the grill beside the main course to be ready at the same time or just before.

You will not be able to bake a loaf of bread on an open barbecue, but, if you have a griddle or heavy cast iron frying pan, try your hand at simple scones.

Any of the butters used below for hot bread or rolls can be spread on the scones while they are still hot.

Hot flavoured breads

Choose wholewheat french loaves or bloomer style loaves. Cut the french loaves into diagonal slices about 4 cm/1½ inches thick; cut bloomers into diagonal slices 2 cm/¾ inch thick.

Spread the slices with flavoured butter and reshape the loaves. Wrap in heavy duty foil or a double thickness of standard weight foil. If the french loaves are very long wrap them in sections.

Place 10-15 cm/4-6 inches over medium coals and cook french breads for 10 minutes, turning several times, and bloomers for 15-20 minutes.

Hot flavoured rolls

Use wholewheat rolls or baps. Split crossways, spread with a savoury butter and reshape. Wrap individually in foil. Cook for 10 minutes over medium coals, turning several times.

Savoury butters for breads and rolls

For 1 large french loaf, 1 bloomer or 8 rolls, use 175 g/6 oz/¾ cup softened butter, plus the flavourings below:

6 tablespoons chopped parsley, 1 crushed garlic clove, 2 teaspoons Worcestershire sauce *or*

4 tablespoons chopped parsley, 4 chopped and pounded anchovy fillets, 1 crushed garlic clove (optional), freshly ground black pepper *or*

2 tablespoons tomato paste, 2 tablespoons chopped parsley, 1 tablespoon chopped basil (or 1 teaspoon dried), pinch cayenne pepper, 1 crushed garlic clove (optional) *or*

2 tablespoons tomato paste, 6 black olives, stoned (pitted) chopped and crushed, 2 tablespoons chopped thyme (or 2 teaspoons dried), 1 crushed garlic clove (optional) *or*

4 tablespoons mango or peach chutney, ½ small onion, grated *or*

2 tablespoons Dijon or French mustard, 6 tablespoons chopped parsley *or*

For blue cheese butter use only 75g/3oz/6 tablespoons unsalted butter plus 75g/3oz/¾ cup grated or crumbled blue cheese, 1 crushed garlic clove, ¼ teaspoon cayenne pepper, 4 tablespoons chopped parsley *or*

4 tablespoons chopped chives, 2 tablespoons chopped parsley, 1 teaspoon mustard powder *or*

1 small grated onion, 50g/2oz/½ cup grated Cheddar or Gruyère cheese, 4 tablespoons chopped parsley (use only 125g/4oz/½ cup butter) *or*

2 tablespoons mild, spiced, granular mustard, 2 tablespoons tomato paste.

PLAIN GRIDDLE SCONES

METRIC/IMPERIAL	AMERICAN
225g/8oz wholewheat flour	2 cups wholewheat flour
½ teaspoon fine sea salt	½ teaspoon fine sea salt
½ teaspoon bicarbonate of soda	½ teaspoon baking soda
50g/2oz butter or vegetable margarine	¼ cup butter or vegetable margarine
150ml/¼ pint natural yoghurt or buttermilk	5floz unflavored yoghurt or buttermilk

Put the flour into a bowl with the salt and bicarbonate of soda (baking powder). Rub in the butter or margarine. Make a well in the centre. Pour in the yoghurt or buttermilk. Mix to a dough. Knead lightly on a floured work surface until smooth. Roll out to a 1.5cm/½inch thick round. Cut into either 8 or 12 wedges.

Place a griddle on the grill 10-15cm/4-6 inches over medium coals. Sprinkle with 1 teaspoon fine sea salt. Rub the salt lightly over the surface of the griddle with a thick pad of kitchen paper. Keep rubbing for about 2 minutes or until the surface is clean. Dust away the salt completely. Continue to heat the griddle for about 15 minutes or until a light sprinkling of flour browns within 3 minutes. Brush the surface of the griddle lightly with oil.

Lay the prepared scones on the griddle and cook for 5 minutes or until well risen and the underneath light brown. Turn and cook for a further 5 minutes, or until the second side is brown and they sound hollow when tapped.

HERB GRIDDLE SCONES Herbs can be added with the salt and bicarbonate of soda (baking soda). Use the following or make your own:
4 tablespoons chopped parsley *or*
2 tablespoons chopped parsley, 2 tablespoons chopped chives *or*
1 tablespoon chopped thyme, 2 chopped sage leaves *or*
2 teaspoons chopped rosemary, 2 teaspoons chopped thyme *or*
1 tablespoon each chopped thyme and marjoram, plus 2 tablespoons chopped parsley *or*
1 teaspoon dill seeds

POTATO GRIDDLE SCONES

METRIC/IMPERIAL

350g/12oz potatoes
75g/3oz butter or vegetable margarine
freshly ground black pepper
¼ teaspoon fine sea salt
175g/6oz wholewheat flour
1 teaspoon bicarbonate of soda
2 tablespoons chopped parsley
2 tablespoons chopped chives

AMERICAN

¾lb potatoes
6 tablespoons butter or vegetable margarine
freshly ground black pepper
¼ teaspoon fine sea salt
1½ cups wholewheat flour
1 teaspoon baking soda
2 tablespoons chopped parsley
2 tablespoons chopped chives

Boil the potatoes in their skins until tender. Drain and peel while they are still warm. Rub through a sieve into a mixing bowl. Beat in the butter or margarine, seasonings and herbs. Mix the flour with the bicarbonate of soda (baking soda). Gradually beat it into the potatoes. Knead the dough in the bowl until smooth. Turn on to a floured board and roll to a thickness of 1.5cm/½inch. Stamp into rounds with a pastry cutter or cut into shapes. There should be about 15. Leave the scones in a warm place while you prepare the griddle as for Plain Griddle Scones.

Bake on the griddle as above.

DESSERTS

Unless the main course has taken a long time to cook, there should be enough life left in the coals for you to complete the meal by cooking the dessert on the barbecue as well. Keep it simple and base it on ingredients that can be cooked quickly.

Fruit makes a perfect light dessert after a meat-based meal. It can be prepared in advance and cooked quickly when needed. Some fruit can be sliced and placed directly on the grill, some can be threaded on kebab skewers and other types stay more juicy if they are first wrapped in foil.

Raw fruits and squares of plain wholewheat cake can be dipped into fondues, or you can simply toast skewers of bread and serve them with a sweet butter or sauce.

Fruits on the grill

If fruit is to be placed directly on the grill, the coals must be medium to hot. You must also make sure that the grill is clean and freshly oiled before laying the fruit on it. You do not want pieces of charred meat or fish clinging to what should be the end to a perfect meal.

To keep it moist and to give flavour, brush the fruit with melted honey, melted sugar-free jam (jelly), apple and pear spread or concentrated apple juice. Flavour by sprinkling lightly with spices such as cinnamon, ground ginger, freshly grated nutmeg or a little mace.

Fruits suitable for placing directly on the grill include: whole bananas, thick apple rings, pineapple wedges or rings, melon wedges, skinned peach halves.

Fruit kebabs

To obtain a pleasing mixture of textures and flavours, cut the mixtures of fruit into even-sized pieces and thread on kebab skewers. Use flat or square skewers and oil them lightly.

Brush the fruit before cooking with a sweetener as above and flavour with spices if wished.

Fruit suitable for kebabs include: bananas, in pieces of about 1 inch, cubed apple, ripe but firm cubed pear, oranges, cut into thick slices with the skin left on and the slices quartered, cubed peaches, halved and stoned apricots or plums, whole large seedless grapes, and whole strawberries.

Cook fruit kebabs 10-15 cm/4-6 inches over hot coals until the fruit is just heated through and beginning to sizzle but still firm enough to handle.

Serve the fruit plainly, or with natural (unflavored) yoghurt or whipped cream; or dip it into a fondue, or use the fondue as a sauce.

Fruit in foil

If all that is left of the fire is the ashes, you can still use it for cooking. Wrap fruit in foil parcels and bury them in it to make use of the last of the heat. When making the parcels, use heavy duty foil or a double thickness of standard weight foil. Oil or butter it lightly.

Foil parcels can also be cooked on the grill over medium to hot coals. This method is more suitable for sliced fruits such as apples which could soften too quickly in the coals.

APPLES: Peel, core and slice. Sprinkle with sweet spices and/or dried fruits such as currants and raisins. Add small fruits such as blackberries or elderberries. Cook on the grill for 12-15 minutes.

Core, and score round the centre. Fill with a sweet dried fruit and nut mixture. Make a foil parcel and cook in the ashes for 30 minutes, or over medium coals for 40-50 minutes.

BANANAS: Peel. Sprinkle with sweet spices. Add honey, Barbados sugar, sugar-free jam (jelly) or apple and pear spread. Grated carob bars can also be used. Sprinkle with nuts, raisins or chopped dates. Spoon over 1 tablespoon rum or liqueur. Cook 8-10 minutes over medium coals.

Alternatively slit the skins and fill with flavourings, reshape and wrap in foil. Cook 5 minutes in the ashes or 8-10 minutes over medium coals. Eat from the skins.

ORANGES: Use large oranges. Cut off peel and pith. Cut into eight crossways slices. Reshape, with a sweetener and/or flavouring between the slices. Add a liqueur if wished. Cook for 10 minutes in the ashes or 20 minutes over hot coals.

PEACHES: Peel, halve and stone. Fill centres with ground nuts and chopped dried fruit if wished or with a sugar-free jam (jelly). Wrap individual halves in foil. Cook over medium coals for 6-8 minutes, turning the packets round several times.

PEARS: Core and treat like stuffed apples or slice and sprinkle with honey and spices such as ginger, cardamom or coriander. Cook for 8-10 minutes over medium coals.

PINEAPPLE: Cut away the husk. Cut the pineapple into four lengthways and remove the core. Brush with honey, sugar-free jam (jelly) or concentrated apple juice. Sprinkle with freshly grated nutmeg or ground cinnamon. 1 tablespoon liqueur can be added if wished. Wrap each piece separately. Cook in the ashes for 8-10 minutes or over hot coals for the same amount of time.

Fondues

Standing round the last of the fire dipping into a fondue pot is one of the most sociable of ways in which to end an evening.

Sweet fondues can be made in advance and reheated very gently over medium-low coals. They should never even come to simmering point. To dip into the fondue provide a selection of fruit, cut up as for fruit kebabs, plus cubes of plain cake. Provide fondue forks or cocktail sticks (wooden picks) for easy dipping and let people help themselves.

Toasted cake

Make two 18cm/7 inch plain sponge cakes, preferably with wholewheat flour. Toast over medium coals for about 5 minutes on each side or until heated through.

Cut into wedges and serve with fresh fruits, fresh fruit salad and/or a warm fondue sauce.

APPLES FILLED WITH WALNUTS AND APRICOTS

METRIC/IMPERIAL	AMERICAN
4 medium cooking apples	4 medium cooking apples
125 g/4 oz shelled walnuts, chopped	1 cup chopped walnuts
50 g/2 oz whole dried apricots	2 oz whole dried apricots
2 tablespoons honey	2 tablespoons honey
pinch ground mace	pinch ground mace
25 g/1 oz butter	2 tablespoons butter

Mince (grind) the walnuts and apricots together or work them in a food processor. Mix in the honey and mace. Core the apples and score round the circumference. Fill with the walnut mixture. Dot the top with butter.

Wrap each apple in a square of lightly buttered foil, bringing the sides of the foil together and twisting them over the top.

Bury the parcels in the hot ashes of the barbecue with the twists of foil above the surface. Leave for 30 minutes. Lift them out by the twists of foil and unwrap each apple on to an individual plate. Serve with natural (unflavored) yoghurt or whipped cream if required. *Note:* To cook on the grill, the coals must be hot. Place the apples 10-15 cm/4-6 inches over the coals and cook for 40-50 minutes.

MARMALADE ORANGES

METRIC/IMPERIAL	AMERICAN
4 large oranges	4 large oranges
150 ml/¼ pint sugar-free marmalade	10 tablespoons sugar-free marmalade
4 tablespoons orange curaçao	¼ cup orange curaçao

Cut the rind and pith from each orange. Cut each orange into eight crossways slices. Take them apart. Reassemble the oranges putting 1 teaspoon sugar-free marmalade between each slice.

Place each orange on a square of heavy-duty foil or a double thickness of standard weight foil. Bring the sides of the foil up and pour 1 tablespoon orange curaçao into each parcel. Twist the sides of the foil together over the top of the orange.

Bury the foil parcels in hot ashes, leaving the twists of foil above the surface. Leave the oranges for 10 minutes. Pull out by the twists of foil.

Unwrap each orange on to an individual plate. Serve with natural (unflavored) yoghurt or whipped cream if required.
Note: To cook on the grill, the coals should still be hot. Cook 10-15 cm/4-6 inches over the coals for 20 minutes.

FLAMED PINEAPPLE

METRIC/IMPERIAL	AMERICAN
1 medium-sized pineapple	1 medium-sized pineapple
8 tablespoons sugar-free apricot jam	½ cup sugar-free apricot jelly
125 ml/4 fl oz kirsch	½ cup kirsch

Remove the top and woody base from the pineapple but do not remove the husk. Cut the pineapple into four lengthways and cut away the cores.

Put each piece on a sheet of lightly oiled heavy duty foil or a double thickness of standard weight foil. Spread the pineapple wedges with the apricot jam (jelly). Bring the edges of the foil together and seal securely.

Cook 10-15 cm/4-6 inches over medium coals for 20 minutes, turning several times. Lay the foil parcels on a heatproof surface such as a metal baking sheet. Open them but do not remove the foil.

Put the kirsch into a small frying pan. Stand it over the coals until just warm. Ignite and pour over the pineapple wedges while still flaming.

BANANA AND WALNUT PARCELS

METRIC/IMPERIAL

4 firm bananas, preferably not speckled
8 teaspoons apple and pear spread
4 tablespoons finely chopped walnuts

AMERICAN

4 firm bananas, preferably not speckled
8 teaspoons apple and pear spread
¼ cup finely chopped walnuts

Slit the skin of each banana from top to bottom. Gently ease it apart. Spoon in 2 teaspoons apple and pear spread. Scatter the walnuts over the top.

Wrap each banana singly in foil, keeping the join over the slit in the skin. Lay the parcels over the hot coals and leave them for 15 minutes.

PEACH AND NECTARINE KEBABS WITH APRICOT FONDUE

METRIC/IMPERIAL

2 peaches
2 nectarines
2 tablespoons sugar-free apricot jam
2 tablespoons white wine or natural
apple juice
fondue
175g/6oz sugar-free apricot jam
3 tablespoons arrowroot
425ml/¾ pint natural apple juice
4 tablespoons apricot brandy (optional)
150ml/¼ pint soured cream

AMERICAN

2 peaches
2 nectarines
2 tablespoons sugar-free apricot jelly
2 tablespoons white wine or natural
apple juice
fondue
6oz sugar-free apricot jelly
3 tablespoons arrowroot
2 cups natural apple juice
¼ cup apricot brandy (optional)
5fl oz dairy sour cream

To make the fondue; gently melt the jam (jelly) in a saucepan. In a bowl, mix the arrowroot with 6 tablespoons of the apple juice. Add the remaining apple juice to the jam (jelly) and warm gently. Stir in the arrowroot and bring the mixture gently to the boil, stirring. Stir until thick and transparent. Take the pan from the heat and stir in the apricot brandy, if using, and the soured cream. Keep the fondue warm on the side of the grill while the kebabs are cooking.

To make the kebabs; scald and skin the peaches and nectarines. Halve and stone (pit) them and cut into 2.5cm/1inch cubes. Divide between four kebab skewers. Melt the jam (jelly) in a small saucepan on a low heat. Mix in the orange juice or wine. Cool the mixture slightly and brush over the fruit. Cook the kebabs 10-15cm/4-6 inches over hot coals for 10 minutes or until beginning to brown, turning several times.

To serve, either dip the kebabs into the fondue or transfer to bowls and spoon the fondue over the top.

CINNAMON TOASTS WITH RASPBERRY SAUCE

METRIC/IMPERIAL	AMERICAN
Twenty 2.5cm/1inch cubes day old wholewheat bread	Twenty 1inch cubes day old wholewheat bread
50g/2oz butter	¼ cup butter
75g/3oz honey	¼ cup honey
1 teaspoon ground cinnamon	1 teaspoon ground cinnamon
sauce	*sauce*
125g/4oz sugar-free raspberry jam	4oz sugar-free raspberry jelly
2 tablespoons arrowroot	2 tablespoons arrowroot
275ml/½ pint red grape juice	1¼ cups red grape juice

Thread the cubes of bread on to four kebab skewers. Put the butter and honey into a saucepan with the cinnamon. Set on a low heat to melt. Brush the mixture over all sides of the bread cubes. Leave for 30 minutes.

To make the sauce, gently melt the jam (jelly) in a saucepan. In a bowl mix the arrowroot with 4 tablepoons/¼ cup of grape juice. Add the remaining grape juice to the jam (jelly) and warm gently. Mix in the arrowroot. Bring the mixture gently to the boil, stirring. Stir until you have a thick, transparent sauce.

Keep the sauce warm on the side of the grill. Lay the bread kebabs over medium coals and toast until each side has crisped, about 10 minutes altogether.

Either let each person dip their bread into the sauce or provide bowls, take the bread off the skewers and pour the sauce over.

BLACKBERRY AND APPLE PARCELS

METRIC/IMPERIAL	AMERICAN
4 small cooking apples	4 small cooking apples
175g/6oz blackberries	6oz blackberries
ground cloves	ground cloves
6 tablespoons Barbados sugar	6 tablespoons Barbados sugar

Peel and core the apples. Cut in half lengthways and then into thin crossways slices. Arrange each apple in the centre of a piece of buttered foil. Sprinkle with a pinch of ground cloves and 1½ tablespoons Barbados sugar. Put the blackberries on top.

Seal the foil parcels. Cook them 10-15cm/4-6 inches over hot coals for 15 minutes or until the apples are soft.

Serve with whipped cream or natural (unflavored) yoghurt.

STRAWBERRY KEBABS WITH CAROB FONDUE

METRIC/IMPERIAL	AMERICAN
450 g/1 lb strawberries	1 lb strawberries
2 tablespoons honey	2 tablespoons honey
juice ½ large orange	juice ½ large orange
fondue	*fondue*
1 tablespoon flour	1 tablespoon flour
75 g/3 oz honey	¼ cup honey
200 ml/7 fl oz natural orange juice	7 fl oz natural orange juice
granted rind 1 large orange	grated rind 1 large orange
1 egg yolk	1 egg yolk
50 g/2 oz butter or vegetable margarine	¼ cup butter or vegetable margarine
two 40 g/1½ oz sugar-free carob bars	two 1½ oz sugar-free carob bars

To make the fondue; put the flour and honey into a saucepan. Set on a low heat and stir in the orange juice and orange rind. Stir until the sauce thickens. Take the pan from the heat. Beat in the egg yolk and butter. Grate in the carob bar. Beat well. Return the pan to a low heat and stir for about 3 minutes, without boiling, until the fondue is thick.

The fondue can be made in advance, put into a fondue pot and left until needed. When you have finished cooking the main course, warm the fondue on the grill, stirring occasionally and making sure that it does not boil.

To make the kebabs; hull the strawberries. Mix together the honey and orange juice. Coat the strawberries in the mixture and leave for 30 minutes.

Thread onto four kebab skewers. Grill over medium coals for 5 minutes or until just warmed through, turning once. Serve on the skewers to be dipped into the fondue. Alternatively, provide bowls so that they can be taken off the skewers and have the fondue poured over the top.

MELON AND GINGER WEDGES

METRIC/IMPERIAL	AMERICAN
1 large honeydew melon	1 large honeydew melon
4 tablespoons syrup from the ginger jar	¼ cup syrup from the ginger jar
4 pieces preserved stem ginger	4 pieces preserved stem ginger
4 tablespoons flaked almonds	¼ cup flaked almonds

Cut the melon into quarters. Remove the seeds. Brush the melon quarters with the ginger syrup. Chop the stem ginger finely and mix it with the almonds.

Cook the melon quarters 10-15 cm/4-6 inches over hot coals for 2-3 minutes each side or until heated through. Fill with the ginger and almond mixture just before serving.

Black Health Bread; Pots of Prawns (Shrimp); Baked Mushrooms; Corn in foil with Green Chillies.

Beef Rib Roast with selection of vegetables in foil, including Rice-stuffed Peppers.

COOKING
IN KETTLE
BARBECUES

Kettles take ordinary barbecuing several steps further. The large, domed cover allows an even heat to circulate all round the food, so enabling you to cook not only chops and steaks, but the largest roasts and even bread and pastries. Covered cooking helps to keep even the smallest cuts of meat moist and juicy with the minimum of shrinkage. Air vents in both cover and base allow you to control the temperature inside the kettle. They will not, however, let in too much air and therefore there is far less risk of a 'flare-up' than there is with an open barbecue. Any food that is cooked in a kettle barbecue will pick up a delicious smoky flavour which enhances even sweet dishes.

Types of kettle barbecue

There are two types of kettle barbecue, round and rectangular. The most popular is round, the base and lid together making almost a complete sphere. It stands on three legs one of which may or may not have a wheel. There are air vents in the base and also in the lid. Charcoal is laid on a lower grill and there is another grill above on which to place the food. Round kettles come in varying sizes, ranging from the smallest which are suitable for table-top cooking through highly portable ones suitable for camping to the largest, which can easily cater for parties. When the lid is removed it can be hung on the side of the base.

Some makes of round kettle have a lever in the base which, when pushed from side to side, will sweep the ash through the bottom vents. This falls into a tray fixed on to the legs of the kettle.

A rectangular kettle barbecue has a hinged grill. It is most usually made from cast iron and mounted on a four-wheeled wagon. These barbecues come in varying sizes to suit the family's needs, but weight and size prohibits their use for camping. There are air vents, on each side of both the base and lid, and grills for the charcoal and on which to put the food.

Cooking on a kettle barbecue

Whichever type you use, the manufacturers always recommend that you cook with the lid on, even when cooking small chops, thin-cut steaks and burgers.

There are two methods of cooking in a kettle. The *direct method* is used for anything that will cook quickly (chops, steaks, burgers, sausages). The charcoal is arranged in an even layer right across the grill. The heat goes directly up to the meat and the cooking time will be relatively short. When cooking kebabs and fish the method is the same, but the charcoal should be arranged more sparsely.

The *indirect method* is used when cooking food that requires a long, slow, even heat, such as large joints of meat or bread. In the round kettle, the charcoal is arranged on either side of the grill with a large gap between. The food is placed over the gap and a drip tray is often placed beneath it when cooking meat to catch the fat and lessen damage to the kettle.

Cooking in Kettle Barbecues 2

When using a barbecue with a hinged grill, the basic principle is the same but instead of being placed in the centre, the food is placed on one side of the barbecue with a drip tray underneath. The charcoal is placed on the other side of the barbecue, beside the drip tray.

With both methods the effect is the same; a good, all-round heat with no scorching.

Fuel and lighting

Charcoal briquettes are the best type of fuel to use in a kettle barbecue. They provide a long-lasting, even heat.

To prepare the kettle for cooking, remove the lid and keep it off until the charcoal is hot enough for food to be placed on the grill.

Choose your fire lighter. Solid, odourless fire lighters or an electric type are the safest to use. If you use a fluid, allow any that spills into the bottom of the kettle to burn away before placing the food on the grill.

For *direct cooking* spread an even layer of charcoal over the charcoal grill. This enables you to know exactly how many briquettes to use. Heap the briquettes into a pyramid and light them. When a layer of grey ash has formed over the briquettes, spread them out again and put the cooking grill into the kettle.

For *indirect cooking* Round kettle: Position the barbecue so that two of the bottom vents are facing into the wind. Place an equal number of briquettes on either side of the charcoal grill. Ignite the briquettes and leave until a grey ash has formed over them. Wait until both sides are burning evenly. Put the drip tray in the centre. Water can be put into the drip tray to keep the air inside the kettle moist. Position the cooking grill.

Rectangular kettle: Position the barbecue so that one of the bottom vents is facing into the wind. Place the briquettes on one side of the charcoal grill and ignite. Never pile them against the sides of the kettle as excessive heat may damage the metal.

Guide to number of briquettes

Size of Kettle	Briquettes each side of start	Add every 50 minutes
67 cm/26½ inch	30	9
56 cm/22 inch	25	8
46 cm/18 inch	16	5
35 cm/14 inch	9	4

Controlling the fire

If the fire gets too intense, as may happen on an excessively windy day, gradually close the air vents until a lower, even heat is attained. To increase the heat make sure all air vents are completely open and that two of the bottom vents of a round kettle or one side vent of a rectangular kettle face into the wind. Make sure the bottom vents are not clogged with ash.

Cooking in Kettle Barbecues 3

Putting out the fire

Completely close all the air vents. Unburnt charcoal can be saved for the next time. Clear out the ash once it is completely cold.

Cooking times

Cooking times are given for all the following recipes, but you should remember that barbecue situations are very different. Weather conditions such as outside temperature and/or wind direction and intensity can alter the heat of the fire slightly. It is best, therefore, to check your food at regular intervals and regulate the air controls if necessary. When cooking large joints of meat and poultry a meat thermometer will help you to know exactly when they are cooked to perfection.

It is always best to start cooking early. If meat or fish is cooked before you need to eat, it can be wrapped in foil and left to stand. If it is necessary to reheat it, place the foil parcel over a gentle, indirect heat. Bread, quiches or puddings can simply be placed in their containers on the grill rack over an indirect heat. Do not wrap them in foil while they are warm or they will become too moist on top.

Maintenance

After use, simply let the cooking grill become cold. The next time you use the kettle, heat the grill over hot coals and brush with a stiff wire brush before placing any food on it.

Enamelled covers such as those on round kettles, should be wiped over with kitchen paper while they are still slightly warm. Always remove ash when it is cold.

Wipe over the inside and outside surfaces of both round and rectangular kettles with a damp cloth when they are cold.

After the kettle has been used four or five times, clean the inside with hot water and a de-greaser or oven cleaner.

Always clean the kettle if it is to be stored for some time. Make sure that it is kept in the dry or that it is protected by a special cover.

Essential accessories

Cooking Foil: Use heavy duty foil or a double thickness of standard foil for wrapping vegetables, fruit and pot roasts. Standard foil can be used to cover meat or fish that is roasting in trays. Use heavy duty foil to make drip trays.

Drip Trays: These must be placed under roasting meats. Meat, fish and other small items such as vegetables and fruits, can be placed inside the trays for cooking. Drip trays are made from heavy duty cooking foil and come in varying sizes. If you cannot buy them you can make your own from heavy duty foil, 45 cm/18 inches wide. Tear off a strip which is at least 7.5 cm/3 inches longer than the meat that you intend to cook. Fold in 4 cm/1½ inches all the way round. Turn the foil over. Score 2.5 cm/1 inch from the edge all the way round. Score from the corners to the point where the scores cross. Fold all edges up along score marks, pinching the corners together and folding them to one side.

Charcoal Rails: These keep the charcoal in position at either side of the charcoal grill.

Tool Hooks: These hang on the side of the round kettles or on the trolleys of rectangular kettles. They are very useful for keeping forks, fish slices and other tools handy.

Roast Holder: This is not absolutely essential but extremely useful. With it, meat can easily be lifted on and off the grill.

Meat Thermometer: If you are not expert at judging the 'doneness' of meat this is a real help, especially if you intend to use your kettle frequently for roasting.

Cover: A must if the kettle is to be kept outside in all weathers, not if it is to be stored indoors.

Non-essential accessories

Potato Baker: Spikes arranged in a circle or semi-circle. Potatoes are placed on spikes for cooking. Corn can sometimes be placed on the same rack.

Shish Kebab Sets: Skewers arranged in rack for easy turning.

Various Racks for holding chops, spare ribs, etc.

Condiment Rack: Fits onto outside of kettle for holding salt and pepper, sauces, etc.

Griddle: Flat metal griddle for frying, available for some models.

Work Tables: For round kettles, will fit on side. Rectangular kettle trolleys usually have these built-in.

FIRST COURSES

Small, tasty first courses can be cooked alongside a slow-cooking main dish in a kettle barbecue, or a little ahead of steaks, chops and fish. Barbecue food is usually very substantial so make them light yet delicious.

CORN ON THE COB

CORN IN FOIL Remove the silk and husks from four corn cobs. Use 75 g/3 oz/6 tablespoons butter to spread over the cobs. Wrap each one in foil and cook over direct heat for 15 minutes.
VARIATIONS: add flavourings to the butter such as:
   1 teaspoon paprika plus ¼ teaspoon chilli powder *or*

Cooking in Kettle Barbecues 5

1 teaspoon paprika plus two finely choped red or green chillies *or*
4 tablespoons chopped parsley *or*
4 tablespoons tomato paste plus paprika and chilli powder or parsley as above.
CORN IN THE HUSK Use this method when the complete husk of the corn cobs is intact. First, carefully peel back the husk and remove the silk. Fold the husk back into position and tie it round at the top with string. Soak the cobs in cold water for 2 hours. Drain but do not dry.

Cook over indirect heat for 30 minutes.

POTS OF PRAWNS (SHRIMP)

METRIC/IMPERIAL	AMERICAN
225 g/8 oz shelled prawns	½ lb shelled shrimp
3 tablespoons soy, tamari or shoyu sauce	3 tablespoons soy, tamari or shoyu sauce
3 tablespoons oil	3 tablespoons oil
1.5 cm/½ inch piece ginger root	½ inch piece ginger root
1 spring onion	1 scallion

Prepare the kettle for indirect cooking.

Mix together the soy sauce and oil. Peel and grate the ginger root. Chop the spring onion (scallion) very finely. Mix them into the oil and sauce. Fold in the prawns (shrimp).

Divide the prawns (shrimp) between four small oven-proof dishes or ramekins. Place on the grill rack in the centre of the kettle.

Cook for 15 minutes or until heated through.

BAKED MUSHROOMS

METRIC/IMPERIAL	AMERICAN
16 small mushrooms, open but not flat	16 small mushrooms, open but not flat
4 tablespoons oil	4 tablespoons oil
75/3 oz Gruyère cheese, finely grated	¾ cup Gruyère cheese, finely grated
3 tablespoons double cream	3 tablespoons heavy cream
2 tablespoons chopped parsley	2 tablespoons chopped parsley
1 tablespoon chopped thyme	1 tablespoon chopped thyme
pinch cayenne pepper	pinch cayenne pepper

Prepare the kettle for indirect cooking.
Lightly brush the mushrooms with oil and lay in a foil tray. Mix together the remaining ingredients. Put small portions of the mixture on each mushroom.

Place the tray in the centre of the kettle and cook for 20 minutes or until the cheese has melted and the mushrooms are heated through and sizzling.

ARTICHOKES FILLED WITH HERBS

METRIC/IMPERIAL	AMERICAN
4 globe artichokes	4 globe artichokes
2 tablespoons white wine vinegar	2 tablespoons white wine vinegar
6 tablespoons olive oil	6 tablespoons olive oil
juice ½ lemon	juice ½ lemon
6 tablespoons chopped parsley	¼ cup chopped parsley
1 tablespoon chopped thyme	1 tablespoon chopped thyme
1 tablespoon chopped marjoram	1 tablespoon chopped majoram
freshly ground black pepper	freshly ground black pepper

Break away the bottom leaves of the artichokes and cut the stalks level with the base. Cut across the top to remove the tips of the leaves. Cut the artichokes into quarters lengthways and remove the chokes using a small, sharp knife. Add the vinegar to a small bowl of water. Dip the artichoke pieces in the water to prevent them turning black. Drain well.

Combine the remaining ingredients to make the dressing. Re-shape each artichoke in the centre of a piece of foil. Put a portion of the herb dressing into each. Wrap the artichokes completely in the foil. Cook, over indirect heat, for 30 minutes, turning once.

BAKED AVOCADOS

METRIC/IMPERIAL	AMERICAN
4 small, firm but ripe avocados	4 small, firm but ripe avocados
2 tablespoons olive oil	2 tablespoons olive oil
1 tablespoon lemon juice	1 tablespoon lemon juice
filling 1	*filling 1*
100g/3½oz tin tuna	3½oz can tuna
4 tablespoons chopped parsley	4 tablespoons chopped parsley
4 black olives	4 black olives
filling 2	*filling 2*
50g/2oz thinly sliced salami	2oz thinly sliced salami
3 tablespoons oil	3 tablespoons oil
1 tablespoon tomato paste	1 tablespoon tomato paste
1 teaspoon paprika	1 teaspoon paprika
1 garlic clove, crushed	1 garlic clove, crushed

Prepare the kettle for indirect cooking.

Halve and stone (pit) the avocados. Mix together the oil and lemon juice. Brush the cut surfaces of the avocados with the mixture. Add filling of choice.

Filling 1: Mash the tuna with 2 tablespoons of its own oil. Mix in the parsley. Fill the cavities of the avocados putting half an olive on top.

Filling 2: Finely chop the salami. Mix it with the other ingredients. Fill the cavities of the avocados.

Place the avocados directly on the grill rack. Cook for 20 minutes or until heated through.

FISH

Fish cooks quickly on a kettle barbecue. The flesh stays moist and the slight hint of smokiness complements the natural flavour. Fish is far more delicate than meat and may break up when overcooked so it is wise to observe a few rules.

If you are cooking directly on the kettle grill, oil the grill well before laying the fish on it. After turning the fish, place it, if you can, on a different part of the grill. This will prevent sticking and will also prevent any small pieces that might be on the grill from spoiling the flavour of the first side.

Fish fillets and steaks are best cooked in a hinged grill. This makes turning easy and definitely prevents any breaking up. Small (pan-sized) fish can also be cooked in this way and larger grills are also available for large, whole fish.

Small whole fish, steaks and fillets can also be sealed completely in a foil parcel and cooked directly over the charcoal. This seals in all the flavour and juices and if herbs are added, their flavour permeates the fish.

Fish can also be cooked in a foil tray using the indirect cooking method. Lay them on a bed of herbs and chopped vegetables for extra flavour. The tray can be left open or can be covered with foil.

Most white fish, especially when cut into fillets or steaks, are best marinated before cooking. Oily fish need only be brushed with an oil and flavouring mixture, but these, too, are made more moist when left for a while. Large and small fish can be stuffed with a savoury breadcrumb mixture. If no stuffing is required, fill the body cavities with herb sprigs and/or slices of lemon and onion.

Cooking Times

WHOLE, SMALL (PAN-SIZED) FISH

Direct heat, coals spread sparsely: 6-8 minutes each side.
Indirect heat, on grill: 7-10 minutes each side.
Indirect heat, in foil tray: 10-15 minutes each side.

FISH FILLETS

Direct heat, coals spread sparsely. In hinged grill: 5 minutes each side.
Wrapped in foil: 5 minutes each side.
Indirect heat, in foil tray: 5-7 minutes each side.

FISH STEAKS

Direct heat, coals spread sparsely: 5-7 minutes each side, depending on thickness.
Indirect heat, in foil tray: 7-10 minutes each side.

WHOLE, LARGE FISH

Direct heat, coals spread sparsely: 8-10 minutes per lb.
Indirect heat, in foil tray: 10-15 minutes per lb.

FISH KEBABS
(fish in 2.5/1 inch cubes)
Direct heat, coals spread sparsely: 10 minutes, turning several times.

PRAWNS (SHRIMP) SHELLED
Indirect heat, in single layer in foil tray: 10 minutes; 6 minutes on thin skewers.

PRAWNS (SHRIMP) IN SHELL
Direct heat: 3-4 minutes each side.

LOBSTER (RAW)
Direct heat, cut-side up: 15-20 minutes or until shell is bright red.

HOT-SMOKED FISH FILLETS
Indirect heat, on kettle grill: 5 minutes to heat through.

MARINADES FOR FISH

These can also be used as basting mixtures if there is no time to marinate.

4 tablespoons oil, juice 1 lemon, 2 tablespoons chopped parsley, 1 tablespoon chopped thyme or tarragon, 1 tablespoon tomato paste (optional) *or*

4 tablespoons oil, grated rind and juice 1 lemon or lime, 1 crushed garlic clove, 1 teaspoon paprika, few drops Tabasco sauce or ¼ teaspoon chilli powder, 2 tablespoons chopped fresh coriander or parsley (optional) *or*

4 tablespoons oil, 2 tablespoons white wine vinegar, 1 teaspoon mustard powder or Dijon mustard, 1 teaspoon grated onion, 1 tablespoon grated horse-radish (best for oily fish) *or*

4 tablespoons oil, 2 tablespoons lemon juice or white wine vinegar, ¼ nutmeg, grated, ¼ teaspoon ground mace, 2 tablespoons chopped parsley *or*

4 tablespoons oil, juice 1 lemon, 2 tablespoons chopped tarragon, 1 tablespoon chopped lemon thyme (best for white fish) *or*

4 tablespoons oil, 2 tablespoon soy sauce, 1 tablespoon tomato paste, 1 crushed garlic clove, 1 teaspoon grated fresh ginger root.

MUSTARD COOKED FISH

METRIC/IMPERIAL	AMERICAN
4 small oily fish, approximately 225g/8oz each	4 small oily fish, approximately ½lb each
1 teaspoon yellow mustard seeds	1 teaspoon yellow mustard seeds
6 tablespoons olive oil	6 tablespoons olive oil
juice 1 lemon	juice 1 lemon
1 teaspoon mustard powder	1 teaspoon mustard powder
4 tablespoons chopped parsley	¼ cup chopped parsley

Cooking in Kettle Barbecues 9

Gut the fish. Remove the heads if wished. Using a pestle and mortar, crush the mustard seeds coarsely. In a large, flat dish mix them with the remaining ingredients. Turn the fish in the mixture, coating them both inside and out. Leave for at least 2 hours at room temperature.

Prepare the kettle for indirect cooking. Cook the fish for 6 minutes on each side or until the flesh flakes when tested with a fork.

FISH STEAKS TOPPED WITH SMOKED CHEESE AND WALNUTS

METRIC/IMPERIAL	AMERICAN
4 white fish steaks	4 white fish steaks
juice 1 lemon	juice 1 lemon
sea salt and freshly ground black pepper	sea salt and freshly ground black pepper
100/4oz smoked Cheddar cheese, grated	1 cup grated smoked Cheddar cheese
50/2oz shelled walnuts, chopped	½ cup shelled walnuts, chopped

Prepare the kettle for indirect cooking.

Brush the fish steaks with the lemon juice. Season, put into a foil tray and leave for 30 minutes. Mix together the cheese and walnuts.

Lay the foil tray in the centre of the kettle and cook the fish for 10 minutes. Turn them over and cook for 5 minutes. Put a portion of the cheese and walnut mixture in the centre of each one. Continue cooking for a further 5 minutes or until the cheese has melted.

PRAWN (SHRIMP) PAELLA

METRIC/IMPERIAL	AMERICAN
125g/4oz prawns in shell	¼lb shrimp in shell
225g/8oz shelled prawns	½lb shelled shrimp
225g/8oz Chorizo sausage	½lb Chorizo sausage
2 red peppers	2 sweet red peppers
1 green pepper	1 sweet green pepper
4 tablespoons oil	¼ cup oil
1 large onion, thinly sliced	1 large onion, thinly sliced
1 garlic clove, finely chopped	1 garlic clove, finely chopped
225g/8oz shelled broad beans (or frozen)	1 cup shelled lima beans (or frozen)
275g/10oz long grain brown rice	1½ cups long grain brown rice
725ml/1¼ pints stock	3¼ cups stock
pinch saffron	pinch saffron

Prepare the kettle for indirect cooking.

Slice the Chorizo thinly. Core and seed the peppers and cut them into 2.5/1 inch strips. Heat the oil in a paella pan on a low heat. Put in the Chorizo and cook for 2 minutes or until the fat begins to run. Add the peppers, onion and garlic and cook, stirring, until the onion begins to soften. Mix in the beans and rice and cook for 2 minutes, stirring. Bring the stock to the boil. Infuse the saffron in 2 tablespoons of the stock. Pour this and the rest of the stock over the rice.

Transfer the paella pan to the kettle. Cook, uncovered but with the cover on the kettle, for 40 minutes.

Mix in the shelled prawns (shrimp) and lay the prawns (shrimp) in shell on top. Cook for a further 20 minutes or until the rice is tender and the stock absorbed.

SMALL FISH WITH TOMATOES

METRIC/IMPERIAL	AMERICAN
4 small white fish	4 small white fish
4 tablespoons olive oil	¼ cup olive oil
juice 1 lemon	juice 1 lemon
2 tablespoons tomato paste	2 tablespoons tomato paste
1 teaspoon paprika	1 teaspoon paprika
¼ teaspoon Tabasco sauce	¼ teaspoon Tabasco sauce
50/2 oz wholewheat flour	½ cup wholewheat flour
4 medium tomatoes, slice into rounds	4 medium tomatoes, sliced into rounds
2 tablespoons chopped parsley	2 tablespoons chopped parsley

Prepare the kettle for indirect cooking.

Gut the fish. The heads may be removed or left on. Beat together the oil, lemon juice, tomato paste and paprika. Brush the mixture over the outside and inside of the fish. Leave for 30 minutes and then coat with the flour.

Cook in the centre of the kettle for 7 minutes on each side, or until the fish are cooked through and the flour browned, laying the tomato slices on the fish for the final 5 minutes.

Serve scattered with parsley.

Note: this recipe may also be used for small oily sea fish (for example herrings or mackerel).

PORK

Pork is an ideal meat for cooking in a kettle barbecue, since the smoky flavour that is acquired complements it well. It is also an economical meat and all cuts can be used from the most expensive piece of leg to the spare ribs.

Quick cooking cuts such as chops, steaks cut from the leg, spare rib chops cut from the shoulder and also offal are best cooked over a direct heat. As pork is such a moist and flavoursome meat, it can be cooked perfectly plainly and still taste superb. However, a marinade or a brushing of herbs or spices will add to this so use them whenever you can.

Cook all the larger cuts of pork, including tenderloin and spare ribs, over indirect heat. They all need to be well done and so a long, slow cooking time will keep them tender. Pork joints can be steeped in a marinade, brushed with herbs and spices before cooking or simply cooked plainly and painted with a glaze for the final 30 minutes of cooking. Spare ribs are always better after marinating.

To add an extra smoky flavour to roast pork or spare ribs, put two soaked hickory or mesquite blocks on to the charcoal at each side of the kettle.

Joints of ham or bacon can be cooked from raw in a kettle barbecue, but most often they are boiled and cooled, then glazed and finished off in a kettle.

Cooking Times

CHOPS

Sear directly over coals for 2 minutes on each side. Then cook over indirect heat.

Thickness	Minutes first side	Minutes second side
2.5 / 1 inch	15-18	15-18
4 / 1½ inches	20-25	18-20
5 / 2 inches	28-30	25-30

STREAKY RASHERS (SLICES)

Sear directly over coals for 3 minutes on each side. Then cook over indirect heat for 45-50 minutes.

TENDERLOIN

Sear directly over coals for 3 minutes on each side. Then cook over indirect heat for 45-50 minutes.

SPARE RIBS

Cook over indirect heat. 1½-2 hours.

PORK ROASTS

(Leg, Shoulder, Loin, Blade, Lean-end belly)
Stand at room temperature for 1½ hours if possible. Cook over indirect heat for 20 minutes per 450g/1lb or to an internal temperature of 75°/170°F. Stand wrapped in foil for 20-30 minutes before carving.

HAM OR BACON JOINTS

Pre-cooked: Indirect heat, 8-10 minutes per 450g/1lb or to an internal temperature of 60°C/140°F.
Uncooked: Indirect heat, 10-15 minutes per 450g/1lb or to an internal temperature of 70°C/160°F. Leave to stand for 30 minutes.

LIVER

Cook over direct heat for 5-6 minutes each side.

KIDNEYS

Halved and cored. Cook over direct heat for 7-8 minutes each side.

MARINADES AND BASTING MIXTURES FOR PORK AND HAM

Crush in a pestle and mortar 1 chopped garlic clove, 4 chopped sage leaves, 1 teaspoon chopped rosemary, ½ teaspoon black peppercorns, ¼ teaspoon sea slat. Rub over chops, spare ribs and steaks *or*

Crush together 1 teaspoon each of black peppercorns, juniper berries, allspice berries and sea salt, plus 1 chopped garlic clove. Rub over outside of roasts *or*

225 ml/8 fl oz/2 cups dry cider, 1 tablespoon honey, 1 tablespoon chopped rosemary, 1 crushed garlic clove. Use for rashers (slices), spare ribs, chops, tenderloin, roasts *or*

125 ml/4 fl oz/½ cup dry white wine, 2 tablespoons white wine vinegar, 1 teaspoon Tabasco sauce, 1 teaspoon paprika, 1 crushed garlic clove. Use for chops, rashers (slices), steaks, tenderloin *or*

275 ml/½ pint/1¼ cups dry cider, 2 tablespoons tomato paste, 4 tablespoons/¼ cup soy sauce, 1 tablespoon honey, 2 tablespoons cider vinegar, 2 teaspoons chopped rosemary. Use for rashers (slices), tenderloin, spare ribs, roasts *or*

4 tablespoons natural pineapple or orange juice, 2 tablespoons concentrated apple juice or honey, 1 tablespoon tomato paste. Use for rashers (slices), tenderloin, spare ribs, roasts.

Glaze for roasts or baked ham. Use only during final 30 minutes of cooking time: 4 tablespoons concentrated apple juice, ¼ teaspoon ground cloves.

FRUITY SPARE RIBS

METRIC/IMPERIAL	AMERICAN
900 g/2 lb pork spare ribs, in one or two pieces	2 lb pork spare ribs, in one or two pieces
250 ml/8 fl oz pineapple juice	1 cup pineapple juice
125 ml/4 fl oz concentrated apple juice	½ cup concentrated apple juice
4 tablespoons cider vinegar	¼ cup cider apple vinegar
1 garlic clove, crushed with pinch sea salt	1 garlic clove, crushed with pinch sea salt
freshly ground black pepper	freshly ground black pepper

Cut the ribs into three-rib pieces. Mix together the pineapple juice, concentrated apple juice, vinegar and garlic. Season well with the pepper. Put the mixture into a large bowl. Put in the pieces of pork and marinate for at least 4 hours at room temperature.

Prepare the kettle for indirect cooking. Cook in the centre of the kettle for 1½ hours, or until the meat is tender and well browned, basting with the marinade for the final 30 minutes.

LOIN OF PORK WITH PRUNES

METRIC/IMPERIAL	AMERICAN
one 1.8-2 kg/4-4½ lb loin of pork, weighed on bone	one 4-4½ lb loin of pork, weighed on bone
16 prunes	16 prunes
275 ml/½ pint natural orange juice	1¼ cups natural orange juice
2 teaspoons mustard powder	2 teaspoons mustard powder
3 sage leaves, chopped	3 sage leaves, chopped
1 tablespoon chopped savory	1 tablespoon chopped savory
2 teaspoons chopped rosemary	2 teaspoons chopped rosemary
2 tablespoons honey or concentrated apple juice	2 tablespoons honey or concentrated apple juice

Soak the prunes for at least 4 hours in the orange juice. Drain them, reserving the juice. Slit lengthways and stone (pit) them.

Prepare the kettle for indirect cooking. Bone the pork and lay it out flat. Mix the mustard powder with 2 tablespoons of the reserved juice to make a paste. Spread over the cut surface of the pork. Scatter the pork with the herbs. Lay the prunes, two abreast, down the centre. Roll the pork and tie it securely with fine string.

Put the pork into a roasting rack or directly on the grill. Cook for 1½ hours. Mix the honey or concentrated apple juice with 4 tablespoons/¼ cup of the reserved juice. Baste the pork. Cook for a further 20-30 minutes or until browned.

PORK CHOPS TOPPED WITH PARMESAN

METRIC/IMPERIAL	AMERICAN
4 loin pork chops	4 loin pork chops
4 sage leaves, chopped	4 sage leaves, chopped
2 teaspoons chopped rosemary	2 teaspoons chopped rosemary
1 garlic clove, finely chopped	1 garlic clove, finely chopped
½ teaspoon black peppercorns	½ teaspoon black peppercorns
2 tablespoons grated Parmesan cheese	2 tablespoons grated Parmesan cheese
2 tablespoons tomato paste	2 tablespoons tomato paste
2 teaspoons dry white wine	2 teaspoons dry white wine

Remove the skin from the chops. Using a pestle and mortar crush together the herbs, garlic and peppercorns to make a rough paste. Spread the paste over both sides of the chops. Leave for at least 1 hour at room temperature. Mix together the Parmesan, tomato paste and wine.

Prepare the kettle for indirect cooking. Cook the chops for 2 minutes on each side directly over the hot coals to sear. Then cook over indirect heat for 20 minutes. Spread the tops with the Parmesan mixture and cook for a further 10 minutes.

PORK AND BEANS

METRIC/IMPERIAL	AMERICAN
225 g/8 oz haricot beans, soaked and cooked for 1 hour	1¼ cups haricot or navy beans, soaked and cooked for 1 hour
450 g/1 lb belly pork rashers	1 lb belly pork slices
4 tablespoons oil	4 tablespoons oil
1 medium onion, finely chopped	1 medium onion, finely chopped
1 garlic clove, finely chopped	1 garlic clove, finely chopped
275 ml/½ pint tomato juice	1¼ cups tomato juice
275 ml/½ pint stock	1¼ cups stock
1 tablespoon molasses	1 tablespoon molasses
2 tablespoons malt vinegar	2 tablespoons malt vinegar
2 sage leaves, chopped	2 sage leaves, chopped
freshly ground black pepper	freshly ground black pepper

Prepare the kettle for indirect cooking.

Drain the beans. Cut the skin and bones from the pork and cut each rasher (slice) in half crossways. Brush with half the oil.

Heat the remaining oil in a frying pan on a low heat. Put in the onion and garlic and soften them. Pour in the tomato juice and stock and bring to the boil. Add the molasses, vinegar and sage and season well with pepper. Put the mixture into a foil tray. Mix in the beans.

Sear the pork for 2 minutes on each side directly over the coals. Put into the tray with the beans. Cover with foil and cook for 1 hour in the centre of the kettle. Remove the foil and cook for a further 30 minutes or until both pork and beans are tender.

BEEF

All cuts of beef can be cooked in a kettle barbecue, from the thinnest steaks and beefburgers to the largest rib roasts.

When cooking the best quality steaks, brush well with a basting mixture before cooking or, better still, leave them for up to 4 hours to marinate. Less tender cuts such as top rump or chuck are best marinated for 4 hours or longer. Cook all steaks over a direct heat with the cover on. If wished, you can sear them for 1 minute each side with the cover off and then cover for the remainder of the cooking time.

Beefburgers are easier to handle if they are put into a hinged grill. This enables you to turn them all at once and prevents their breaking up.

Small, lean, roasting cuts of beef keep moist and flavoursome if they are marinated before cooking. For these, use an indirect heat.

Large beef joints, such as a standing rib or rolled rib maintain their moisture without marinating. They can be basted from time to time but even this may not be necessary. As they are cooked for a longer time than the smaller cuts, they pick up more of that delicious, characteristic smoky kettle flavour which really makes any other flavouring unnecessary. To enhance this, add two soaked wood blocks to the charcoal on each side. Oak blocks are particularly good with beef.

If you have a small, very lean joint such as aitchbone or rolled rump, a beef pot-roast is a good idea. Sear the meat first and then wrap it in a single layer of heavy duty foil, or a double thickness of standard foil, along with flavourings such as diced carrot, celery and onion, herbs, 2 tablespoons oil and about 4 tablespoons wine. Cook on the grill over indirect heat for about 30 minutes per 450g/1lb or until well done.

Cooking Times

STEAKS

Brush with basting mixture or marinate. Snip fat at regular intervals round edges. Cook over direct heat.

	Minutes per side					
Thickness	*Rare*		*Medium*		*Well done*	
	1st side	*2nd side*	*1st side*	*2nd side*	*1st side*	*2nd side*
2.5cm/1inch	2	3	4	4	5	6
4cm/1½inch	5	6	7	8	9	10
5cm/2inches	7	8	9	9	10	11

If searing, cook for 1 minute each side uncovered. Take 1 minute each side off the covered cooking time.
Less tender steaks such as top rump, chuck or topside are best cooked to medium or well done.

BEEF FILLET (TENDERLOIN)

If one piece or halved crossways, 45 minutes to 1 hour depending on whether it is required to be rare (60°C/140°F) or medium (70°C/160°F).

BEEF ROASTS

If possible, stand them at room temperature for 1½-2 hours before cooking. If using a meat thermometer insert it in the centre of the thickest lean part. Use indirect heat. Place fat side up in a roast holder or on the grill.

Cut	Minutes per 450g/1lb		
	Rare (65°C/150°F)	*Medium* (70°C/160°F)	*Well done* (75°C/170°F)
Topside, top rump, rolled rump, aitchbone, silverside	—	18-22	20-22
Rolled rib	16-18	18-22	20-22
Rolled brisket	—	—	20-22
Standing rib (on bone)	18-20	20-25	25-30

Thin rib (short ribs): total time approximately 1½ hours. When done, wrap the joint in foil and leave to stand for 20-30 minutes.

BURGERS

Thickness	Minutes per side		
	Rare	*Medium*	*Well done*
2cm/¾inch	3	4	5
2.5cm/1 inch	4-5	5-6	6-7

KEBABS
Rare: 5-6 minutes; Medium: 6-7 minutes; Well done: 8-10 minutes.

BASTING MIXTURES FOR BEEF ROASTS

These can also be used as marinades for steaks and small joints and for sealing up in foil parcels with pot roasts.

3 tablespoons olive oil, 3 tablespoons dry white wine, 1 tablespoon tomato paste *or*

3 tablespoons olive oil, 3 tablespoons dry red wine, 1 crushed garlic clove, 2 tablespoons fresh, chopped mixed herbs *or*

3 tablespoons olive oil, 3 tablespoons dry red wine, 1 teaspoon Dijon or French mustard *or*

3 tablespoons olive oil, 2 tablespoons malt vinegar, 1 teaspoon mustard powder *or*

3 tablespoons sesame oil, 2 tablespoons soy sauce, 1 teaspoon freshly grated ginger root, 1 crushed garlic clove *or*

2 tablespoons olive oil, 4 tablespoons dry red wine, juice and grated rind ½ orange, 1 tablespoon each chopped thyme and marjoram.

POT ROAST BEEF WITH SPICED PLUM SAUCE

METRIC/IMPERIAL	AMERICAN
1.15 kg/3 lb piece rolled rib or blade of beef	3 lb piece rolled rib, blade or chuckroast
450 g/1 lb dark cooking plums	1 lb dark cooking plums
2 red chillies	2 red chilies
6 cloves	6 cloves
1 bay leaf	1 bay leaf
125 ml/4 fl oz malt vinegar	½ cup malt vinegar

Prepare the kettle for indirect cooking.

Halve and stone (pit) the plums. Core, seed and finely chop the chillies.

Sear the meat for 20 minutes directly over the coals, turning it frequently. Put the meat into a foil tray. Surround it with the plums. Put in the chillies, cloves and bay leaf, and pour in the vinegar. Cover the tray completely with foil.

Cook over indirect heat for 1½ hours or until completely tender. Take out the meat and wrap in foil to keep warm. Rub the contents of the tray through a sieve. Skim if necessary and reheat in a heavy pan over direct heat. Carve the beef and serve the sauce separately.
Note: Both beef and sauce can be served cold if wished.

RED WINE MARINADE FOR BEEF ROASTS

Use for topside, silverside, aitchbone, top rump and rolled rib joints.

METRIC/IMPERIAL	AMERICAN
425 ml/¾ pint dry red wine	2 cups dry red wine
6 tablespoons olive oil	6 tablespoons olive oil
2 tablespoons red wine vinegar	2 tablespoons red wine vinegar
1 onion, chopped	1 onion, chopped
1 large carrot, chopped	1 large carrot, chopped
2 celery sticks, chopped	2 celery sticks, chopped
1 garlic clove, chopped	1 garlic clove, chopped
2 teaspoons black peppercorns	2 teaspoons black peppercorns
2 sprigs each parsley, thyme, marjoram, sage	2 sprigs each parsley, thyme, marjoram, sage
2 bay leaves	2 bay leaves

Put all the ingredients into a saucepan. Bring to just below boiling point, cover, and keep at that temperature for 5 minutes. Take the pan from the heat and cool the marinade completely, still covered.

Put the marinade into a deep dish big enough to take your joint of beef. Add the beef and turn it to make sure that it is well coated.

Leave in the refrigerator for 48 hours, turning it twice daily. Roast according to instructions.

GRILLED STEAK WITH CHIVES

METRIC/IMPERIAL	AMERICAN
900 g/2 lb rump steak in four even-sized pieces	2 lb rum steak in four even-sized pieces
or four sirloin steaks	or four sirloin steaks
6 tablespoons olive oil	6 tablespoons olive oil
2 tablespoons dry red wine	2 tablespoons dry red wine
freshly ground black pepper	freshly ground black pepper
6 tablespoons chopped chives	6 tablespoons chopped chives
125 g/4 oz curd or cream cheese	½ cup curd or cream cheese
pinch sea salt	pinch sea salt

In a flat dish mix together the oil and wine. Season with pepper and mix in half the chives. Turn the pieces of steak in the mixture, making sure that each one is well coated. Leave for at least 1 hour at room temperature.

Beat the remaining chives into the cheese and season to taste with pepper. Cook the steak over direct heat for the time required, spooning the cheese on top for the final 2 minutes of cooking. It should heat through and begin to soften.

BEEF LOAF

METRIC/IMPERIAL	AMERICAN
450 g/1 lb minced beef	1 lb ground beef
125 g/4 oz fresh wholewheat breadcrumbs	1 cup fresh wholewheat breadcrumbs
6 tablespoons stock	6 tablespoons stock
2 tablespoons Worcestershire sauce	2 tablespoons Worcestershire sauce
1 small onion, fine grated	1 small onion, finely grated
1 small carrot, finely grated	1 small carrot, finely grated
125 g/4 oz mushrooms, finely chopped	¼ lb mushrooms, finely chopped
2 tablespoons chopped parsley	2 tablespoons chopped parsley
1 tablespoon chopped thyme	1 tablespoon chopped thyme
2 sage leaves, chopped	2 sage leaves, chopped

Prepare the kettle for indirect cooking.

Put the beef into a large bowl. Soak the breadcrumbs in the stock and Worcestershire sauce for 10 minutes. Mix into the beef. Add the remaining ingredients and mix well, squeezing the mixture together with your fingers.

Put the mixture into a 450 g/1 lb foil loaf tin, heaping it up in the centre. Cook for 1 hour, or until it is firm and cooked through, checking at 50 minutes.

Either serve hot or cool completely in the tin before turning out and slicing.

LAMB

When lamb is cooked in a kettle barbecue, the natural moisture of the meat is maintained, while at the same time the fat is allowed to drip away.

Chops and steaks cut from the leg or chump end can be cooked quickly over direct heat, while large joints should be roasted slowly over indirect heat. Most cuts of lamb can be cooked to rare, medium or well done, so refer to the charts and take your choice.

Lamb is a meat which quickly becomes flavoured with herbs and spices. You can simply brush it with oil and lay herbs above and below it while cooking, or let it stand for a time in a tasty marinade. Most large roasting cuts can be boned and filled with a savoury stuffing before reshaping and tying.

Breast of lamb can be a fatty cut and so barbecuing over indirect heat suits it well. Cut into small pieces about 2.5 cm by 7.5 cm/1 inch by 3 inches first, and always tenderise it in a marinade for at least 6 hours.

Liver, and kidneys that have been split and cored, should be brushed well with oil, seasoned and sprinkled with herbs before cooking. Kidneys in their own fat are delicious if simply placed on the grill over an indirect heat.

Cooking Times
LAMB ROASTS

Bring to room temperature for 1½ hours before cooking over indirect heat.

Cut	Minutes per 450 g/1 lb		
	Rare (60°C/140°F)	Medium (65°C/150°F)	Well done (75°C/170°)
Leg, whole	18-22	22-28	28-33
Leg, chump end	18-22	22-28	28-33
Leg, shank end	22-28	28-33	33-38
Shoulder, on bone	—	22-28	28-35
Shoulder, rolled	—	33-38	38-43
Loin (rib) 675-900 g/ 1½-2 lb	30-35	35-40	40-45
Loin (rib) 900 g-2.7 kg/ 2-6 lb	25-30	30-35	35-40
Crown roast	28-33	33-38	38-43

Wrap in foil and leave to stand for 20 minutes before serving.

LIVER

Cut into 1 cm/⅜ inch thick slices. Cook over direct heat, 5 minutes per side.

KIDNEY

Split and cored: cook over direct heat, 10 minutes per side.
In fat: cook over direct heat, 45 minutes total time.

LEG, BUTTERFLIED

Cook over direct heat, 20-25 minutes per side.

CHOPS AND STEAKS
Direct heat

Thickness	Minutes per side		
	Rare	Medium	Well done
2.5 cm/1 inch	5-6	7	8
4 cm/1½ inch	7	8-9	10
5 cm/2 inches	8-9	10-12	12-14

BREAST (cut into spare ribs)

Cook over indirect heat 1½ hours, or until crisp and brown.

MARINADES AND FLAVOURINGS FOR LAMB

Spread chops with a mixture of 3 tablespoons Dijon mustard and 1 tablespoon rosemary leaves. Cook over indirect heat with a halved garlic clove on each one. The same mixture can be spread inside a boned piece of loin or shoulder *or*

Grated rind and juice 1 medium orange, 150 ml/¼ pint/5 fl oz dry white wine, 1 small chopped onion, 2 tablespoons chopped thyme, ¼ teaspoon cayenne pepper. Use for chops or double the quantity for roasts *or*

Sprinkle cut surface of boned roasts with chopped garlic, chopped mint and turmeric *or*

Marinade for roasts and breast: 150 ml/¼ pint/5 fl oz natural (unflavored) yoghurt, grated rind and juice 1 lemon, 2 tablespoons chopped mint, 1 crushed garlic clove, freshly ground black pepper *or*

As above, substituting 2 tablespoons each chopped parsley and marjoram and 2 teaspoons chopped rosemary for the mint *or*

150 ml/¼ pint/5 fl oz natural (unflavored) yoghurt, grated rind and juice 1 lemon, 1 tablespoon tomato paste, 2 teaspoons curry powder, 1 teaspoon turmeric, 1 crushed garlic clove *or*

Grated rind and juice or 2 limes, ½ pint natural (unflavored) yoghurt, 2 teaspoons paprika, ½ teaspoon cayenne pepper, 2 tablespoons chopped fresh coriander, 1 garlic clove, crushed with pinch sea salt.

SHOULDER OF LAMB WITH CURRANT STUFFING

METRIC/IMPERIAL	AMERICAN
½ shoulder of lamb, boned	½ shoulder of lamb, boned
15 g/½ oz butter	1 tablespoon butter
1 medium onion, finely chopped	1 medium onion, finely chopped
50 g/2 oz currants	¼ cup currants
50 g/2 oz fresh wholewheat breadcrumbs	1 cup fresh wholewheat breadcrumbs
1 tablespoon chopped lemon thyme	1 tablespoon chopped lemon thyme
1 tablespoon chopped rosemary	1 tablespoon chopped rosemary
2 tablespoons chopped parsley	2 tablespoons chopped parsley
grated rind and juice ½ lemon	grated rind and juice ½ lemon
for basting	*for basting*
juice ½ lemon	juice ½ lemon
4 tablespoons oil	¼ cup oil
1 teaspoon Dijon mustard	1 teaspoon Dijon mustard

Prepare the kettle for indirect cooking.

Melt the butter in a frying pan on a low heat. Put in the onion and soften it. Add the currants and take the pan from the heat. Mix in the breadcrumbs, herbs, lemon rind and juice.

Lay the lamb out flat. Spread the stuffing mixture over the cut surface. Roll up the meat and tie it with fine string. Place the lamb in a meat rack or directly on the grill. Beat together the lemon juice, oil and mustard. Brush the mixture over the lamb.

Cook for 2½-3 hours, basting every 30 minutes. It should be cooked through, registering 75°C/170°F on a meat thermometer. Wrap in foil and leave to stand for 30 minutes before serving.

LAMB CHOPS WITH APRICOTS

METRIC/IMPERIAL	AMERICAN
8 small loin lamb chops, or 4 lamb steaks	8 small loin lamb chops, or 4 lamb steaks
150 ml/¼ pint natural yoghurt	5 fl oz unflavored yoghurt
1 teaspoon curry powder	1 teaspoon curry powder
1 garlic clove, crushed	1 garlic clove, crushed
4 tablespoons chopped fennel	¼ cup chopped fennel
8 apricots	8 apricots

Trim the chops of any excess fat if necessary. Mix together the yoghurt, curry powder, garlic and fennel. Put the mixture into a flat dish. Turn the chops in the marinade, cover and leave for at least 1 hour at room temperature.

Prepare the kettle for indirect cooking.

Stone (pit) the apricots and cut into slices lengthways. Take the chops from the marinade. Sear directly over the hot coals. Cook over indirect heat for 15 minutes. Turn the chops and arrange the apricot slices on top. Cook for a further 10-15 minutes or until cooked through and the apricots are soft and beginning to 'melt' into the meat.

POULTRY AND GAME

Chicken, capon and turkey, birds which can all become dry when cooked in a conventional oven, retain all their moisture and flavour when cooked in a kettle barbecue. A duck or goose will stay moist while losing most of its fat, and game, which can sometimes be slightly tough, benefits from the slow, indirect form of cooking.

Chicken can be cooked whole or jointed. A whole chicken need only be basted as it cooks, joints are best marinated, if only for a short time, or at least brushed well with an oil and herb or spice mixture before cooking. A whole turkey, turkey pieces or a rolled turkey breast can all be cooked successfully over indirect heat. Baste them well as they cook.

To give a duck or goose a crispy, browned skin, prick it all over with a fork and then rub the skin with fine sea salt. It will need no basting for the first hour of cooking after which it can be brushed with a glaze.

Small game birds may need to be covered with bacon rashers (slices) to keep them moist. Larger ones, such as pheasant or guinea-fowl, can be cooked whole, jointed, or spatchcocked (split down the back, rib cage removed and bird opened out flat). They need to be well brushed with a flavoured oil mixture before cooking and basted as they cook.

If a stuffing is added to any bird approximately 20 minutes extra should be added to the cooking time. To flavour poultry and game without using a stuffing fill the body cavity with sliced orange or lemon, or chopped apple, plus a bouquet of herbs of your choice.

Truss all poultry and game before cooking and, if possible, place it in a roasting rack on the grill. Cut the string two-thirds of the way through cooking time to ensure that the thicker parts cook well. After cooking, whole birds should be wrapped in foil and allowed to stand for 20 minutes before serving.

Cooking Times

CHICKEN, *whole*
Cook over indirect heat to well done, 85°C/185°F.

350-575 g/12 oz-1 lb 4 oz — 65 minutes
900 g-1.35 kg/2-3 lb — 70-80 minutes
1.35 kg-1.8 kg/3-4 lb — 1½-1¾ hours

CHICKEN, *jointed*
Cook over indirect heat, 30 minutes each side.

CAPON
2.25 kg-3.2 kg/5-8 lb
Cook over indirect heat, 2-2½ hours to well done 85°C/185°F.

DUCK
Cook over indirect heat, 12-15 minutes per 450 g/1 lb or to 85°C/185°F.

GOOSE
Cook over indirect heat, 20-30 minutes per 450 g/1 lb or 85° C/185° F.

TURKEY
Cook over indirect heat to 85°C/185°F.
2.7-3.2 kg/6-7 lb — 2-2¾ hours
3.2-5.4 kg/7-12 lb — 2½-3¾ hours
5.4-7.2 kg/12-16 lb — 3½-4 hours
7.2-9 kg/16-20 lb — 4½-5 hours.

TURKEY BREAST, *rolled*
Cook over indirect heat, 1-1½ hours to 80°C/175°F.

GAME BIRDS
Cook over indirect heat.
Pheasant — 25-35 minutes per 450 g/1 lb
Partridge — 60-80 minutes total
Pigeon — 45-60 minutes total
Quail — 20-25 minutes total
Guinea-fowl — 70 to 80 minutes total.

RABBIT, *jointed*
Cook over indirect heat, 1 hour (must be marinated or well basted).

VENISON
Roasts: 25-30 minutes per 450 g/1 lb or to 65°C/150°F.
Steaks: 2.5 cm/1 inch, 4-5 minutes per side; 4 cm/1½ inches, 7-8 minutes per side; 5 cm/2 inches, 8-9 minutes per side.

MARINADES AND BASTING MIXTURES FOR CHICKEN

Crush together 20 juniper berries and 20 black pepper corns. Rub into the chicken skin. Baste with olive oil or a mixture of 4 tablespoons/¼ cup each dry red wine and olive oil *or*

Tandoori marinade: 275 ml/½ pint/1¼ cups natural (unflavored) yoghurt, juice ½ lemon, 15 g/½ oz fresh ginger root, grated, 1 crushed garlic clove, 2 teaspoons cumin seeds, 2 teaspoons ground coriander, 2 teaspoons ground turmeric. Marinate whole chicken for at least 24 hours *or*

Curried Apricot Basting Mixture: 4 tablespoons olive oil, juice ½ lemon, 2 tablespoons sugar-free apricot jam (jelly), 1 teaspoon curry powder, 1 crushed garlic clove *or*

Tarragon Basting Mixture (use also as a marinade): 6 tablespoons olive oil, 2 tablespoons tarragon vinegar, 2 tablespoons chopped tarragon, freshly ground black pepper, 1 crushed garlic clove, optional *or*

Hot Spiced Mixture (use also as a marinade): 4 tablespoons olive oil, juice ½ lemon, 1 tablespoon tomato paste, 1 teaspoon paprika, ¼-½ teaspoon cayenne pepper, ½ teaspoon ground cinnamon, 1 crushed garlic clove.

AROMATIC CHICKEN

METRIC/IMPERIAL	AMERICAN
1.575 kg/3½ lb roasting chicken	3½ lb roasting chicken
225 ml/8 fl oz dry white wine	1 cup dry white wine
4 tablespoons olive oil	¼ cup olive oil
freshly ground black pepper	freshly ground black pepper
4 large bay leaves, torn into small pieces	4 large bay leaves, torn into small pieces
2 tablespoons chopped celery leaves	2 tablespoons chopped celery leaves
twelve 7.5 cm/3 inch fennel stalks fresh or dried	twelve 3 inch fennel stalks, fresh or dried

Joint the chicken. Mix together the wine and oil and season with the pepper. Put the mixture into a flat dish. Add the bay and celery leaves. Turn the chicken pieces in the mixture. Leave them in the dish, with fennel stalks above and below them. Cover and leave for at least 6 hours at room temperature.

Prepare the kettle for indirect cooking.

Brush all the herbs from the chicken. Lay the fennel stalks on the grill rack. Put the chicken pieces on top, skin side down and cook for 30 minutes. Turn and cook for a further 30 minutes, or until the juices run clear when the meat is pierced with a fork.

STUFFED LEMON CHICKEN

METRIC/IMPERIAL

1.575 kg/3½ lb roasting chicken
stuffing
75 g/3 oz fresh wholewheat breadcrumbs
25 g/1 oz shelled walnuts, finely chopped
25 g/1 oz chopped parsley
grated rind and juice ½ lemon
125 ml/4 fl oz natural yoghurt
for basting
4 tablespoons olive oil
juice ½ lemon
1 garlic clove, crushed

AMERICAN

3½ lb roasting chicken
stuffing
¾ cup fresh wholewheat breadcrumbs
2 tablespoons shelled walnuts, finely chopped
½ cup chopped parlsey
grated rind and juice ½ lemon
½ cup unflavored yoghurt
for basting
¼ cup olive oil
juice ½ lemon
1 garlic clove, crushed

Prepare the kettle for indirect cooking.

Mix together the stuffing ingredients. Stuff and truss the chicken. Brush it with the basting mixture.

Set the chicken on the grill over the drip tray. Cook for 1¾ hours, basting frequently and testing with a fork at 1¼ and 1½ hours.

Carve and serve with the stuffing.

GLAZED DUCK WITH LEMON

METRIC/IMPERIAL

1.8-2 kg/4-4½ lb duckling
2 teaspoons fine sea salt
1 lemon
bouquet garni, which includes mint sprig
2 tablespoons red currant jelly
2 tablespoons dry red wine
2 tablespoons chopped mint

AMERICAN

4-4½ lb duckling
2 teaspoons fine sea salt
1 lemon
bouquet garni, which includes mint sprig
2 tablespoons red currant jelly
2 tablespoons dry red wine
2 tablespoons chopped mint

Prepare the kettle for indirect cooking.

Slice half the lemon thinly and put the slices inside the duck with the bouquet garni. Prick the skin all over with a fork and rub with the salt. Truss the duck and put into a roasting rack. Cook in the centre of the kettle for 1½ hours.

While the duck is cooking, put the red currant jelly and wine into a saucepan and set on a low heat for the jelly to melt. Slice the remaining half lemon thinly.

Brush the glaze over the duck. Lay the lemon slices down the breast. Scatter the chopped mint over the rest of the skin. Cook for a further 30 minutes or until shiny and brown.

VEGETABLES

Whichever vegetable you choose, you can be sure that it can be cooked in a kettle barbecue. Some can be cooked over direct or indirect heat, directly on the grill. Many are best wrapped in foil so that they steam naturally in their own juices, so preserving much of their goodness and natural flavour.

Use heavy duty foil or a double thickness of standard weight foil. Cook over indirect heat.

ARTICHOKES, GLOBE: Remove stems and trim the leaves. Place singly in lightly buttered or oiled foil. Add either 3 tablespoons water or 2 tablespoons each water and oil. Cook 1 hour.

ARTICHOKES, JERUSALEM: Peel. Slice or dice. Place in buttered or oiled foil, 225 g/8 oz per packet. Add 2 tablespoons water or stock. Dot with butter. Sprinkle, if wished, with chopped parsley and/or mustard powder. Cook 30 minutes.

AUBERGINES (EGGPLANT): *Direct method:* Cut into 1.5 cm/½ inch thick slices. Put into colander, sprinkle with sea salt and leave to drain for 20 minutes. Wash with cold water and dry with kitchen paper. Brush with oil and season with freshly ground black pepper. Cook directly over the charcoal for 10 minutes, basting and turning once.
Foil method: Cut into 2.5 cm/1 inch dice. Salt, drain and dry as before. Place in foil either sprinkled with oil or dotted with butter, one medium aubergine per packet. Cook 30-40 minutes.

SPICED BASTING MIXTURE FOR AUBERGINES (EGGPLANT)

for 450 g/1 lb

METRIC/IMPERIAL	AMERICAN
6 tablespoons olive oil	¾ cup olive oil
juice 1 lemon	juice 1 lemon
1 tablespoon tomato paste	1 tablespoon tomato paste
½ teaspoon ground cinnamon	½ teaspoon ground cinnamon
½ teaspoon ground cumin	½ teaspoon ground cumin
pinch chilli powder	pinch chili powder
1 garlic clove, crushed	1 garlic clove, crushed

Beat together in a large bowl. Turn the slices or cubes of aubergine in the mixture. Leave for 30 minutes if possible. Cook by direct or foil method.

ASPARAGUS: Trim ends, scrape any tough skin from the stems. Leave stems whole. Place in buttered foil, one serving per packet. Add 2 tablespoons water. Dot with butter. If wished add chopped parsley or grated Parmesan cheese. Cook 10-20 minutes, checking at 10 minutes.

BEANS, BROAD (Lima): Place in buttered or oiled foil, 225 g/8 oz per packet. Add 4 tablespoons water, dry cider or stock. Dot with butter or sprinkle with oil. If wished add 2 tablespoons chopped parsley or 1 tablespoon chopped savory. Cook 15-20 minutes. Frozen beans can be used in the same way.

BEANS, FRENCH (Green, French style): Top and tail. Leave whole or cut into short lengths. Place in buttered or oiled foil, no more than 225 g/8 oz per packet. Add 2 tablespoons water. Dot with butter or add 1 tablespoon oil. Flavour with 1 tablespoon chopped thyme or savory and/or a little grated nutmeg. If wished 25 g/1 oz diced bacon can also be added. Cook 15-20 minutes.

BEANS, RUNNER (Green): Trim tops and edges. Slice. Place in buttered or oiled foil, 175 g/6 oz per packet. Add 1 tablespoon water, and 1 tablespoon oil. Flavour, if wished, with chopped parsley, thyme or savory. Diced bacon can be added if wished. Cook 15-20 minutes.

BEETROOT (Beets): Use small, round beetroot. Trim stems to 1 cm/½ inch but leave root. Wash, but do not peel. Place in oiled foil, four per packet. Add 1 tablespoon water. Cook 30-40 minutes. Peel before serving.

BROCCOLI: Trim stalks to 5 cm/2 inches. Scrape any tough skin from stalk. Place in buttered foil, four to six heads per packet. Add 2 tablespoons water plus either 1 tablespoon oil or 15 g/½ oz butter. A squeeze of lemon juice may be added, or a sprinkling of grated Cheddar, Gruyère or Parmesan cheese. Cook 15-20 minutes.

BRUSSELS SPROUTS: Trim stems and outer leaves if necessary. Place in buttered or oiled foil, 175 g/6 oz per packet. Add 2 tablespoons water or stock. If wished, mix ½ teaspoon Dijon or a spiced granular mustard with the liquid. Dot with butter or add 1 tablespoon oil. Cook 20-25 minutes.

CABBAGE: Shred finely. Place in buttered or oiled foil, 225 g/8 oz per packet. Add 2 tablespoons water and either 1 tablespoon oil or dot with butter. Season with freshly ground black pepper. Cook 20 minutes.

Spiced Cabbage Mixture: For 1 medium cabbage: 10 black peppercorns, 8 juniper berries, 8 allspice berries, 1 chopped garlic clove, pinch fine sea salt. Crush all together. Mix into shredded cabbage before putting into the foil.

CARROTS: Keep small new carrots whole. Slice large carrots or cut into matchstick pieces. Place in buttered or oiled foil, 225 g/8 oz per packet. Add 2 tablespoons water. Dot with butter. Sprinkle with freshly grated nutmeg or chopped parsley, chervil or marjoram. Cook 30-45 minutes.

CAULIFLOWER: Break into florets (flowerets). Place in buttered or oiled foil, 1 small cauliflower per packet. Add 2 tablespoons water or stock. Dot with butter or sprinkle with oil. A small squeeze of lemon juice can be added if wished, also chopped parsley, thyme or lemon thyme, or a sprinkling of grated Parmesan cheese. Cook 15-20 minutes.

CELERY: Cut into 2.5-5 cm/1-2 inch pieces. Place in buttered or oiled foil, 225 g/8 oz per packet. Add 1 tablespoon water or stock plus 1 tablespoon oil. Sprinkle with freshly grated nutmeg and/or add 2 chopped sage leaves. Cook 10-15 minutes.

COURGETTES (ZUCCHINI): *Direct method:* If small, halve lengthways or keep whole. If large, slice 1.5 cm/½ inch thick. Brush with oil and season with freshly ground black pepper. Cook over charcoal on grill rack for 10 minutes, or until soft, turning and basting once.

Foil method: Halve lengthways and then crossways if small. If large, slice 1 cm/⅜ inch thick. Coat with oil and freshly ground black pepper. Place in foil, 175 g/6 oz per packet. Cook for 20 minutes.

Marinade for Courgettes: Use for sliced or quartered courgettes in foil; sliced courgettes to be cooked on direct heat. Enough for 675 g/1½ lb. 4 tablespoons olive oil, juice ½ lemon, 2 tablespoons soured cream, 1 teaspoon Dijon mustard, 2 tablespoons chopped thyme. Mix all together. Leave courgettes in mixture for 30 minutes.

CUCUMBER: Cut into quarters, lengthways. Peel and remove seeds. Cut into 2.5 cm/1 inch lengths. Put into a colander and sprinkle with salt. Leave to drain for 20 minutes. Wash with cold water and dry with kitchen paper. Place in foil, half a large cucumber per packet. Dot with butter or sprinkle with 2 tablespoons oil. Add chopped parsley, fennel or dill weed or a sprinkling of dill seeds. Cook 10-15 minutes.

FLORENCE FENNEL: Slice or chop. Place in buttered or oiled foil, 225 g/8 oz per packet. Add 2 tablespoons oil mixed, if wished, with 1 tablespoon tomato paste, plus chopped parsley. Cook 30 minutes.

MUSHROOMS: Leave button mushrooms whole or slice thinly. Slice open mushrooms thinly. Place in foil, 225 g/8 oz per packet. Dot with butter or add 2 tablespoons oil. Pour on juice ½ lemon. Season, if wished, with 1 tablespoon Worcestershire sauce. Add 2 tablespoons chopped parsley. Cook 15-20 minutes.

ONIONS: Large: Wrap singly in buttered foil. Make a cross cut in top placing a piece of butter on top. 1 tablespoon chopped parsley can be added. Cook 50-60 minutes.

PEAS: Use shelled, fresh or frozen. Place in buttered foil, 225 g/8 oz per packet. Dot with butter and add 1 tablespoon water. Instead of water 4 tablespoons/¼ cup double (heavy) cream may be used. Chopped parsley or chopped mint can be added, also chopped spring onions (scallions).

PEPPERS, SWEET: Core and seed. Cut into 2.5 cm/1 inch strips. Place in buttered or oiled foil, two large peppers per packet. Add a thinly sliced small onion, or 1 crushed garlic clove and chopped parsley or thyme if wished. Cook 15-20 minutes.

POTATOES: *Direct method:* Scrub and dry even-shaped, medium-sized potatoes. Prick them twice on each side with a fork. Brush

RICE STUFFED PEPPERS

METRIC/IMPERIAL	AMERICAN
4 green or red peppers, or a mixture	4 sweet green or red peppers, or a mixture
3 tablespoons oil	3 tablespoons oil
1 medium onion, thinly sliced	1 medium onion, thinly sliced
1 garlic clove, finely chopped	1 garlic clove, finely chopped
1 teaspoon ground turmeric	1 teaspoon ground turmeric
pinch chilli powder	pinch chili powder
200 g/7 oz long grain brown rice	1 cup long grain brown rice
575 ml/1 pint stock	2½ cups stock
pinch sea salt	pinch sea salt
75 g/3 oz peanuts	½ cup peanuts

Heat the oil in a saucepan on a low heat. Add the onion and soften it. Stir in the turmeric and chilli powder and cook for ½ minute. Add the rice and stir for 1 minute more. Pour in the stock and bring to the boil. Season with the salt. Cover and cook for 40-45 minutes or until the rice is tender and all the liquid absorbed. Mix in the peanuts.

Cut the tops from the peppers and remove the cores. Fill the peppers with the rice, pressing down well. Wrap each pepper separately in a sheet of oiled foil.

Cook in the centre of the kettle for 45-50 minutes.

---

with oil. Place directly over the charcoal for about 20 minutes, or until soft in the centre, turning once. The skins will darken but the taste is superb. Potatoes can also be placed on potato spikes (available from barbecue accessory shops).

Indirect method: Scrub, make slits in the potatoes at regular 1 cm/⅜ inch intervals, not going completely through. Top with butter and wrap in buttered foil; or baste with oil. Sprinkle with a little paprika if wished. Cook 45-60 minutes.

POTATOES, SWEET: Cook as ordinary potatoes. For potatoes in foil, Barbados sugar and/or rum can be added.

PUMPKIN: Cut into 2.5 cm/1 inch chunks. Place in oiled foil, 225 g/8 oz per packet. Spoon over a mixture of 2 tablespoons oil plus 1 tablespoon tomato paste or soy sauce and 1 crushed garlic clove. Cook 20-30 minutes.

SQUASH: Halve small squash and remove seeds. Fill centres with diced bacon, chopped onion and a sprinkling of Barbados sugar. Wrap each half separately in oiled foil. Cook 50-60 minutes.

SWEETCORN: See under first courses (page).

TOMATOES: Cook over direct heat. Slice in half either lengthways or crossways. Season if wished.

Toppings for tomato halves: chopped basil or parsley; chopped anchovy fillets; halved small black or green olives; thin slices of cheese; pinch celery salt or garlic salt. Place on grill rack. Cook for 5-7 minutes or until heated through and beginning to soften but still firm enough to be lifted with tongs.

DESSERTS

The most popular desserts for cooking on any type of barbecue are those based on fresh fruit. Cooking fruit in a kettle barbecue retains flavour, goodness and a firm texture. Fruit can be cooked in foil trays, in parcels of foil or threaded on kebab skewers.

Fruit, however, is not the only type of dessert that can be cooked in a kettle barbecue. Because the kettle allows heat to circulate all round any food that is put into it, it is quite possible to make baked pies, puddings and crumbles.

APPLES: Core and score the skins round the circumference with a sharp knife. Fill with dried fruits moistened with fruit juice, ground nuts sweetened with honey, or with Barbados sugar and butter. Wrap singly in foil. Cook for 30-40 minutes.

APRICOTS: Halve and stone. Slice if wished. Place on buttered foil, six apricots (one serving) per packet. Sprinkle with Barbados sugar, melted honey or sugar-free jam (jelly). Cinnamon and/or nutmeg can also be added. Cook for 30 minutes.

BANANAS: Peel. Slice into four diagonal pieces and reshape. Place singly on buttered foil. Add Barbados sugar, melted honey, apple and pear spread or sugar-free jam (jelly). Scatter with 1 tablespoon dried sultanas (golden raisins) or raisins if wished. 1 tablespoon rum or sweet sherry can also be added. Cook for 10-15 minutes.

FRUIT KEBABS: Cut fruit into even-sized pieces, leaving small fruits such as grapes, cherries and strawberries whole. Thread on to slender kebab skewers. Brush with sweetener dissolved in lemon juice, spirit or liqueur. Sprinkle sparingly with ground sweet spices such as cinnamon, nutmeg or cardamom. Cook directly over charcoal for about 5 minutes or until lightly browned all over.

GRAPEFRUIT: Halve, leave in shell and separate the segments. Sprinkle with Barbados sugar, or spoon over some melted honey, apple and pear spread, concentrated apple juice or sugar-free jam (jelly). Sprinkle with a small amount of ground cinnamon. Add 1 tablespoon sherry or marsala if wished. Dot with butter. Place in foil tray. Bake for 30 minutes or until heated through and glazed.

ORANGES: Peel, cut into 1 cm/⅜ inch thick slices. Lay in a foil tray, only slightly overlapping. Spoon over melted honey and orange liqueur or any of the flavourings for grapefruit. Cook in centre of kettle for 20 minutes or until heated through and glazed.

PEACHES: Halve, skin and stone (pit). Lay in foil tray. Top with melted honey, sugar-free jam (jelly) or apple and pear spread. Scatter with chopped nuts if wished. Cook for 25 minutes or until heated through and beginning to soften.

PEARS: Peal, core and slice. Place each one separately in buttered foil. Sprinkle with cinnamon, nutmeg or ground cardamom. Spoon over sugar, honey, sugar-free jam or apple and pear spread. Cook for 30 minutes.

PINEAPPLE: Peel. Either cut into slices and core, or quarter lengthways and core. Lay in foil tray. Sprinkle with honey and rum, sherry or liqueur. Cook for 30-40 minutes or until heated through.

ALMOND STUFFED PEACHES

METRIC/IMPERIAL	AMERICAN
4 peaches, ripe but firm	4 peaches, ripe but firm
125 g/4 oz ground almonds	¾ cup ground almonds
4 tablespoons sugar-free raspberry jam	¼ cup sugar-free raspberry jelly
oil for greasing	oil for greasing

Prepare the kettle for indirect cooking.

Halve and stone (pit) the peaches. Mix together the almonds and jam. Pile the mixture on top of the peaches. Arrange them in a lightly oiled foil tray.

Cook in the centre of the kettle for 25 minutes or until heated through and beginning to soften.

OATY PLUM CRUMBLE

METRIC/IMPERIAL	AMERICAN
900 g/2 lb red cooking plums	2 lb cooking plums
75 g/3 oz raisins	½ cup raisins
75 g/3 oz Barbados sugar	½ cup Barbados sugar
225 g/8 oz rolled oats	2 cups rolled oats
50 g/2 oz sunflower seeds	6 tablespoons sunflower seeds
25 g/1 oz sesame seeds	3 tablespoons sesame seeds
4 tablespoons oil	¼ cup oil

Prepare the kettle for indirect cooking.

Halve and stone (pit) the plums. Put into a 23 × 28 cm/9 × 11 inch baking tin or foil tray. Scatter with the raisins and sugar. Mix together the oats, sunflower and sesame seeds. Add the oil and mix, making sure that the oats and seeds are well coated. Cover the plums with the mixture.

Cook in the centre of the kettle for 45 minutes or until the top is beginning to brown. Serves 6.

BAKING

Bread, both savoury and sweet, is deliciously moist and soft when cooked in a kettle barbecue and the crispy crust has a very slightly smoky flavour.

Even a quiche can be baked over indirect heat in the kettle. The pastry will be crisp and the filling will taste slightly smoky, especially if it contains fish, bacon or ham.

TUNA AND CORN QUICHE

METRIC/IMPERIAL	*AMERICAN*
shortcrust pastry made with 175 g/6 oz wholewheat flour	shortcrust pastry made with 1½ cups wholewheat flour
100 g/3½ oz tin tuna	3½ oz can tuna
175 g/6 oz tin sweetcorn	6 oz can corn
1 green pepper	1 sweet green pepper
2 tablespoons oil	2 tablespoons oil
1 small onion, thinly sliced	1 small onion, thinly sliced
1 garlic clove, finely chopped	1 garlic clove, finely chopped
3 eggs	3 eggs
50 g/2 oz curd cheese	¼ cup curd cheese

Prepare the kettle for indirect cooking.

Use the pastry to line a 20 cm/8 inch diameter foil tart tin. Drain and flake the tuna. Drain the sweetcorn. Mix them together. Core and seed the pepper and cut into 2.5 cm/1 inch strips.

Heat the oil in a frying pan on a low heat. Add the onion, pepper and garlic and soften them. Take the pan from the heat and mix in the corn and tuna. Spread the mixture evenly over the pastry base.

Beat the eggs and gradually beat them into the cheese so that you have a thick, smooth mixture. Pour it over the filling.

Carefully place the quiche in the centre of the kettle. Cook for 50 minutes, checking at 30 and 40 minutes. The top will set but not brown and the pastry should be crisp but not coloured.

HEALTH BREAD

METRIC/IMPERIAL	*AMERICAN*
350 g/12 oz wholewheat flour	3 cups wholewheat flour
75 g/3 oz medium oatmeal	¾ cup medium oatmeal
25 g/1 oz bran	¾ cup bran
1 teaspoon bicarbonate of soda	1 teaspoon baking soda
1 teaspoon fine sea salt	1 teaspoon fine sea salt
6 tablespoons oil	6 tablespoons oil
275 ml/1 pint natural yoghurt or buttermilk	1¼ cups unflavored yoghurt or buttermilk

Prepare the kettle for indirect cooking.

In a bowl, mix together the flour, oatmeal, bran, bicarbonate of soda (baking soda) and salt. Make a well in the centre and put in the oil and yoghurt or buttermilk. Mix to a dough.

Put the dough into an oiled 450 g/1 lb loaf tin. Cook the loaf in the centre of the kettle for 50-60 minutes or until it sounds hollow when tapped, and a skewer inserted in the centre comes out clean.

Smoker. Top left: Smoky Baked Beans; top right: Mesquite-Smoked Pork; bottom left: Smoked Salt Pork Rashers; bottom right: Smoked Sausages.

Smoker. Top: Smoked Peppered Turkey; bottom right: Smoky Barbecued Chicken Portions; bottom left: Smoky Stuffed Peppers.

SMOKE COOKERY

Wood smoke gives food a delicious rich flavour and deep golden brown colour. The cooking process is long and slow, allowing meat to become very tender and fish soft and flaky. The type of smoking that can be done on charcoal grills is hot smoking, a process which produces food that is ready to eat and which requires no further cooking.

Equipment

Food can be smoked effectively in a kettle barbecue or in a special charcoal smoker. Most smokers consist of a tall metal cylinder with a rounded base and domed lid. In the base there is a rack which holds the charcoal. On a rack above there are fitments which hold a water bowl. Boiling water is put into this to keep the atmosphere inside the smoker moist and steamy. Directly above the water bowl is the grill for holding the food. Many models have an additional rack above the first. This enables you to cook smaller pieces of meat or fish, which do not require such a high heat, at the same time as large birds or joints. Most purpose-built smokers have air vents in the lid and base and a small door in the side for you to add more charcoal to the fire.

If you are using a kettle barbecue, place a drip tray in the centre of the charcoal rack and fill this with boiling water. You need less fuel in a kettle barbecue but this must be replenished regularly with hot coals. It is therefore a good idea to have a smaller, open barbecue on which to keep the lighted coals ready. You will also need long-handled tongs with which to handle the charcoal.

Fuel

The main heat for cooking the food will come from the charcoal. Use briquettes for their slow burning qualities. The smoke for flavouring is provided by hardwood. Too much smoke will spoil the food so only a small amount of wood is necessary. Hardwood is used rather than softwood because of its slow burning qualities. Do not use pine or any other resinous woods as these give an unpleasant flavour to the food. Green, unseasoned wood gives more smoke than dry, but it must not be too new or it will not burn at all. Hardwood that has been cut about 2 months is ideal. Older wood can be used, but it must be soaked in water for about 2 hours before using.

Woods that are suitable for smoking include oak, hickory, mesquite, beech, apple, cherry, peach, pecan, and buttonwood. You can provide these yourself, cutting them into small chunks about 7.5 cm/3 inches square. You can also buy ready-cut wood chunks or chips specially packed for the barbecue.

Whether you are using a special smoker or a kettle barbecue, you will need four chunks to give the right flavour to your food. These should be soaked in water, ideally for 2 hours, before being added to the charcoal. They will burn for 2 or more hours. If your cooking process is going to be longer than this, have other pieces ready soaking. You need about a 225 ml / 8 fl. oz / 1 cup measure of wood chips. Soak them for 30 minutes. They should last 1 to 1½ hours so have extra ones soaking.

Method

If you are using a special smoker, light the manufacturer's recommended amount of charcoal. Pile it in a pyramid to light it and spread it out before cooking. Add the wood chips or blocks to the fire when it has reached the grey ash stage. Pour boiling water into the water bowl. Place the food on the rack and put on the cover. Open the air vents and leave the food to smoke, adding charcoal and more wood when necessary.

The temperature inside the smoker should be between 55 and 60°C/140 and 150°F. Check this by putting a meat thermometer on the rack beside the meat or by using the special gauge which is fitted to some smokers.

To use a kettle barbecue, first light twelve charcoal briquettes on a small barbecue. In the kettle, put the drip tray in the centre of the charcoal grill. When the charcoal has reached the grey ash stage, put four briquettes on either side of the drip tray. Put two wood chunks on each side or scatter the chips over. Pour boiling water into the drip tray. Put the grill in place and put the food directly over the drip tray with no part over the charcoal. Cover the kettle and open all air vents.

The temperature inside the kettle should also be 55-60°C/140-150°F. Again check by placing a thermometer beside or on top of the meat. In order to maintain a steady heat, place fresh briquettes round the four that you have left on the small barbecue. Add extra hot briquettes to those in the kettle about every hour, and keep replenishing the spares so you have a constant supply.

It is best not to smoke in a high wind as this will burn the charcoal too quickly.

Food can be hot smoked by this method until it is completely cooked through. The process, especially for the larger pieces of meat and large birds such as turkeys, is a long one. You can, therefore, transfer them when they are flavoured and golden brown, to a preheated 170°C/325°F/gas mark 3 oven until the required internal temperature is reached. Another method is to parboil meats first and then finish them in the smoker.

Food for smoking

Most foods, from cream cheese to turkeys and even vegetables, can be given the flavour of wood smoke. Fish can be smoked whole, filleted or in cutlets. Meat can be in large joints or cut into slices. Sausages, frankfurters (although these are already slightly smoked) and even burgers can also be smoked. Nothing could look better on the table than a golden smoked chicken or turkey. You can also smoke chicken or turkey pieces.

Preparing food for smoking

Food can be placed directly in the smoker with no additional flavourings whatsoever and still come out tasting delicious. However, you can add to the flavour by marinating it first or steeping it in brine. This will be a slightly spicy flavour and also improve its keeping qualities.

Poultry can be filled with herbs and sliced citrus fruits. Other meats can be rubbed with spices.

To add extra flavour while the food is smoking, the marinade can be added to the water in the bowl or drip tray. If there is no marinade, add herbs, spices, thinly-pared lemon or orange rind or liquids such as red or white wine, beer, cider or fruit juice.

Serving smoked food

Smoked food can be served hot or cold and is equally delicious either way. Generally speaking smaller cuts such as joints of poultry, sausages, burgers and slices of meat are best hot. Large joints of meat and whole birds are best if they are cooled, sliced thinly and served with a salad. White fish is best hot. Oily fish can be served hot or cold. Hard cheese should be cooled completely. Cream cheese can be served warm or chilled.

Sugar-smoking

This is a technique adapted from a Chinese method of cooking. The food is cooked in a kettle barbecue at the normal temperature over indirect heat. The smoky flavour is derived from a bed of brown sugar and China tea leaves over which the food is placed before being completely enclosed in foil.

Cooking Times

FISH

Whole, small fish, 1½-2 hours
Small fillets, 1-1¼ hours
thick fillets, 1¼-1½ hours

BEEF

Steak, 2-3 hours
Burgers, 1½-2 hours
Roasts, 1.35-1.8 kg/3-4 lb, 5 hours *or* 3 hours in smoker and 45 minutes in oven
2.25-3.15 kg/5-7 lb, 6-7 hours, *or* 3 hours in smoker and 1¼-1½ hours in oven

PORK

Chops, 3-4 hours
Roast, 1.8-3.15 kg/4-7 lb, 6-7 hours *or* 3 hours in smoker and 1-1½ hours in oven
Spare ribs, 4-5 hours *or* 3 hours in smoker and 45 minutes in oven
Sausages, 1½-2 hours

LAMB

Leg, 6-7 hours *or* 3 hours in smoker and 1-1½ hours in oven

CHICKEN

Chicken, 1.575 kg/3½ lb, 6-7 hours *or* 2-2½ hours in smoker and 45 minutes in oven   Jointed, 4-5 hours *or* 2 hours in smoker and 30 minutes in oven

DUCK

1.8-2.25 kg/4-5 lb, 7-8 hours *or* 2½ hours in smoker and 1 hour in oven

TURKEY

4.5 kg/10 lb, 8-10 hours *or* 4-4½ hours in smoker and 2½-3 hours in oven

Notes: Where oven and smoker are used the oven should be 170°C/325°F/gas mark 3 As the temperature inside smokers and kettles inevitably varies slightly, cooking times are only approximate. To be certain that poultry and large cuts of meat are cooked through use an oven thermometer. Push it into the meat at the thickest part, not touching the base.

Required Internal Temperature of Meats:

	Rare	*Medium*	*Well done*
Beef	65°C/150°F	70°C/160°F	75°C/170°F
Pork	—	—	75°C/170°F
Lamb	60°C/140°F	65°C/150°F	75°C/170°F
Chicken	—	—	85°C/185°F
Turkey	—	—	85°C/185°F
Duck	—	—	85°C/185°F

SMOKY MIXED NUTS

METRIC/IMPERIAL	*AMERICAN*
125 g/4 oz shelled walnuts	1 cup shelled walnuts
125 g/4 oz shelled hazelnuts	1 cup shelled hazelnuts
125 g/4 oz shelled almonds	1 cup shelled almonds
125 g/4 oz shelled brazil nuts	1 cup shelled brazil nuts
575 ml/1 pint water	2½ cups water
125 g/4 oz non-iodised salt	⅓ cup non iodised salt

Mix the salt into the water. Leave until dissolved. Soak the nuts in the brine for 30 minutes. Drain and dry.

Prepare a kettle barbecue or smoker using mesquite chips or blocks. If using a smoker, spread a large sheet of well-perforated foil over the grill. Spread the nuts over it and smoke for no longer than 1 hour. Make sure that there is not too much smoke or they may burn.

If using a kettle barbecue, put the nuts into a foil tray. Smoke for 2 hours.

PAPRIKA SMOKED CHEESE

METRIC/IMPERIAL	AMERICAN
450 g/1 lb cheese such as Cheddar, Gruyère or another firm, hard cheese	1 lb cheese such as Cheddar, Gruyère or another firm, hard cheese
2 tablespoons paprika	2 tablespoons paprika
575 ml/1 pint bitter beer, optional	2½ cups beer, optional

Cut the cheese into 4 cm/1½ inch cubes. Rub them with paprika. Prepare a kettle barbecue or smoker using oak chips or blocks. If wished, add the beer to the water in the water holder or drip tray.

Lay the pieces of cheese on the grill. Smoke for 40 minutes. If it looks like melting at any time, move it to the coolest part of the grill.

Wrap the cubes in foil and leave for 1 hour in a cool place before serving.

SMOKED CREAM CHEESE

METRIC/IMPERIAL	AMERICAN
four 85 g/3 oz packs Philadelphia cream cheese (or similar)	four 3 oz packs Philadelphia cream cheese (or similar)
6 tablespoons tomato juice	6 tablespoons tomato juice
1 garlic clove, crushed	1 garlic clove, crushed
pinch cayenne pepper	pinch cayenne pepper

The cheese should be in blocks about 2.5 cm/1 inch thick. Mix together the tomato juice, garlic and cayenne pepper. Brush the cheese portions with the mixture. Prepare a kettle barbecue or smoker using oak chips or blocks. Lay a sheet of foil over the coolest part of the grill. Put the cheese on the foil. Smoke for 50 minutes.

The cheese can be served warm with crackers or can be wrapped and chilled.

Note: Cream cheese can also be smoked without the flavourings, in which case it can be served with fresh fruits and fruit salad.

SMOKED SOY EGGS

METRIC/IMPERIAL	AMERICAN
8 eggs, hard boiled	8 hard-cooked eggs
275 ml/½ pint China tea	1¼ cups China tea
4 tablespoons soy, tamari or shoyu sauce	¼ cup soy, tamari or shoyu sauce

Remove the shells from the eggs. Mix together the tea and soy sauce. Put the eggs into the mixture and leave for 1 hour. Take out and pat dry.

Prepare a kettle barbecue or smoker using oak chips or blocks. Lay the eggs on the grill and smoke for 1 hour.

Cool. Wrap each one in clingfilm (plastic wrap) and chill for 1 hour. Serve as a first course, as a light meal with a salad, or sliced on bread rolls or biscuits as part of a buffet.

Note: The eggs can be smoked without being marinated first.

OAK-SMOKED OILY FISH

METRIC/IMPERIAL	AMERICAN
4 small oily fish, 175-225g/6-8oz each	4 small oily fish, 6-8oz each
850ml/1½ pints water	3¾ cups water
125g/4oz non-iodised salt	⅓ cup non-iodised salt
juice and thinly-pared rind 1 lemon	juice and thinly-pared rind 1 lemon
1 tablespoon grated horse-radish	1 tablespoon grated horseradish

Clean the fish and remove the heads and fins. Fillet if wished. Dissolve the salt in the water and add the lemon juice. Put the brine into a deep dish long enough to take the fish without bending. Add the fish and leave for 2 hours at room temperature. Take them out and place on a wire rack for 30 minutes to dry naturally.

Prepare a kettle barbecue or smoker using oak chips or blocks. Add the lemon rind and horse-radish to the water in the foil tray or water bowl.

Smoke whole fish for 2 hours, or until they flake easily when tested with a fork, turning once.

Fillets need 60-70 minutes.

SUGAR-SMOKED FISH

METRIC/IMPERIAL	AMERICAN
675g/1½lb white fish fillets	1½lb white fish fillets
4 tablespoons soy, tamari or shoyu sauce	¼ cup soy, tamari or shoyu sauce
4 tablespoons oil	¼ cup oil
pinch salt	pinch salt
3 tablespoons Barbados sugar	3 tablespoons Barbados sugar

Skin the fish and cut into even-sized serving pieces. Mix together the soy sauce, oil and salt and marinate the fish pieces for 1 hour at room temperature.

Prepare the kettle for normal direct cooking. Sprinkle the brown sugar in a large foil tray. Lay a rack over the top. Put the fish on the rack and cover with foil. Place the tray on the grill rack of the kettle. Cook the fish for 20 minutes or until they flake when tested with a fork.

HERB-SMOKED WHITE FISH

METRIC/IMPERIAL	AMERICAN
900g/2lb white fish fillets	2lb white fish fillets
875ml/1½ pints water	3¾ cups water
125g/4oz non-iodised salt	⅓ cup non-iodised salt
4 tarragon sprigs	4 tarragon sprigs
4 thyme sprigs	4 thyme sprigs
150ml/¼ pint dry white wine, optional	5fl.oz dry white wine, optional

Dissolve the salt in the water. Add the fish and leave for 30 minutes at room temperature. Take the fish out. Put on a wire rack and leave to dry naturally for 30 minutes.

Prepare a kettle barbecue or smoker using hickory chips or blocks. Add the herbs and white wine to the water in the foil tray or water bowl.

Lay the fish on the grill in a single layer, if possible without touching. Smoke for 2-3 hours or until they flake easily when tested with a fork.

SPICY SMOKED PRAWNS (SHRIMP)

METRIC/IMPERIAL	AMERICAN
450g/1lb peeled prawns	1lb peeled shrimp
150ml/¼ pint tomato juice	5fl.oz tomato juice
2 teaspoons Worcestershire sauce	2 teaspoons Worcestershire sauce
1 tablespoon soy, tamari or shoyu sauce	1 tablespoon soy, tamari or shoyu sauce

Mix together the tomato juice, Worcestershire sauce and soy sauce. Turn the prawns (shrimp) in the mixture. Lay them in a single layer in a foil tray.

Prepare a kettle barbecue or smoker using oak chips or blocks. Smoke for 1 hour or until gently flavoured.

Serve as a first course.

SMOKED SAUSAGES AND FRANKFURTERS

Sausages and frankfurters can be smoked and cooked through in a relatively short time.

If using a smoker, put them on the upper grill. If using a kettle barbecue, make sure that they are not directly over the coals. Hickory, mesquite or oak chips or blocks can be used. Smoke for 1¾ hours or until cooked through.

PAPRIKA-SMOKED BEEF

METRIC/IMPERIAL	AMERICAN
1.35 kg/3 lb topside, top rump or silverside of beef rolled and tied	3 lb topside, top rump or round of beef rolled and tied
2 tablespons paprika	2 tablespoons paprika
½ teaspoon cayenne pepper	½ teaspoon cayenne pepper
2 garlic cloves, crushed	2 garlic cloves, crushed
1 teaspoon caraway seeds	1 teaspoon caraway seeds

Mix together the paprika, cayenne pepper and garlic. Rub the mixture into the surface of the beef. Leave overnight in the refrigerator.

Prepare a kettle barbecue or smoker using oak chips or blocks. Add the caraway seeds to the water in the foil tray or water bowl.

Smoke for 5-6 hours or until the internal temperature is 70°C/160°F for medium, 75°/170°F for well done. Leave to stand for 20 minutes before serving.

Alternatively smoke until dark brown, about 3 hours. Put into a preheated 170°C/325°F/gas mark 3 oven for 60 minutes, or until the same internal temperature is reached.

SALTY SMOKED LEG OF LAMB

METRIC/IMPERIAL	AMERICAN
1 leg of lamb	1 leg of lamb
2.3 litres/4 pints water	5 cups water
225 g/8 oz salt	⅔ cup salt
2 teaspoons allspice berries, crushed	2 teaspoons allspice berries, crushed
2 teaspoons juniper berries, crushed	2 teaspoons juniper berries, crushed
2 teaspoons black peppercorns, crushed	2 teaspoons black peppercorns, crushed
2 garlic cloves, chopped	2 garlic cloves, chopped
2 bay leaves, crumbled	2 bay leaves, crumbled

In a large earthenware or plastic container, mix together the water and salt and add half the crushed spices, half the garlic and 1 bay leaf. Add the leg of lamb. Leave for 12 hours in a cool place. Take out and pat dry.

Prepare a kettle barbecue or smoker using oak chips or blocks and add the remaining spices, garlic and bay leaf to the water in the foil tray or water bowl.

Smoke for 7 hours or until the lamb reaches an internal temperature of 75°C/170°F for well done. Alternatively, smoke for 3 hours or until golden and finish in a preheated 170°C/325°F/gas mark 3 oven for 1-1½ hours.

DRY SALTING MIXTURE FOR SMOKED PORK

METRIC/IMPERIAL	AMERICAN
225 g/8 oz fine sea salt	⅔ cup fine sea salt
125 g/4 oz Barbados sugar	½ cup Barbados sugar
1 tablespoon cloves, crushed	1 tablespoon cloves, crushed
2 teaspoons juniper berries, crushed	2 teaspoons juniper berries, crushed
2 teaspoons allspice berries, crushed	2 teaspoons allspice berries, crushed
2 teaspoons black peppercorns, crushed	2 teaspoons black peppercorns, crushed
2 bay leaves, crushed	2 bay leaves, crushed

Mix all the ingredients together. Rub them into the surface of a 900 g/1.85 kg/2-4 lb joint of pork (leg, shoulder or belly). Leave the pork, covered with a lid or greaseproof paper, in a non-corrosible dish, for 3 days in a cool place. Rub it with the mixture (which will turn to a syrupy brine) twice a day.

Rinse the pork under cold water. Dry it with kitchen paper. Smoke it for the required time.

MESQUITE-SMOKED PORK

METRIC/IMPERIAL	AMERICAN
1.35 kg/3-4 lb rolled shoulder pork	3-4 lb rolled shoulder pork
marinade	*marinade*
425 ml/¾ pint pineapple juice	2 cups pineapple juice
1 tablespoons soy, tamari or shoyu sauce	2 tablespoons soy, tamari or shoyu sauce
2 tablespoons white wine vinegar	2 tablespoons white wine vinegar
1 tablespoon tomato paste	1 tablespoon tomato paste
1 garlic clove, crushed	1 garlic clove, crushed

Mix the ingredients for the marinade. Put the pork in a plastic bag (make sure that it has no holes). Pour in the marinade and seal the bag tightly. Leave in the refrigerator for 12 hours, turning several times if possible. Lift out the pork and place on a wire rack for 30 minutes to dry naturally. Reserve the marinade.

Prepare a kettle barbecue or smoker using mesquite chips or blocks. Add the marinade to the water in the foil tray or water bowl.

Place the pork on the grill. Smoke for 6-7 hours or until it reaches an internal temperature of 70°C/170°F. Alternatively, smoke for 3 hours or until golden brown and finish in a preheated 170°/325°F/ gas mark 3 oven for 1¼ hours, or until the required internal temperature is reached.

SMOKED SALT PORK SLICES

METRIC/IMPERIAL	AMERICAN
1.35 kg/3 lb belly of pork in one piece	3 lb belly of pork in one piece
brine	*brine*
2.3 litres/4 pints water	5 pints water
225 g/8 oz sea salt	⅔ cup sea salt
1 teaspoon cloves, bruised	1 teaspoon cloves, bruised
1 teaspoon juniper berries, bruised	1 teaspoon juniper berries, bruised
1 teaspoon black peppercorns, crushed	1 teaspoon black peppercorns, crushed
2 bay leaves	2 bay leaves
1 garlic clove, bruised	1 garlic clove, bruised
boiling	*boiling*
1 onion, halved not peeled	1 onion, halved, not peeled
1 carrot, roughly chopped	1 carrot, roughly chopped
1 celery stick, broken	1 celery stick, broken
1 bay leaf	1 bay leaf
1 sprig sage	1 sprig sage
1 teaspoon black peppercorns	1 teaspoon black peppercorns
1 teaspoon cloves	1 teaspoon cloves
smoking	*smoking*
275 ml/½ pint dry cider	1¼ cups dry cider
1 onion, quartered	1 onion, quartered
1 carrot, roughly chopped	1 carrot, roughly chopped
1 celery stick, broken	1 celery stick, broken
1 teaspoon cloves, bruised	1 teaspoon cloves, bruised
1 teaspoon juniper berries, bruised	1 teaspoon juniper berries, bruised
1 teaspoon black peppercorns, bruised	1 teaspoon black peppercorns, bruised
1 bay leaf	1 bay leaf
1 sprig sage	1 sprig sage

To make the brine dissolve the salt in the water. Add the remaining ingredients. Put the brine into an earthenware or plastic container. Add the pork. Cover and leave in a cool place for 2 days.

Remove the salt pork, place in a large saucepan and cover with water. Bring gently to the boil. Drain, rinse with cold water and drain again. Add more cold water to cover plus the remainder of the boiling ingredients. Bring to the boil again, cover and simmer for 1 hour. Cut off the skin and pull out the bones. Cut the pork into 2 cm/¾ inch thick slices.

Prepare a kettle barbecue or smoker using hickory chips or blocks and putting all the smoking ingredients into the foil tray or water bowl with the water.

Lay the slices on the grill. Smoke for 2 hours or until golden and cooked through.

Serve with Smoky Baked Beans.

HERB-SMOKED CHICKEN

METRIC/IMPERIAL

1.575 kg/3½ lb roasting chicken
½ lemon, thinly sliced
2 sprigs each thyme, marjoram, parsley
and rosemary
150 ml/¼ pint dry white wine
1 onion, quartered

AMERICAN

3½ lb roasting chicken
½ lemon, thinly sliced
2 sprigs each thyme, marjoram, parsley
and rosemary
5 fl. oz dry white wine
1 onion, quartered

Truss the wings underneath the chicken but leave the legs untied to allow the smoke to circulate. Fill the body cavity with the lemon and one sprig each of the herbs.

Prepare a kettle barbecue or smoker using oak chips or blocks. Add the remaining herb sprigs, wine and onion to the water in the foil tray or water bowl.

Smoke for 7 hours until the chicken reaches an internal temperature of 85°C/185°F. Alternatively, smoke for 2-2½ hours or until golden and finish in a preheated 170°C/325°/gas mark 3 oven for 45 minutes, or until the required internal temperature is reached.

SZECHUAN SMOKED CHICKEN

METRIC/IMPERIAL

1.575 kg/3½ lb roasting chicken
2 tablespoons Szechuan pepper or black
peppercorns
1 tablespoon salt
4 tablespoons Barbados sugar
2 tablespoons China tea leaves
2 teaspoons ground ginger
2 tablespoons sesame oil

AMERICAN

3½ lb roasting chicken
2 tablespoons Szechuan pepper or black
peppercorns
1 tablespoon salt
4 tablespoons Barbados sugar
2 tablespoons China tea leaves
2 tablespoons ground ginger
2 tablespoons sesame oil

Prepare the kettle for indirect cooking. Place the peppercorns in a frying pan. Put the pan on the grill rack and stir the peppercorns for 3 minutes. Remove from the heat. Crush them coarsely, using a pestle and mortar. Mix with the salt. Rub the pepper mixture over both the inside and outside of the chicken.

Mix together the sugar, tea leaves and ginger. Put the mixture into a foil tray. Put a rack in the tray and set the chicken on top. Cover both the chicken and the tray with foil.

Put the tray on the barbecue grill and cook for 1½ hours or until the juices run clear when pierced with a fork. The chicken can be served hot or cold. Brush with the sesame oil before serving.

SMOKY BARBECUED CHICKEN PORTIONS

METRIC/IMPERIAL	AMERICAN
4 chicken portions	4 chicken portions
barbecue sauce	*barbecue sauce*
450 g/1 lb ripe tomatoes	1 lb ripe tomatoes
1 medium onion	1 medium onion
1 tablespoon oil	1 tablespoon oil
1 garlic clove, chopped	1 garlic clove, chopped
½ teaspoon chilli powder	½ teaspoon chili powder
½ teaspoon mustard powder	½ teaspoon mustard powder
2 tablespoons Worcestershire sauce	2 tablespoons Worcestershire sauce
2 tablespoons soy, tamari or shoyu sauce	2 tablespoons soy, tamari or shoyu sauce
2 tablespoons Barbados sugar	2 tablespoons Barbados sugar
2 tablespoons malt vinegar	2 tablespoons malt vinegar

Chop the tomatoes and onion. Heat the oil in a saucepan on a low heat. Add the onion and garlic and soften them. Add all the remaining ingredients. Bring to the boil and simmer gently, uncovered, for 30 minutes. Rub the sauce through a sieve. Return it to the rinsed pan and simmer gently for about 15 minutes or until thick. Cool.

Brush the sauce thickly over the chicken pieces. Leave for 30 minutes at room temperature.

Prepare a kettle barbecue or smoker using hickory chips or blocks. Smoke for 4-5 hours or until cooked through, basting with the sauce twice. Alternatively, smoke for 2 hours, basting once. Baste again and finish in a preheated 170°C/325°F/gas mark 3 oven for 30-45 minutes.

SMOKED PEPPERED TURKEY

METRIC/IMPERIAL	AMERICAN
4.5kg/10lb turkey	10lb turkey
2 tablespoons black peppercorns, coarsely crushed	2 tablespoons black peppercorns, coarsely crushed
2 bay leaves	2 bay leaves
2 sprigs each thyme, marjoram, tarragon, parsley	2 sprigs each thyme, marjoram, tarragon, parsley
½ small orange, thinly sliced	½ small orange, thinly sliced
150ml/¼ pint dry white wine	5fl oz dry white wine

Truss the wings of the turkey, but leave the legs free to allow the smoke to circulate. Place 1 tablespoon of the crushed peppercorns, 1 bay leaf, 1 each of the herb sprigs and the orange inside the cavity.

Prepare a kettle barbecue or smoker using hickory or oak chips or blocks. Add the wine, the remaining peppercorns and herbs to the water in the foil tray or water bowl.

Smoke for 8 hours or until it reaches an internal temperature of 85°C/185°F. Alternatively, smoke for 4-4½ hours or until golden and finish in a preheated 170°C/325°F/gas mark 3 oven for 2½-3 hours or until the required temperature is reached.

ORANGE MARINATED SMOKED DUCK

METRIC/IMPERIAL	AMERICAN
1.8-2.25kg/4-5lb duck	4-5lb duck
275ml/½ pint orange juice, preferably freshly squeezed	1¼ cups orange juice, preferably freshly squeezed
thinly-pared rind 1 large orange	thinly-pared rind 1 large orange
150ml/¼ pint dry white wine	5fl.oz dry white wine
1 small onion, grated	1 small onion, grated
1 garlic clove, crushed	1 garlic clove, crushed
2 small cooking apples, quartered	2 small cooking apples, quartered
2 medium onions, quartered	2 medium onions, quartered
2 celery sticks, roughly chopped	2 celery sticks, roughly chopped

Mix together the orange juice and rind, white wine, grated onion and crushed garlic. Put into a deep dish or large bowl. Turn the duck in the mixture and leave for 4 hours at room temperature, turning several times (alternatively, leave overnight in the refrigerator).

Remove the duck. Fill the cavity with 1 quartered apple, 1 quartered onion and 1 roughly chopped celery stick.

Prepare a kettle barbecue or smoker, using oak chips or blocks. Add the marinade plus the remaining apple, onion and celery stick to the water in the foil tray or water bowl.

Smoke for 7-8 hours or until it reaches an internal temperature of 85°C/185°F, or until the legs move freely in the joints. Alternatively, smoke for 2½ hours or until golden and finish in a preheated 170°C/325°F/gas mark 3 oven for 1 hour or until the required internal temperature is reached.

SMOKY STUFFED PEPPERS

METRIC/IMPERIAL	AMERICAN
4 large red peppers	4 large sweet red peppers
3 tablespoons oil	3 tablespoons oil
1 medium onion, thinly sliced	1 medium onion, thinly sliced
1 garlic clove, finely chopped	1 garlic clove, finely chopped
1 teaspoon paprika	1 teaspoon paprika
200g/7oz long grain brown rice	1 cup long grain brown rice
575ml/1 pint stock	2½ cups stock
pinch sea salt	pinch sea salt
125g/4oz garlic sausage	4oz garlic sausage

Heat the oil in a saucepan on a low heat. Add the onion and garlic and soften them. Add the paprika and rice and stir for 1 minute. Pour in the stock and bring to the boil. Add the salt. Cover and simmer for 40-45 minutes or until the rice is tender and all the liquid absorbed. Cool. Chop the garlic sausage finely and mix with the rice.

Cut the tops from the peppers and remove the cores. To make them stand upright, you may have to take a thin slice from the bottom but make sure that this does not go all the way through thus making a hole in the bottom. Bring a large pan of water to the boil. Add the peppers and cook for 1 minute. Drain, plunge into cold water and drain again. Fill the peppers with the rice mixture.

Prepare a kettle barbecue or smoker using whichever chips or blocks are most suited to your meat or fish. Smoke for 1¾ hours, or until soft.

SMOKY BAKED BEANS

METRIC/IMPERIAL

two 450 g/1 lb tins baked beans
2 tablespoons Worcestershire sauce
2 tablespoons soy, tamari or shoyu sauce
2 tablespoons tomato paste

AMERICAN

two 1 lb cans Boston baked beans
2 tablespoons Worcestershire sauce
2 tablespoons soy, tamari or shoyu sauce
2 tablespoons tomato paste

Mix the beans with the remaining ingredients. Put into a foil tray. Smoke cook in a kettle barbecue or smoker for 1½ hours.

SMOKY BAKED BEANS AND HAM

To turn baked beans into a meal cut 675 g/1½ lb ham steaks into 2.5 cm/1 inch squares. Add to the beans and cook as above.

Teenage Party for 12. Cheese & Boston Brown Bread; right: Mildly Spicy Burgers; left: Beef & Bacon Burgers; Salad; Hot Tomato & Corn Relish; Blue Cheese Dressing; Mild Mustard Dressing; Tomato Mayonnaise; Jacket Potatoes with Curd Cheese Topping; Barbecued Spare Ribs.

Eastern Style Barbecue for Eight. Top left: Korean Style Barbecued Meat; top right: Grilled Pineapple with Coconut Sauce; centre: Spiced Rice; right: Grilled Aubergine Rings; Peppers on Skewers; front: Indonesian Spiced Eggs with Cooked Vegetable Salad.

BARBECUE
PARTIES

At any barbecue party you are combining superb food with a relaxed and happy atmosphere which surely must be the recipe for success. Barbecued food can be as sumptuous or as plain as you wish, and it can cater for all tastes from the smallest children to adults that you are keen to impress. Barbecue parties can take place at any time of the day: try a mid-morning brunch, Sunday lunch, a children's party in the late afternoon or a more formal party in the evening.

As with any party, a little planning ahead helps a great deal. Buy your food at least a day in advance, and make sure that you have enough things like paper napkins and tablecloths, kitchen paper and foil. Check your barbecue equipment and buy enough charcoal to see you through the evening.

When you plan a barbecue menu, try to make it as easy on the cook as possible. Do not cook all the food on the barbecue and make other dishes that can be prepared in advance. If some food has to be cooked in or on a conventional stove, make sure that there will be a time when you can leave the barbecue without spoiling anything, to attend to it.

Wherever the barbecue is sited, you should have enough light round it so that you can see to cook and your guests can see what they are eating. Place a large table near the barbecue to hold all your ingredients and utensils. On another table place plates, cutlery and side dishes.

Work out a simple timetable for yourself, and make a list of all the dishes which you are to cook in the order in which they are going to be placed on the barbecue or put into the oven.

Remember that the charcoal will take up to 45 minutes to be ready for cooking so light it well in advance and provide snacks such as nuts or small pieces of raw vegetables for your guests to nibble while they are waiting for the meal.

Put on your apron before you start cooking to avoid ruining your best clothes, pour yourself a drink, and begin.

BRUNCH PARTY FOR SIX

Grapefruit and Orange Cup
Bacon and Sausage Kebabs
Spiced Kidneys with Yoghurt Sauce
Wholewheat Rolls or Wholewheat French Bread
Apple Pancakes

A good hearty brunch after an extra hour or two in bed at the weekend will leave you free to dig the garden or to go out and enjoy yourself for the rest of the day.

With this menu most of the food can be prepared on the day before. Only the grapefruit and orange cup and the yoghurt sauce need to be put together as near to serving as possible.

Barbecue Parties 2

GRAPEFRUIT AND ORANGE CUP

METRIC/IMPERIAL	AMERICAN
6 large oranges	6 large oranges
3 pink grapefruit	3 pink grapefruit
75g/3oz honey	¼ cup honey
6 tablespoons orange curaçao (or other similar liqueur)	6 tablespoons orange curaçao (or other similar liqueur)
6 maraschino cherries	6 maraschino cherries
6 mint leaves	6 mint leaves

Cut the peel and pith from the oranges and grapefruit. Cut the segments away from the skin. Leave the orange segments whole. Halve the grapefruit segments. Put into a bowl.

Place the honey in a small saucepan. Melt gently without letting it boil. Cool completely. Stir in the liqueur. Gently fold the mixture into the fruits.

Spoon the fruits into glasses and top each one with a maraschino cherry and mint leaf.

SPICED KIDNEYS WITH YOGHURT

Note: Kidneys are very small and shrink further on cooking. There is therefore a danger that they may slip through the grill on to the charcoal. If possible, use a hinged wire grill to cook them in. If one is not available, perforate a large sheet of foil and lay it on the grill. Get it hot before laying the kidneys on it.

METRIC/IMPERIAL	AMERICAN
12 lamb's kidneys	12 lamb's kidneys
6 tablespoons oil	6 tablespoons oil
1 small onion, grated	1 small onion, grated
1 garlic clove, crushed	1 garlic clove, crushed
1 teaspoon ground cumin	1 teaspoon ground cumin
1 teaspoon ground coriander	1 teaspoon ground coriander
1 teaspoon paprika	1 teaspoon paprika
sauce	*sauce*
275ml/½ pint natural yoghurt	1¼ cups unflavored yoghurt
2 tablespoons chopped parsley	2 tablespoons chopped parsley
¼ cucumber, finely chopped	¼ cucumber, finely chopped

Halve the kidneys and snip out the cores. Mix together the oil, onion, garlic and spices. Turn the kidneys in the mixture and leave overnight in the refrigerator. To make the sauce, mix the yoghurt with the parsley and cucumber.

Cook the kidneys 10-15cm/4-6 inches over hot coals for 10-15 minutes or until cooked through but still soft, turning once.

BACON AND SAUSAGE KEBABS

METRIC/IMPERIAL	AMERICAN
12 large pork sausages	12 large pork sausages
12 lean back bacon rashers	12 lean Canadian bacon slices
12 button mushrooms	12 button mushrooms

Cut each sausage in half crossways. Cut the rind from the bacon and roll up each piece. Trim the mushrooms if necessary and leave them whole.

Alternate the pieces of sausage, bacon rolls and mushrooms on six kebab skewers.

Cook 10-15 cm/4-6 inches over hot coals, turning several times, for 10-15 minutes or until cooked through.

APPLE PANCAKES

METRIC/IMPERIAL	AMERICAN
175 g/6 oz wholewheat flour	2 cups wholewheat flour
pinch salt	pinch salt
½ teaspoon ground cinnamon	½ teaspoon ground cinnamon
2 eggs	2 eggs
225 ml/8 fl. oz milk	1 cup milk
225 ml/8 fl. oz water	1 cup water
2 tablespoons oil	2 tablespoons oil
filling	*filling*
675 g/1½ lb cooking apples	1½ lb cooking apples
1 cinnamon stick	1 cinnamon stick
2 thinly pared strips lemon rind	2 thinly pared strips lemon rind
150 g/5 oz honey	6 tablespoons honey
25 g/1 oz butter	2 tablespoons butter
4 tablespoons cider or water	¼ cup cider or water
natural yoghurt or soured cream for serving	unflavored yoghurt or dairy sour cream for serving

For the pancakes, put the flour into a bowl with the salt and cinnamon. Make a well in the centre and add the eggs. Gradually stir in the flour from the sides of the well. Mix the milk and water together. Beat half the mixture into the flour. Beat in the oil and remaining milk and water. Beat well until bubbles appear on the surface. Leave the batter in a cool place for 30 minutes.

To cook, heat 1 tablespoon oil in an 18 cm/7 inch frying pan on a high heat. Put in 3 tablespoons of the batter mixture. Tip the pan to spread it out. Cook the pancake until it is golden brown on one side. Turn it and cook the other side. Tip the pancake on to a plate. Cook the others in the same way to make twelve. Cool completely.

Core the apples and chop without peeling. Place in a saucepan with the cinnamon stick, lemon rind, honey, butter and cider or water. Cover tightly and set on a low heat for 15 minutes, or until they can be beaten to a purée. Rub through a sieve. Cool completely.

Put a portion of the apple purée in a line down one side of each pancake. Roll up the pancakes and put in an ovenproof dish. Cover the dish with foil and leave overnight in a cool place. To reheat, put into a preheated 180°C/350°F/gas mark 4 oven for 20 minutes.

Serve straight from the dish and serve the yoghurt or cream separately.

BARBECUE PICNIC OR BEACH PARTY FOR 8 PEOPLE

Hot Pickled Prawns (Shrimp)
Sweet Curried Drumsticks
Devilled Frankfurters
Potato, Bean and Beetroot (Beet) Salad
Green Salad with Herb Dressing
Wholewheat French Bread
Fruity Ginger Cake with Cheese and Fresh Fruit

The food for any picnic needs to be portable, easy to eat and no trouble to cook.

Take the prawns (shrimp) and the drumsticks in sealed containers still in their marinades, and the frankfurters ready prepared. Each person can cook his own prawns (shrimp) while waiting for the frankfurters and chicken.

The potato, bean and beetroot (beet) salad can be made at home. For the green salad, take washed and prepared salad vegetables all mixed in a sealed container and carry the dressing separately, to be folded in at the last minute.

Wholewheat French bread is easy to carry. It can be split and buttered beforehand if wished, or the butter can be taken separately.

Make the ginger cake at home and provide several different types of cheese and a good selection of fresh fruit.

HOT PICKLED PRAWNS (SHRIMP)

METRIC/IMPERIAL	AMERICAN
900 g/2 lb prawns in shell	2 lb shrimp in shell
4 tablespoons pickling spice	¼ cup pickling spice
2 tablespoons chopped celery leaves	2 tablespoons chopped celery leaves
1 teaspoon celery seed	1 teaspoon celery seed
225 ml/8 fl. oz white wine vinegar	1 cup white wine vinegar
¼ teaspoon Tabasco sauce	¼ teaspoon Tabasco sauce
125 ml/4 fl. oz oil	½ cup oil

Put the pickling spice, celery leaves and seeds and vinegar into a saucepan, cover, bring gently to the boil and simmer for 5 minutes. Cool completely. Mix in the oil.

Put the marinade mixture into a container. Add the prawns (shrimp). Stir them around to coat well and leave for at least 4 hours at room temperature.

To cook, provide each person with a long skewer. The prawns (shrimp) should be secured singly and held over hot charcoal for about 1 minute or until heated through.

SWEET CURRIED DRUMSTICKS

METRIC/IMPERIAL	AMERICAN
16 chicken drumsticks	16 chicken drumsticks
125 ml/4 fl. oz oil	½ cup oil
1 large onion, finely chopped	1 large onion, finely chopped
1 garlic clove, crushed	1 garlic clove, crushed
1 tablespoon curry powder	1 tablespoon curry powder
1 teaspoon ground turmeric	1 teaspoon ground turmeric
125 ml/4 fl. oz stock	½ cup stock
125 ml/4 fl. oz mango chutney	½ cup mango chutney

Heat the oil in a saucepan on a low heat. Add the onion and garlic and cook until the onion is soft. Stir in the curry powder and turmeric. Cook gently for 1 minute. Pour in the stock and bring to the boil. Simmer for 2 minutes. Take the pan from the heat and stir in the chutney. Cool the mixture completely.

Put the marinade into a container. Turn the drumsticks in it to coat them. Leave for at least 4 hours at room temperature.

Cook the drumsticks over medium heat for 30 minutes, or until the juices run clear when the thickest part of the flesh is pierced with a fork.

DEVILLED FRANKFURTERS

METRIC/IMPERIAL	AMERICAN
36 frankfurters	36 frankfurters
6 tablespoons tomato paste	6 tablespoons tomato paste
4 tablespoons mild American mustard	4 tablespoons mild American mustard
2 tablespoons paprika	2 tablespoons paprika

Mix together the tomato paste, mustard and paprika. Make lengthways slits in the frankfurters about three-quarters of the way through. Spread the slits with the tomato and mustard mixture.

Cook 10-15 cm/4-6 inches over hot coals for 10 minutes, turning several times.

POTATO, BEAN AND BEETROOT (BEET) SALAD

METRIC/IMPERIAL	AMERICAN
900g/2lb firm potatoes, cooked	2lb firm potatoes, cooked
225g/8oz haricot beans, soaked and cooked	1¼ cups haricot beans, soaked and cooked
350g/12oz beetroot, cooked	¾lb beets, cooked
4 large pickled gherkins	4 large pickled gherkins
225g/8oz low fat soft cheese	1 cup low fat soft cheese
175ml/6fl oz mayonnaise	¾ cup mayonnaise
juice 1 lemon	juice 1 lemon
freshly ground black pepper	freshly ground black pepper

Dice the beetroot (beets) and potatoes and mix with the beans. Chop the gherkins finely and add to the rest.

Beat together the remaining ingredients to make the dressing. Fold into the salad.

GREEN SALAD WITH HERB DRESSING

METRIC/IMPERIAL	AMERICAN
dressing	*dressing*
175ml/6fl oz olive or sunflower oil	¾ cup olive or sunflower oil
6 tablespoons white wine vinegar	6 tablespoons white wine vinegar
1 garlic clove, crushed	1 garlic clove crushed
4 tablespoons chopped parsley	¼ cup chopped parsley
2 tablespoons chopped thyme	2 tablespoons chopped thyme
2 tablespoons chopped marjoram	2 tablespoons chopped marjoram
4 sage leaves, chopped	4 sage leaves, chopped
2 tablespoons chopped tarragon	2 tablespoons chopped tarragon
1 tablespoon chopped basil	1 tablespoon chopped basil
freshly ground black pepper	freshly ground black pepper

Beat all the ingredients together. Put into a watertight container for carriage.

Salad: Take washed and shredded lettuce, sliced cucumber, prepared mustard and cress and watercress, chopped chicory (Belgian endive), leaves of corn salad (lamb's tongues or field lettuce) and any other green salad vegetable that you may have, mixed together in a salad container. Fold in the dressing just before serving.

FRUITY GINGER CAKE

METRIC/IMPERIAL	AMERICAN
225g/8oz butter or vegetable margarine	1 cup butter or vegetable margarine
175g/6oz Barbados sugar	¾ cup Barbados sugar
3 eggs, beaten	3 eggs, beaten
150g/5oz molasses or black treacle	¾ cup dark molasses
150g/5oz honey	¾ cup honey
450g/1lb wholewheat flour	4 cups wholewheat flour
1 teaspoon bicarbonate of soda	1 teaspoon baking soda
2 teaspoons ground ginger	2 teaspoons ground ginger
2 teaspoons ground mixed spice	2 teaspoons ground mixed spice
150ml/¼ pint natural yoghurt	5fl oz unflavored yoghurt
125g/4oz sultanas	¼lb golden raisins
225g/8oz raisins	½lb raisins

Heat the oven to 170°C/325°F/gas mark 4. Line a 20 × 30cm/8 × 12 inch and 5cm/2 inches deep cake tin with buttered greaseproof (waxed) paper.

Cream the butter or margarine with the sugar. Gradually beat in the eggs, molasses or treacle and honey. Mix the flour with the bicarbonate of soda (baking soda), ginger and mixed spice. Fold into the mixture using a metal spoon. Beat in the yoghurt. Fold in the dried fruits.

Put the mixture into the prepared tin. Bake for 1 hour or until a skewer inserted in the centre comes out clean. Turn the cake on to a wire rack to cool completely.

Cut the cake into slices or squares before packing.

FAMILY REUNION OR ANNIVERSARY PARTY (16 PEOPLE)

(Cooked in a kettle barbecue)

Turkey with Herbs
Stuffed Mushrooms
Grilled Tomatoes
Mixed Cabbage Salad
Scalloped Potatoes
Fondue with Cake and Fresh Fruit

A family party for 16 people is made easy by cooking a large turkey in a kettle barbecue and preparing much of the other food in advance. As a hot garnish for the turkey, stuffed mushrooms and tomatoes can be quickly cooked on the grill. The fondue can be heated gently on the dying coals.

Salad vegetables can be shredded or chopped a day in advance

Barbecue Parties 8

and stored in plastic bags in the bottom of the refrigerator. The potatoes can also be prepared a day in advance and reheated if wished.

The cake can be made up to two days before the party and the fondue the day before. The fruit, however, is best prepared as near to the serving time as possible.

TURKEY WITH HERBS

METRIC/IMPERIAL	AMERICAN
one 7.2-9 k/16-20 lb turkey	one 16-20 lb turkey
freshly ground black pepper	freshly ground black pepper
1 lemon, thinly sliced	1 lemon, thinly sliced
1 orange, thinly sliced	1 orange, thinly sliced
2 large sprigs each parsley, thyme, marjoram, tarragon, sage	2 large sprigs each parsley, thyme, marjoram, tarragon, sage
basting:	*basting:*
125 g/4 oz butter	½ cup butter
grated rind and juice ½ lemon	grated rind and juice ½ lemon
grated rind and juice 1 medium orange	grated rind and juice 1 medium orange
4 tablespoons chopped parsley	¼ cup chopped parsley
2 tablespoons chopped thyme	2 tablespoons chopped thyme
2 tablespoons chopped marjoram	2 tablespoons chopped marjoram
2 tablespoons chopped tarragon	2 tablespoons chopped tarragon

Prepare a kettle for indirect cooking. Season the body cavity of the turkey. Fill it with the sliced lemon and orange and the herb sprigs. Secure the wings under the back. Tie the legs and tail together. Insert a meat thermometer into the thickest portion of the thigh with the point away from the bone.

Put the turkey either in a roast holder or directly on the barbecue grill. Brush it with the basting mixture. Cook for 4½-5 hours, basting frequently and adding extra briquettes to the fire when necessary. The internal temperature should be 80°C/180°F.

Lift out the turkey and wrap it in foil. Leave it to stand for 20-30 minutes before carving.

GRILLED TOMATOES

METRIC/IMPERIAL	AMERICAN
32 tomatoes	32 tomatoes
celery salt	celery salt

Cut each tomato in half crossways. Sprinkle lightly with celery salt.

Cook, cut side up, directly over the coals in the kettle barbecue for 5-7 minutes or until heated through and beginning to soften, but still firm enough to be lifted with tongs.

STUFFED MUSHROOMS

METRIC/IMPERIAL	AMERICAN
32 open mushrooms about 6 cm/2½ inches across	32 open mushrooms about 2½ inches across
125 ml/4 fl. oz oil	¼ cup oil
75 g/3 oz lean bacon	3 oz lean bacon
15 g/½ oz butter	1 tablespoon butter
1 large onion, finely chopped	1 large onion, finely chopped
175 g/6 oz wholewheat breadcrumbs	6 oz wholewheat breadcrumbs
125 ml/4 fl. oz dry white wine or cider	½ cup dry white wine or cider
6 tablespoons chopped parsley	6 tablespoons chopped parsley
2 tablespoons chopped thyme	2 tablespoons chopped thyme

Lightly brush the mushrooms with the oil. Lay in foil trays.

Chop the bacon finely. Place in a frying pan with the butter and set on a low heat until cooked through and beginning to brown. Take the pan from the heat. Mix in the breadcrumbs, wine and herbs. Fill the mushrooms with the mixture. Cook in the kettle barbecue over indirect heat for 20 minutes or until they are heated through and sizzling.

SCALLOPED POTATOES

METRIC/IMPERIAL	AMERICAN
2.25 kg/5 lb small potatoes	5 lb small potatoes
25 g/1 oz butter	2 tablespoons butter
3 large onions, thinly sliced	3 large onions, thinly sliced
25 g/1 oz parsley, finely chopped	½ cup finely chopped parsley
12 sage leaves, finely chopped	12 sage leaves, finely chopped
sea salt and freshly ground black pepper	sea salt and finely ground black pepper
freshly grated nutmeg	freshly grated nutmeg
ground mace	ground mace
6 bay leaves	6 bay leaves
850 ml/1½ pints milk	3¾ cups milk
500 ml/16 fl. oz soured cream	2 cups dairy sour cream

Heat the oven to 200°C/400°F/gas mark 6. Melt the butter in a frying pan on a low heat. Add the onions and soften them. Take the pan from the heat.

Layer the potatoes and onions in two or three oven-proof dishes, scattering the herbs between, seasoning lightly with salt but well with pepper, and adding a very little grated nutmeg and ground mace. Mix together the milk and soured (dairy sour) cream. Pour the mixture into the dishes. Put two bay leaves in each dish.

Bake the potatoes for 1 hour, pushing them under the surface of the liquid after the first 30 minutes.

MIXED CABBAGE SALAD

METRIC/IMPERIAL	AMERICAN
1 medium white cabbage	1 medium white cabbage
450 g/1 lb carrots	1 lb carrots
2 heads celery	2 heads celery
3 crisp dessert apples	3 crisp dessert apples
3 large oranges	3 large oranges
450 g/1 lb green grapes	1 lb green grapes
225 g/8 oz shelled peanuts	½ lb shelled peanuts
125 ml/4 fl. oz mayonnaise	½ cup mayonnaise
125 ml/4 fl. oz natural yoghurt	½ cup unflavored yoghurt
2 tablespoons Dijon mustard	2 tablespoons Dijon mustard

Shred the cabbage finely. Grate the carrots. Chop the celery finely. Core and slice the apples. Cut the rind and pith from the oranges. Cut the flesh into quarters lengthways and slice it thinly. Halve and seed the grapes. Mix all these in a large bowl and add the peanuts.

Beat the remaining ingredients together to make the dressing and fold into the salad.

LEMON AND APRICOT FONDUE WITH LEMON CAKE AND FRESH FRUITS

Choose a variety of fruits in season, both commonplace and exotic, for example, apples, pears, plums, bananas, strawberries, cherries, grapes, apricots, pineapple, mangoes, paw-paws. Cut the larger fruits into 2.5 cm/1 inch cubes: halve and stone (pit) plums and apricots; keep strawberries whole; stone (pit) cherries; keep grapes whole, or halve and seed if wished. If possible, prepare only 1 hour before serving. To prevent those such as apples and pears from turning brown after cutting, coat in a liquid made from pineapple juice and lemon juice, using 275 ml/½ pint/1¼ cups pineapple juice to the juice of 1 lemon. If possible, cut up bananas just before serving. Put each fruit in a separate bowl.

LEMON CAKE: Make this the day before and store it in a cool place wrapped in cling film (plastic wrap).

METRIC/IMPERIAL	AMERICAN
450 g/1 lb wholewheat flour	4 cups wholewheat flour
2 teaspoons bicarbonate of soda	2 teaspoons baking soda
grated rind and juice 2 lemons	grated rind and juice 2 lemons
450 g/1 lb vegetable margarine	2 cups vegetable margarine
350 g/12 oz honey	1 cup honey
8 eggs, beaten	8 eggs, beaten

Heat the oven to 180°C/350°/gas mark 4. Mix the flour with the bicarbonate of soda (baking soda) and lemon rind. Beat the margarine with the honey. Add the flour alternately with the eggs. Beat in the lemon juice.

Put the mixture into a 20 × 30 cm/8 × 12 inch, 5 cm/2 inch deep cake tin. Bake the cake for 40 minutes or until a skewer inserted in the centre comes out clean. Turn it on to a wire rack to cool completely.

To serve, cut the cake into 2.5 cm/1 inch cubes.

APRICOT FONDUE: This can also be prepared in advance.

METRIC/IMPERIAL	AMERICAN
900 g/2 lb dried whole apricots	2 lb dried whole apricots
1.15 litres/2 pints water	5 cups water
juice 2 lemons	juice 2 lemons
275 ml/½ pint double cream, lightly whipped	1¼ cups heavy cream, lightly whipped

Put the apricots into a saucepan with the water and lemon juice. Bring to the boil and simmer for 4 minutes. Take the pan from the heat and leave the apricots to soak for 4 hours. Liquidise them with the liquid in a blender or food processor. If preparing in advance, stop here. Put the mixture into a bowl and leave in the refrigerator or in a cool place.

Bring the mixture back to room temperature. Divide between two fondue pots or two small saucepans. Fold in the cream. Set the fondue pots over their burners or put the saucepans on the barbecue over low coals. Stir for 3-4 minutes or until just heated through. Leave the fondue over the burner or on the grill to keep warm.

Serving: Put out the fruit in separate bowls and the cubes of cake piled on a plate. Provide small plates or bowls and plenty of cocktail sticks (wooden picks). Each person can help themselves, skewering a piece of fruit or cake on a cocktail stick (wooden pick) and dipping it into the fondue.

FAMILY SUNDAY LUNCH

for 6 people
Butterflied Leg of Lamb
Carrots with Nutmeg and Thyme
Cauliflower with Parsley
Potato Skewers
Date-filled Apples with Cider Syllabub

A leg of lamb will cook far more quickly on an open barbecue than it will in a conventional oven if it is boned and opened out. Cook carrots and potatoes on the barbecue and cook the cauliflower indoors. While you are eating, cook apples in the ashes of the fire and serve them with a cider syllabub that should be chilling in the refrigerator.

BUTTERFLIED LEG OF LAMB

METRIC/IMPERIAL

one whole leg of lamb
150 ml/¼ pint dry red wine
4 tablespoons olive oil
1 tablespoon rosemary leaves
1 garlic clove, crushed
freshly ground black pepper

AMERICAN

one whole leg of lamb
5 fl. oz dry red wine
¼ cup olive oil
1 tablespoon rosemary leaves
1 garlic clove, crushed
freshly ground black pepper

Slit leg of lamb down one side through to the bone. Working with the knife close to the bone, open out the other side of the leg. Remove the bone. The meat should now be in one piece and when laid flat will be in a butterfly shape.

Mix together the remaining ingredients and put into a large flat dish. Turn the lamb in the marinade and leave, cut side down, for at least 1 hour at room temperature.

Light the barbecue and arrange the coals so as to achieve an even heat. Lay the lamb on the grill, outer side down for 10 minutes. Turn and continue cooking for 35-40 minutes, or until cooked through, turning several times.

CARROTS WITH NUTMEG AND THYME

METRIC/IMPERIAL

675 g/1½ lb carrots
50 g/2 oz butter or vegetable margarine
freshly ground nutmeg
2 tablespoons chopped thyme
9 tablespoons water

AMERICAN

1½ lb carrots
¼ cup butter or vegetable margarine
freshly grated nutmeg
2 tablespoons chopped thyme
9 tablespoons water

Cut the carrots into matchstick pieces. Thickly butter three pieces of heavy duty foil or double thicknesses of standard weight foil. Divide the carrots between the three pieces.

Sprinkle the carrots with nutmeg and thyme. Add 3 tablespoons water per packet and dot with the remaining butter. Bring the sides of the foil together and seal the ends.

If possible, while the lamb is cooking, move it to one side and let it continue to cook over medium to low coals. Make a bed of coals on one side or in the centre of the barbecue. Lay the packets of carrots over these coals and cook for 30 minutes, turning several times.

CAULIFLOWER WITH PARSLEY

METRIC/IMPERIAL	AMERICAN
1 large cauliflower	1 large cauliflower
275ml/½ pint stock	1¼ cups stock
6 tablespoons chopped parsley	6 tablespoons chopped parsley

Break the cauliflower into florets (flowerets). Put the stock into a saucepan and bring to the boil on a high heat. Add the cauliflower and scatter the parsley over. Cover and cook gently for 15 minutes or until the cauliflower is tender and most of the liquid evaporated.

POTATO SKEWERS

METRIC/IMPERIAL	AMERICAN
6 medium sized potatoes	6 medium sized potatoes
50g/2oz butter	¼ cup butter

Cut the potatoes into 2.5cm/1 inch cubes. Thread on to kebab skewers. Melt the butter in a small pan on the side of the grill. Brush it over the potatoes.

If there is room, cook the potatoes alongside the carrots. If not, cook the carrots first and put to one side to keep warm. Cook the potato skewers over hot coals for 20-30 minutes, turning several times. They should be browned on the outside and soft in the middle.

DATE-FILLED APPLES WITH CIDER SYLLABUB

METRIC/IMPERIAL	AMERICAN
6 medium size cooking apples	6 medium size cooking apples
225g/8oz stoned dates	½lb pitted dates
butter for greasing	butter for greasing
275ml/½ pint double cream	1¼ cups heavy cream
125ml/4fl oz dry cider	½ cup dry cider
50g/2oz honey	1 tablespoon honey

Core the apples. Score round the circumference with a sharp knife. Chop the dates finely and stuff them into the apples. Wrap each apple in a piece of buttered foil and seal it securely. Bury the apple parcels in the hot ashes of the fire and leave for 10-15 minutes or until soft. Unwrap each one on to a separate plate and serve the syllabub separately.

Make the syllabub at least one hour in advance. Whip the cream stiffly. Whip in the cider and honey. Pile the syllabub in a bowl and put in the refrigerator until needed.

TEENAGE PARTY FOR 12

Beef and Bacon Burgers
Mildly Spicy Burgers
Barbecued Spare Ribs
Hot Tomato and Corn Relish
Salads with a Choice of Dressings
Jacket Potatoes with Curd Cheese Topping
Boston Brown Bread with Cheese and Fresh Fruit

Teenagers like to consider themselves daring, but on the other hand, are often highly conservative in their tastes. Burgers and spare ribs are often favourites. Make the burgers slightly different by adding bacon to some of the beef and mild spices to the rest. The amounts given in the recipes are enough for one of each type per person. The simply made, colourful relish is served hot and can either be spooned on top of the burgers or served on the side.

If you wish to cut down on the time that you spend by the barbecue the spare ribs can be cooked in the oven along with the jacket potatoes.

Put out a mixture of attractively prepared beetroot (beet) on one plate, diced celery or cucumber surrounded by tomato slices on another, shredded lettuce with a rosette of mustard and cress in the centre. Put the dressings in separate bowls.

Provide wholewheat baps or rolls and let the guests help themselves. Burger, salad, relish and dressing can all be put into one roll, or the burger can be put on a plate and the salad in a roll, or whatever they like.

Boston Brown bread is a semi-sweet, dark brown bread that can either be steamed on the stove or cooked in a kettle barbecue.

Put out fairly plain cheeses, such as Edam or Cheddar, cut into wedges or slices, and a large bowl of fresh fruit; apples, pears, bananas, grapes or any popular fruit in season.

BEEF AND BACON BURGERS

METRIC/IMPERIAL	*AMERICAN*
1 kg/2 lb 4 oz lean minced beef	2¼ lb lean ground beef
350 g/12 oz lean bacon	¾ lb lean bacon
1 medium onion	1 medium onion
4 tablespoons chopped parsley	4 tablespoons chopped parsley
2 tablespoons chopped thyme	2 tablespoons chopped thyme

Mince (grind) or chop the bacon very finely. Mix it with the beef. Grate in the onion and add the herbs. Mix well, squeezing with your fingers so the mixture becomes well incorporated.

Barbecue Parties 15

Divide the mixture into 12 portions. Form each one into a round, flat burger. Put on to a flat plate and refrigerate for at least 30 minutes, or until they set into shape.

Cook in hinged wire grills 10-15 cm/4-6 inches over hot coals for 6 minutes on each side for medium, 8-10 minutes for well done; or, in a kettle barbecue, over direct heat for 5 minutes each side for medium, 7 minutes for well done.

MILDLY SPICY BURGERS

METRIC/IMPERIAL	AMERICAN
1.35 kg/3 lb lean minced beef	3 lb lean ground beef
1 medium onion	1 medium onion
3 tablespoons Worcestershire sauce	3 tablespoons Worcestershire sauce
1 teaspoon paprika	1 teaspoon paprika
1 teaspoon curry powder	1 teaspoon curry powder

Put the beef in a bowl. Grate in the onion, add the Worcestershire sauce and spices. Mix well, squeezing with your fingers to incorporate everything. Form the mixture into 12 round flat burgers (using a burger press if possible). Put on to a flat plate and refrigerate for at least 30 minutes to set into shape.

Cook in hinged wire grills 10-15 cm/4-6 inches over hot coals for 6 minutes on each side for medium, 8-10 minutes for well done; or, in a kettle barbecue, over direct heat, for 5 minutes on each side for medium, 7 minutes for well done.

BARBECUED SPARE RIBS

METRIC/IMPERIAL	AMERICAN
1.8 kg/4 lb pork spare ribs	4 lb pork spare ribs
125 ml/4 fl oz tomato juice	½ cup tomato juice
125 ml/4 fl oz pineapple juice	½ cup pineapple juice
4 tablespoons oil	¼ cup oil
4 tablespoons soy, tamari or shoyu sauce	¼ cup soy, tamari or shoyu sauce
2 tablespoons white wine vinegar	2 tablespoons white wine vinegar

Mix together the tomato and pineapple juices, oil, soy sauce and vinegar. Put the mixture into a large, flat dish. Turn the ribs in the marinade and leave for at least 2 hours at room temperature.

Either cook for 1 hour over low to medium coals on an open barbecue, or for the same time over indirect heat in a kettle barbecue, or put the ribs on racks in roasting tins in a preheated 190°C/375°F/gas mark 5 oven for 1 hour or until well browned.

HOT TOMATO AND CORN RELISH

METRIC/IMPERIAL

two 400g/14oz tins tomatoes in juice
3 tablespoons Worcestershire sauce
2 tablespoons soy, tamari or shoyu sauce
2 tablespoons malt vinegar
2 teaspoons Barbados sugar
two 350g/12oz tins sweetcorn, drained

AMERICAN

two 14oz cans tomatoes in juice
3 tablespoons Worcestershire sauce
2 tablespoons soy, tamari or shoyu sauce
2 tablespoons malt vinegar
2 teaspoons Barbados sugar
two ¾lb cans sweetcorn, drained

Liquidise the tomatoes with their juice. Put into a saucepan with the Worcestershire and soy sauces, vinegar and sugar. Bring to the boil, simmer, uncovered, for 15-20 minutes or until reduced by one-third. Stir in the sweetcorn. Serve hot.

MILD MUSTARD SALAD DRESSING

METRIC/IMPERIAL

125ml/4fl oz mayonnaise
125ml/4fl oz natural yoghurt
1-2 tablespoons mild American mustard

AMERICAN

½ cup mayonnaise
½ cup unflavored yoghurt
1-2 tablespoons mild American mustard

Beat together the mayonnaise, yoghurt and 1 tablespoon of the mustard. Taste. Add more mustard if required.

TOMATO MAYONNAISE

METRIC/IMPERIAL

125ml/4fl oz mayonnaise
125ml/4fl oz natural yoghurt
2 tablespoons tomato paste

AMERICAN

½ cup mayonnaise
½ cup unflavored yoghurt
2 tablespoons tomato paste

Beat all the ingredients together.

OIL AND VINEGAR DRESSING

METRIC/IMPERIAL

125ml/4fl oz sunflower oil
4 tablespoons white wine vinegar
pinch cayenne pepper
1 garlic clove, crushed, optional

AMERICAN

½ cup sunflower oil
¼ cup white wine vinegar
pinch cayenne pepper
1 garlic clove, crushed, optional

Beat all the ingredients together.

BLUE CHEESE DRESSING

METRIC/IMPERIAL	AMERICAN
50g/2oz soft blue cheese	2oz soft blue cheese
oil and vinegar dressing as above	oil and vinegar dressing as above

Finely grate or crumble the cheese in a bowl. Gradually beat in the oil and vinegar dressing.

JACKET POTATOES WITH CURD CHEESE TOPPING

METRIC/IMPERIAL	AMERICAN
12 medium to large potatoes	12 medium to large potatoes
450g/1lb curd cheese	2 cups curd cheese
150ml/¼ pint natural yoghurt	5fl oz unflavored yoghurt
6 tablespoons chopped chives	6 tablespoons chopped chives

Heat the oven to 200°C/400°F/gas mark 6. Scrub the potatoes. Prick on both sides with a fork. Lay directly on the oven rack and cook for 1¼ hours or until the outsides are crisp and the middles soft.

Put the cheese in a bowl and beat until smooth. Gradually beat in the yoghurt. Mix in the chives.

Serve the potatoes on a large tray covered with paper napkins. Serve the sauce separately.

BOSTON BROWN BREAD

METRIC/IMPERIAL	AMERICAN
225g/8oz whole rye flour	2 cups wholemeal rye flour
225g/8oz wholewheat flour	2 cups wholewheat flour
225g/8oz cornmeal	2 cups corn meal
2 teaspoons bicarbonate of soda	2 teaspoons baking soda
2 teaspoons fine sea salt	2 teaspoons fine sea salt
125ml/4fl oz oil	½ cup oil
450g/1lb molasses	1lb molasses
450ml/16fl oz natural yoghurt or buttermilk	2 cups unflavored yoghurt or buttermilk

Mix together the flour, cornmeal, bicarbonate of soda (baking soda) and salt. Make a well in the centre and add the oil, molasses and yoghurt or buttermilk. Mix to a thick batter.

If cooking in a kettle barbecue, do it before the party begins so that the bread is still just warm when it is served. Prepare the kettle for indirect cooking. Divide the mixture between four oiled 425ml/¾ pint/1½ cup foil pudding tins. Cook in the centre of the kettle for 50-60 minutes or until a skewer inserted in the centre comes out clean.

If you do not have a kettle barbecue, divide the mixture between four 425 ml/¾ pint/1½ cup or two 850 ml/1½ pint/3 cup pudding basins. Cover with greaseproof (waxed) paper and foil and secure with string. Lower into saucepans of boiling water and steam for 1½-2 hours or until a skewer inserted in the centre comes out clean.

Whichever way you cook, turn the bread out of the moulds as soon as it is done. Leave on wire racks to cool slightly.

EASTERN STYLE BARBECUE FOR 8

Indonesian Spiced Eggs with Cooked Vegetable Salad
Korean Style Barbecued Meat
Spiced Rice
Grilled Aubergine (Eggplant) Rings
Peppers on Skewers
Grilled Pineapple with Coconut Sauce

This barbecue, full of Eastern flavours, has an egg and vegetable salad that is served as a first course with a light pineapple dessert, both providing a refreshing contrast with the spiced meats and rice.

The eggs can be cooked a few hours in advance but, if possible, do not prepare the vegetables for the salad more than 1 hour before serving. The marinades and dip for the meats can all be made ahead of time and the rice, which is cooked on top of an ordinary stove, can be cooked and reheated if wished.

Cut the pineapples and leave them in covered containers. Prepare the ingredients for the baste in a small pan so they can be heating while you eat the main course. The coconut topping can be prepared beforehand and kept in the refrigerator until needed.

INDONESIAN SPICED EGGS WITH COOKED VEGETABLE SALAD

METRIC/IMPERIAL	AMERICAN
8 eggs, hard boiled	8 hard cooked eggs
1 tablespoon oil	1 tablespoon oil
1 small onion, grated	1 small onion, grated
1 garlic clove, crushed	1 garlic clove, crushed
½ teaspoon ground ginger	½ teaspoon ground ginger
1 stem lemon grass, bruised *or* 2 thinly pared strips lemon rind	1 stem lemon grass, bruised *or* 2 thinly pared strips lemon rind
4 tablespoons soy sauce	¼ cup soy sauce
150 ml/¼ pint water	5 fl oz water
salad	*salad*
175 g/6 oz bean sprouts	6 oz bean sprouts
1 Chinese cabbage, shredded	1 Chinese cabbage, shredded
225 g/8 oz carrots, cut into matchstick pieces	½ lb carrots, cut into matchstick pieces
1 cucumber, thinly sliced	1 cucumber, thinly sliced
4 tablespoons crunchy peanut butter	¼ cup crunchy peanut butter
125 ml/4 fl oz peanut oil	½ cup peanut oil
juice 1 lemon	juice 1 lemon
1 garlic clove, crushed	1 garlic clove, crushed
pinch chilli powder	pinch chili powder
1 small onion, very finely chopped, optional	1 small onion, very finely chopped, optional

Shell the eggs, and score them lightly all over with a fork. Heat the oil in a wok or frying pan over a low heat. Add the onion and garlic and cook until very soft. Stir in the ginger and cook for ½ minute, stirring. Add the lemon grass or strips of lemon rind and soy sauce. Pour in the water and bring to the boil. Add the eggs. Simmer, turning frequently, for about 20 minutes or until all the water has evaporated. Take out the eggs and cool completely.

Bring three separate pans of lightly salted water to the boil. Put the beansprouts into one, cook for 1 minute. Drain, run cold water through them and drain again. Put the Chinese cabbage into another. Cook for 1½ minutes. Drain, run cold water through them and drain again. Put the carrots into the remaining pan. Cook for 2 minutes. Drain, run cold water through them and drain again.

For the dressing, put the peanut butter into a bowl. Gradually beat in the oil. Stir in the lemon juice, garlic, chilli powder and onion, if using.

Quarter the eggs lengthways and put in the centre of a large serving plate. Surround with the beansprouts, then a ring of carrots, the Chinese cabbage and then the cucumber.

Serve the dressing separately.

KOREAN STYLE BARBECUED MEAT

To serve 8

METRIC/IMPERIAL	AMERICAN
1.575 kg/3½lb roasting chicken	3½lb roasting chicken
675 g/1½lb lean pork, cut from the leg or shoulder	1½lb lean pork, cut from the leg or shoulder
675 g/1½lb rump or sirloin steak	1½lb rump or sirloin steak
275 ml/½ pint tamari, shoyu or soy sauce	1¼ cups tamari, shoyu or soy sauce
10 spring onions, very finely chopped or minced	10 scallions, very finely chopped or ground
50 g/2 oz fresh ginger root, peeled and grated	2 oz fresh ginger root, peeled and grated
2 garlic cloves, crushed	2 garlic cloves, crushed
3 tablespoons tahini (sesame paste)	3 tablespoons tahini (sesame paste)
2 tablespoons sesame oil	2 tablespoons sesame oil
freshly ground black pepper	freshly ground black pepper
2 teaspoons chilli sauce	2 teaspoons chili sauce
2 teaspoons black bean paste	2 teaspoons black bean paste
vinegar dip	*vinegar dip*
3 tablespoons tahini (sesame paste)	3 tablespoons tahini (sesame paste)
6 tablespoons white wine vinegar	3 fl. oz white wine vinegar
6 tablespoons tamari, shoyu or soy sauce	3 fl. oz tamari, shoyu or soy sauce
6 tablespoons sesame oil	3 fl oz sesame oil

Cut the chicken into ten small serving pieces (each leg into two, the wings separate and the breast into four). Slice the pork about 1.5 cm/½ inch thick and cut it into serving pieces. Cut the beef into serving pieces.

Mix together the sauce, onions, ginger and garlic. Add the tahini and beat well. Add the oil and beat again. Season with the pepper. Divide the mixture into three. Keep one portion as it is, mix the chilli sauce into the second portion and the black bean paste into the third.

Put the plain mixture into a flat dish. Turn the chicken in it so it becomes well coated. Put the chilli mixture into a bowl and mix in the pork. Put the bean paste mixture into another flat dish and use it to coat the beef. Leave the meats for 15 minutes.

Mix together the ingredients for the dip and put into a small serving bowl.

On an open barbecue, cook the steak 10-15/4-6 inches over hot coals for 7-12 minutes on each side, depending on whether you require it medium or well done. This marinade is not really suited to rare steak. Cook the pork over medium heat for a total of 30 minutes. Cook the chicken over medium heat for 30-40 minutes.

If using a covered barbecue, cook the steaks directly over the coals for 7-11 minutes on each side; cook the pork over indirect heat for 18 minutes on each side; cook the chicken over indirect heat for a total of 1 hour.

SPICED RICE

METRIC/IMPERIAL	AMERICAN
4 tablespoons oil	4 tablespoons oil
1 large onion, thinly sliced	1 large onion, thinly sliced
1 garlic clove, finely chopped	1 garlic clove, finely chopped
2 teaspoons ground cumin	2 teaspoons ground cumin
2 teaspoons ground ginger	2 teaspoons ground ginger
pinch chilli powder	pinch chili powder
450 g/1 lb long-grain brown rice	2 cups long-grain brown rice
1.15 ml/2 pints chicken stock	2½ cups chicken stock
12 spring onions, finely chopped	12 scallions, finely chopped

Heat the oil in a saucepan on a low heat. Add the onion and garlic and cook until they begin to brown. Stir in the spices and rice and cook, stirring, for 2 minutes. Pour in the stock and bring to the boil. Cover and simmer for 40 minutes or until all the stock is absorbed and the rice tender.

Mix in the spring onions (scallions) just before serving.

GRILLED AUBERGINE (EGGPLANT) RINGS

METRIC/IMPERIAL	AMERICAN
4 medium aubergines	4 medium eggplant
2 tablespoons sea salt	2 tablespoons sea salt
175 ml/6 fl oz oil	¾ cup oil
juice 1 lemon	juice 1 lemon
1 teaspoon ground coriander	1 teaspoon ground coriander
1 teaspoon ground turmeric	1 teaspoon ground turmeric

Cut the aubergines (eggplant) into 1.5 cm/⅝ inch thick slices. Put them in a colander and sprinkle with sea salt. Leave for 20 minutes to drain. Rinse with cold water and dry with kitchen paper.

Beat the remaining ingredients together in a large bowl and add the aubergine (eggplant) slices. Turn to coat them.

Cook the aubergines (eggplants) 10-15 cm/4-6 inches over hot coals for 6-8 minutes turning once, so they are soft and beginning to brown.

To cook in a kettle barbecue, cook directly over hot coals for the same time, turning once.

GRILLED PINEAPPLE WITH COCONUT SAUCE

<table>
<tr><td>METRIC/IMPERIAL</td><td>AMERICAN</td></tr>
<tr><td>3 medium pineapples</td><td>3 medium pineapples</td></tr>
<tr><td>225 ml/8 fl oz pineapple juice</td><td>1 cup pineapple juice</td></tr>
<tr><td>2 tablespoons honey</td><td>2 tablespoons honey</td></tr>
<tr><td>4 cardamom pods, bruised</td><td>4 cardamom pods, bruised</td></tr>
<tr><td>225 g/8 oz fresh coconut</td><td>½ lb fresh coconut</td></tr>
<tr><td>425 ml/¾ pint natural yoghurt</td><td>2 cups unflavored yoghurt</td></tr>
<tr><td>8 pieces preserved stem ginger, finely chopped</td><td>8 pieces preserved stem ginger, finely chopped</td></tr>
<tr><td>almonds or walnut halves</td><td>almonds or walnut halves</td></tr>
</table>

Prepare the coconut mixture for the topping in advance. Grate the coconut finely, and mix it with the yoghurt and ginger.

Cut the husk from the pineapples. Cut the flesh into 1.5 cm/⅝ inch thick slices. Stamp out the cores.

Put the pineapple juice, honey and cardamom pods into a small pan. Heat gently on the side of the barbecue grill for 15 minutes, without boiling. Take the pan from the heat. Dip the pineapple rings in the mixture.

Before cooking, make sure that the barbecue grill is clean and that the coals are hot. Cook the pineapple rings 10-15 cm/4-6 inches over the hot coals for 4 minutes each side or until heated through but not dried.

Put the cooked pineapple rings on to a large serving plate. Spoon a portion of the coconut mixture on each one and top with an almond or walnut half.

SPECIAL OCCASION BARBECUE FOR 8 PEOPLE

Cheese and Yoghurt Dip with Crudités
Mixed Meats on Skewers
Hot Rolls with Two Butters
Spiced Bananas with Rum and Raisin Sauce

No barbecue is ever absolutely formal, but this one could certainly be served to guests that you want to impress. It could also be served at a family birthday celebration. The food will look and taste superb but the whole meal is easy to prepare, leaving the cook plenty of time to talk to guests or join in the party.

The vegetables are served as a first course with a tasty low-fat dip. Make sure that you buy the best quality possible as they are to be eaten raw. They can be prepared up to 2 hours before serving and kept in covered containers in the refrigerator. The dip can be prepared well in advance and chilled until needed.

The kebabs and basting sauce can all be prepared ahead of time. Instead of potatoes, serve rolls with two different savoury butters. These can be made, wrapped in foil and kept at room temperature until you are ready to put them on the barbecue.

The meal is ended with spiced bananas with rum and raisin sauce. The sauce can be made the day before and warmed gently on the barbecue. Prepare the bananas about an hour before the guests arrive.

CHEESE AND YOGHURT DIP WITH CRUDITÉS

METRIC/IMPERIAL	AMERICAN
350 g/12 oz low fat soft cheese	½ lb low fat soft cheese
150 ml/¼ pint natural yoghurt	5 fl. oz unflavored yoghurt
4 tablespoons chopped parsley	¼ cup chopped parsley
3 tablespoons chopped chives	3 tablespoons chopped chives
1 tablespoon chopped basil	1 tablespoon chopped basil
1 teaspoon chopped tarragon	1 teaspoon chopped tarragon
¼ teaspoon Tabasco sauce	¼ teaspoon Tabasco sauce
40 g/1½ oz grated Parmesan cheese	3 tablespoons grated Parmesan cheese
1 tablespoon French mustard	1 tablespoon French mustard
raw vegetables for serving	raw vegetables for serving

Cream the cheese in a bowl and gradually work in the yoghurt. Beat in the herbs, Tabasco sauce, Parmesan cheese and mustard.

Put a small portion of the dip in the centre of eight small plates. Surround it with raw vegetables, such as fingers of celery, carrot, cucumber and sweet green or red pepper; small cauliflower florets (flowerets); button mushrooms in superb condition; and whole radishes.

A plate of savoury biscuits can also be placed in the centre of the table.

MIXED MEATS ON SKEWERS

METRIC/IMPERIAL	AMERICAN
225 g/8 oz beef fillet	½ lb beef fillet
225 g/8 oz veal fillet	½ lb veal fillet
225 g/8 oz pork tenderloin	½ lb pork tenderloin
225 g/8 oz lamb's liver	½ lb lamb's liver
8 lamb's kidneys	8 lamb's kidneys
1 tablespoon paprika	1 tablespoon paprika
2 teaspoons curry powder	2 teaspoons curry powder
salt	salt

METRIC/IMPERIAL	AMERICAN
8 streaky bacon rashers	8 lean bacon slices
3 large onions	3 large onions
1 red pepper	1 sweet red pepper
baste	*baste*
125 g/4 oz butter	4 oz butter
2 tablespoons tomato paste	2 tablespoons tomato paste
4 tablespoons stock	¼ cup stock
1 tablespoon paprika	1 tablespoon paprika
2 teaspoons curry powder	2 teaspoons curry powder

Cut the beef, veal, pork and liver into 2.5 cm/1 inch cubes. Halve the kidneys crossways and snip out the cores. Keep all the meats separate and sprinkle them with paprika, curry powder and a little salt. Peel the onions and cut them into round slices. Core and seed the pepper and cut into 2.5 cm/1 inch squares. Cut each bacon rasher (slice) in half. Stretch the halves slightly and roll them up.

Alternate pieces of meat, liver, kidney, bacon, onion and pepper on kebab skewers. For the baste, melt the butter in saucepan on a low heat. Stir in the tomato paste, stock, paprika and curry powder. Brush the mixture over the meats.

Cook the kebabs 10-15 cm/4-6 inches over hot charcoal for about 20 minutes, turning and basting several times, until the meats are browned and cooked through. In a covered barbecue, cook sparsely arranged charcoal for the same amount of time.

HOT ROLLS WITH TWO BUTTERS

METRIC/IMPERIAL	AMERICAN
16 wholewheat baps or rolls	16 wholewheat baps or rolls
anchovy and olive butter	*anchovy and olive butter*
175 g/6 oz butter, softened	¾ cup butter, softened
8 anchovy fillets	8 anchovy fillets
8 black olives	8 black olives
3 tablespoons tomato paste	3 tablespoons tomato paste
1 garlic clove, crushed	1 garlic clove, crushed
cheese and mustard butter	*cheese and mustard butter*
125 g/4 oz butter, softened	½ cup butter, softened
75 g/3 oz Cheddar cheese, grated	¾ cup grated Cheddar cheese
1 tablespoon Dijon mustard	1 tablespoon Dijon mustard
6 tablespoons chopped parsley	6 tablespoons chopped parsley

Split the rolls crossways. For the anchovy butter use a blender or food processor. Put in the butter, chopped anchovies, stoned (pitted) and chopped olives and tomato paste. Work to a smooth mixture. If making by hand, pound the anchovies to a paste with the olives using a pestle and mortar. Beat these and the tomato paste into the butter.

For the cheese and mustard butter, put the butter into a bowl and beat in the cheese. Add the mustard and parsley and mix well.

Spread half the rolls with the anchovy and olive butter and the other half with the cheese and mustard butter. Reshape and wrap separately in foil.

Heat the rolls over medium coals for 20 minutes, turning them several times. In a covered barbecue, heat them over an indirect heat for the same time.

SPICED BANANAS WITH RUM AND RAISIN SAUCE

METRIC/IMPERIAL	AMERICAN
8 bananas	8 bananas
butter for greasing	butter for greasing
8 tablespoons Barbados sugar	½ cup Barbados sugar
ground mixed spice	ground mixed spice
sauce	*sauce*
450 ml/16 fl oz natural orange juice	2 cups natural orange juice
2 tablespoons arrowroot	2 tablespoons arrowroot
125 g/4 oz raisins	¼ lb raisins
125 ml/4 fl oz rum	½ cup rum

Peel the bananas. Lay each one on a piece of buttered foil. Scatter 1 tablespoon sugar over the top and sprinkle with a little ground mixed spice. Bring the sides of the foil together and seal. Seal the ends.

To make the sauce, mix 125 ml/4 fl oz/½ cup of the orange juice in a bowl with the arrowroot. Put the remaining orange juice into a saucepan with the raisins. Bring to the boil on a medium heat. Stir in the orange juice and arrowroot to make sure no arrowroot is stuck in the bottom of the bowl and then add to the saucepan. Stir the sauce until it is thick and transparent, about 1½ minutes. Take the pan from the heat and stir in the rum.

Lay the banana packets on the grill 10-15 cm/4-6 inches over hot coals for 8 minutes, turning once. At the same time, warm the sauce on the grill.

To serve, put each banana on a separate dish or plate. Pour the sauce into a jug and serve it separately, providing a spoon for pouring it over the bananas.

ENTERTAINING THE IN-LAWS

An impressive meal for 6

Hummus with Tomatoes and Pitta Bread
Whole Fish with Orange and Lemon Yoghurt Hollandaise
French Beans with Thyme
Jacket Potatoes with Parsley and Chive Butter
Grilled Camembert with Chicory, Orange and Walnuts
Fresh Fruit

When entertaining your in-laws you need to make everything run as smoothly as possible, so this is certainly not a time for cooking absolutely everything on the barbecue. It is also a good idea to have the fish completely cooked before you start the first course, so that the cook does not have to keep leaving the table to attend to it. Leave it wrapped in foil to keep warm.

The first course, the yoghurt hollandaise, the butter for the potatoes and the salads can all be prepared ahead of time. The beans can be topped and tailed ready for last minute cooking, while the potatoes can look after themselves in the oven.

No one minds waiting for the cheese after they have enjoyed a superb main course, so when the table has been cleared, make sure that everyone's glass is filled and leave to quickly cook the camembert, first making sure that the grill is absolutely clean.

A bowl of attractively arranged fruits will complete the meal.

HUMMUS WITH PITTA BREAD

METRIC/IMPERIAL	AMERICAN
hummus	*hummus*
225 g/8 oz chick peas, soaked and cooked until soft	1 cup Garbanzo beans, soaked and cooked until soft
2 garlic cloves, crushed with pinch sea salt	2 garlic cloves, crushed with pinch sea salt
juice 2 lemons	juice 2 lemons
4 tablespoons tahini (sesame paste)	¼ cup tahini (sesame paste)
125 ml/4 fl oz olive oil	½ cup olive oil
6 tablespoons chopped parsley	6 tablespoons chopped parsley
freshly ground black pepper	freshly ground black pepper
serving	*serving*
3 black olives, halved and stoned	3 black olives, halved and pitted
6 tomatoes	6 tomatoes
6 wholewheat pitta breads	6 wholewheat pitta breads

Put the chick peas through the fine blade of a vegetable mill or rub them through a sieve. Beat in the garlic and lemon juice. Add the tahini, 1 tablespoon at a time, then gradually beat in the oil. Add the parsley and pepper and mix well.

To serve, put a portion of the hummus into the centre of six small plates. Top with an olive half. Slice the tomatoes and arrange them round the edge.

The pitta breads can be served cold or they can be gently warmed on the barbecue for about 2 minutes on each side.

WHOLE FISH WITH ORANGE AND LEMON

KETTLE BARBECUE METHOD

METRIC/IMPERIAL	AMERICAN
one 1.8 kg/4 lb fish (salmon, sea bass)	one 4 lb fish (salmon, sea bass)
1 large orange	1 large orange
½ lemon	½ lemon
1 large onion	1 large onion
2 teaspoons dill seed	2 teaspoons dill seed
9 sprigs lemon thyme (or common thyme)	9 sprigs lemon thyme (or common thyme)
150 ml/¼ pint dry white wine	5 fl oz dry white wine

Prepare the kettle for indirect cooking.

Clean the fish. Leave the head on if wished. Slice the orange, lemon and onion thinly.

Put half the orange slices and one-third of the onion slices in the bottom of a foil tray. Scatter with ½ teaspoon dill seeds and put 3 lemon thyme sprigs on top. Lay the fish on the orange and onion slices.

Scatter 1 teaspoon dill seeds inside the body cavity of the fish, then add the lemon slices, one-third of the onion slices and 3 lemon thyme sprigs. Scatter the remaining dill seeds on the fish and put the remaining orange and onion slices on top. Pour the white wine over.

Cook, uncovered, in the centre of the kettle for 1 hour or until the fish flakes easily with a fork.

OPEN BARBECUE METHOD

METRIC/IMPERIAL	AMERICAN
one 1.8 kg/4 lb fish (salmon, sea bass)	one 4 lb fish (salmon, sea bass)
juice 1 large orange	juice 1 large orange
juice ½ lemon	juice ½ lemon
½ small onion, grated	½ small onion, grated
2 teaspoons dill seed	2 teaspoons dill seed
3 tablespoons chopped lemon thyme (or common thyme)	3 tablespoons chopped lemon thyme (or common thyme)
150 ml/¼ pint dry white wine	5 fl oz dry white wine
4 tablespoons oil	¼ cup oil
extra oil for greasing	extra oil for greasing

Mix together all the ingredients except the fish. Clean the fish. If possible, cook it in a large, hinged, fish-shaped grill. Measure the size against the grill. If the fish is too long, cut off the head; if not, leave the head on. Cut three diagonal slashes in either side of the fish running backwards and downwards from head to tail.

Brush the fish well with the orange and lemon mixture, inside the slits and body cavity as well as over the outside. Put in a flat dish and pour in any remaining mixture. Leave for 30 minutes at room temperature.

Oil the hinged grill and the barbecue grill. Put the fish into the grill if using. If not, lay it directly on the barbecue grill. Cook 10-15 cm/4-6 inches over medium coals for 45 minutes, or until the flesh flakes easily with a fork, turning it and basting it three times during cooking.

Lift the fish on to a serving plate. Remove the skin from one side. Take the flesh away from the bone in sections on that side. Turn the fish over and repeat.

YOGHURT HOLLANDAISE

METRIC/IMPERIAL	AMERICAN
275 ml/½ pint natural yoghurt	1¼ cups unflavored yoghurt
2 eggs, beaten	2 eggs, beaten
1 teaspoon made English mustard	1 teaspoon made English mustard
juice ½ lemon	juice ½ lemon
2 tablespoons chopped parsley	2 tablespoons chopped parsley

In a small saucepan, mix together the yoghurt, eggs, mustard and lemon juice. Set the pan on a low heat and stir with a wooden spoon without letting it boil, until the mixture is like a thick custard.

Immediately take the pan from the heat and stir in the parsley. Ideally the sauce should be served hot. If you have made it in advance, reheat it in a double saucepan or in a bowl standing in a saucepan of water. Set on a low heat and stir, without letting the water underneath it boil. This can be done successfully on the barbecue grill.

FRENCH BEANS WITH THYME

METRIC/IMPERIAL	AMERICAN
675 g/1½ lb french beans	1½ lb french style green beans
25 g/1 oz butter	2 tablespoons butter
225 ml/8 fl oz water (or use half water and half dry white wine)	1 cup water (or use half water and half dry white wine)
3 tablespoons chopped thyme	3 tablespoons chopped thyme

Top and tail the beans. Put the butter and water in a saucepan and set on a medium heat for the butter to melt and the water to boil. Add the beans and thyme.

Cover and cook on a low heat for 15 minutes or until the beans are just tender and most of the liquid has evaporated. Drain if necessary.

JACKET POTATOES WITH PARSLEY AND CHIVE BUTTER

METRIC/IMPERIAL	*AMERICAN*
6 medium to large potatoes	6 medium to large potatoes
175g/6oz butter, softened	¾ cup butter, softened
4 tablespoons chopped parsley	4 tablespoons chopped parsley
3 tablespoons chopped chives	3 tablespoons chopped chives
½ teaspoon mustard powder	½ teaspoon mustard powder

The butter can be made well in advance. Put the butter in a bowl and beat in the herbs and mustard powder. Form into a roll and wrap in greaseproof (waxed) paper. Chill until firm. Cut into round pats for serving and arrange them attractively on a plate garnished, if wished, with a parsley sprig.

For the potatoes, heat the oven to 200°C/400°F/gas mark 6. Scrub the potatoes. Prick on both sides with a fork. Lay on the oven rack and cook for 1¼ hours or until the outsides are crisp and the middles soft.

GRILLED CAMEMBERT WITH CHICORY, ORANGE AND WALNUTS

METRIC/IMPERIAL	*AMERICAN*
6 portions Camembert	6 portions Camembert
40g/1½oz medium oatmeal	⅓ cup medium oatmeal
3 small heads chicory	3 small heads Belgian endive
3 medium oranges	3 medium oranges
50g/2oz shelled walnuts	⅔ cup shelled walnuts
4 tablespoons olive or walnut oil	¼ cup olive or walnut oil
2 tablespoons red wine vinegar	2 tablespoons red wine vinegar
1 garlic clove, crushed with pinch sea salt	1 garlic clove, crushed with pinch sea salt
pinch cayenne pepper	pinch cayenne pepper

Coat each portion of Camembert in oatmeal. Trim the chicory (endive) heads and cut them into quarters lengthways. Arrange two quarters on either side of six medium-sized plates. Cut the peel and pith from the oranges and cut the segments away from the skin. Arrange the segments by the chicory (endive). Chop the walnuts finely. Beat together the oil, vinegar, garlic and cayenne pepper. Spoon the dressing over the chicory (endive) and scatter the walnuts over the top.

Put the Camembert portions in a hinged wire grill. Cook over medium coals for 1½ minutes on each side, or until they are beginning to soften but not melt. Put a portion in the centre of each plate.

CHILDREN'S PARTIES

The whole fun of having a barbecue party for children is in the children doing as much of the cooking as possible themselves. Make sure that an adult is always there, however, to supervise the lighting and tending of the fire and to make sure that there are no squabbles or absolute catastrophes.

Children enjoy cooking but most of them are not at all keen on preparation, so before the party prepare the food indoors up to the cooking stage. Make sauces which can be heated in old saucepans, dips for salads or any marinades or basting mixtures that you think suitable.

Ask any child what his favourite barbecued food is and you can be more or less certain that he will say burgers and sausages. Make up 125 g/4 oz/quarter pound burgers for them, if possible using a burger press. To be on the safe side, use only a hint of flavouring. To every 1.35 kg/3 lb minced (ground) beef use 1 medium onion, finely grated, 1½ teaspoons dried mixed herbs and a little freshly ground black pepper.

Provide wholemeal buns or baps, ready split so that the burger can be inserted as soon as it is cooked. In separate bowls provide grated cheese, chopped onion, tomato ketchup (you can buy a sugar-free variety from health food shops), mayonnaise and chopped salad vegetables. Keep the vegetables to tomatoes, lettuce, cucumber and beetroot (beet). Grated carrot can also be included. Burgers are finger food, so provide a pile of napkins.

Buy good quality sausages, that are brownish rather than pink in colour, with a high proportion of meat and not too highly spiced. Keep some as they are. For the more adventurous children, slit some lengthways, insert a little sweet chutney and wrap the sausage round with a de-rinded bacon rasher (slice). Bacon rashers can also be provided as they are.

An excellent topping for burgers or accompaniment to sausages is the old favourite — baked beans. Give them a barbecue flavour by adding 3 tablespoons each tomato paste and soy sauce and up to 2 tablespoons Worcestershire sauce per 447 g/15¾ oz tin (can). Put them into an old saucepan to be heated on the barbecue.

Jacket potatoes are always popular. If you are providing food for half the school class (which it will often seem like), it is probably best to cook them indoors. Split or halve them before serving. These can be topped with grated cheese, tomato ketchup or baked beans. Provide butter or vegetable margarine as well.

Many children will be satisfied with all this. Older ones may like to have a salad as well. Provide a large bowl of thick dressing and fingers of salad vegetables and offer them while the children are cooking the rest of the meal. They will probably be so hungry at this point that most of them will want at least one dip. Make the dressing by mixing together equal quantities of mayonnaise and natural yoghurt and flavouring it with a little tomato paste, chopped parsley or creamed blue cheese if you think this will be acceptable. Put the dip into a bowl and surround it with fingers of carrot, celery and beetroot (beet), cauliflower florettes (flowerets), whole radishes and wedges of tomato. Small wholewheat biscuits can be put out with the dip.

As for a dessert, provide a home-made ice-cream or buy one of good quality. Offer fresh fruit and home-made cake to go with it. Alternatively if it is a chilly day, make the Spicy Apple Pudding below.

SPICY APPLE PUDDING

METRIC/IMPERIAL	AMERICAN
675g/1½lb cooking apples	1½lb cooking apples
125g/4oz stoned dates	¼lb pitted dates
2 teaspoons mixed spice	2 teaspoons mixed spice
225g/8oz honey	⅔ cup honey
225g/8oz wholewheat flour	2 cups wholewheat flour
1 teaspoon bicarbonate of soda	1 teaspoon baking soda
4 eggs, beaten	½ cup corn oil
125ml/4fl oz natural orange or apple juice	4 eggs, beaten
	½ cup natural orange or apple juice

Peel, core and chop the apples. Chop the dates finely. Mix with 1 teaspoon of the spice and 50g/2oz/2 tablespoons honey.

Put the flour into a bowl with the bicarbonate of soda (baking soda) and the remaining teaspoon mixed spice. Make a well in the centre. Add the remaining honey and the oil and gradually begin to beat in flour from the sides of the well. Add the beaten eggs, a little at a time. Beat in the fruit juice. Beat until you have a smooth, thick batter.

Put the apple mixture into a 23 × 28 cm/9 × 11 inch foil tray or baking tin. Pour the batter over the top.

If using a kettle barbecue, bake the pudding in the centre of the kettle over indirect heat for 45 minutes or until the top has browned lightly and a skewer inserted in the centre comes out clean. If using a conventional oven, cook at a preheated temperature of 180°C/350°F/gas mark 4 for 40 minutes.

GAS & ELECTRIC BARBECUES

Gas and electric barbecues are not quite as exciting, or such fun to use, as charcoal barbecues, but they are easy to light, quick to heat up and clean, and even without a 'live' fire a characteristic barbecue flavour will still be achieved.

Gas Barbecues

Most gas barbecues are designed to be used like kettle barbecues with the cover on. Some can also be used like a brazier type barbecue. Like kettle barbecues, they can be rectangular or round in shape, with a domed, ventilated lid.

The heat comes from a gas burner fuelled by butane gas. Depending on the shape of the barbecue, the burner can be either round or oval in shape. A few types of rectangular gas barbecue have twin burners. Most gas barbecues can be fitted to a standard gas bottle such as used for a camp stove. Others, such as the Weber, have their own design of bottle.

A burner can be regulated, thus providing you with instant high, low and in some cases, medium heat.

Above the burner is a rack on which is placed a single layer of volcanic rock. This comes in the form of small dark grey chunks looking rather like coal and roughly the same size as charcoal briquettes. The rock heats up and provides enough heat to cook most foods from burgers to a large turkey. The food is placed on a rack above these rocks.

Gas barbecues are designed for use outside and should not be used indoors because of dangerous fumes.

Lighting. Always light the gas barbecue with the lid off. Make sure that the gas bottle is connected properly. If you are using a Weber barbecue or any other with an 'Indirect' cooking position (see below) turn the control knob to 'Indirect'.

Open the gas bottle valve. Insert a lighted match into the air slot under the burner, or wherever recommended in the manufacturer's instructions. Turn the gas control knob to high. Put on the cover and leave at a high setting for 10 minutes for the rocks to heat up. If there is a Direct/Indirect setting on your barbecue, use the Direct setting for this heating up time.

If the gas does not ignite immediately, turn off the control knob. Remove the cover and wait 3-5 minutes before trying again.

Cooking. All food that can be cooked in a kettle barbecue can be cooked in a gas barbecue. As a general rule, trim away all but 5 mm/¼ inch of fat from foods such as chops and steaks and make sure that roasts do not consist of too much fat.

Small cuts of meat (chops, steaks, kebabs, burgers, chicken joints, pork rashers (slices), offal, sausages) can all be cooked directly over the hot rocks. Whole birds and large joints of meat are best placed on a rack in a foil tray or ordinary cooking tray.

Some gas barbecues have Direct and Indirect heat settings. The Direct heat setting allows the flames from the gas to rise directly up through the rocks to the cooking food. The Indirect setting spreads the heat outwards leaving an area in the centre of the barbecue that is cool. If you are using such an appliance, cook the smaller pieces of meat over a direct heat. For birds and large joints, place a drip tray in the centre of the barbecue directly over the cool rocks. Place the food on the grill rack directly over the drip tray. This method is also suitable for vegetables and other items such as quiches or breads which are cooked in foil trays or tins.

Small cuts of meat, or any foods that require a short cooking time, cook in the same time in a covered barbecue over gas-heated rocks as they do in a charcoal heated kettle barbecue. If you have a gas barbecue with Direct and Indirect settings, roasting times over indirect heat are the same as those for a kettle barbecue with charcoal on either side of a drip tray. In most other types of gas barbecue, roasting times over the direct heat on a low setting will be slightly shorter. If meats look as though they are cooking too quickly, cover them completely with foil. A little fat falling on the hot rocks will not harm them and it is the small amount of smoke that this creates that gives the food its barbecued flavour. However, should too much fat drip down, you may cause a flare-up. This may be corrected by moving the food to a cooler part of the grill or by turning the grill to a lower setting. If it persists, take the food off the grill, replace the cover and turn the gas to high until all the fat has been burned away.

After cooking, put on the cover and turn the heat to high for 10 minutes to burn any fat from the rocks.

Storing. After cleaning the rocks, turn off the gas and leave the barbecue to cool completely. Turn off the gas bottle valve. Remove the gas bottle from the grill and store it outside in a well-ventilated place, such as a garden shed. The grill may be stored indoors if wished. If it is outside, make sure that it has a cover.

Cleaning. Periodically clean the inside and outside of the base and lid with a kitchen degreaser. The grills can be cleaned simply by getting them hot the next time the barbecue is lit and rubbing them with a wire brush.

Cooking Times

FISH

Steaks, high/direct heat, 5-7 minutes each side
Whole, small, high/direct heat, 6-8 minutes each side
Whole, large (in foil tray), low/indirect heat, 10-15 minutes per lb
Prawns (shrimp) in shell, high/direct heat, 3 minutes each side
Lobster, raw, high/direct heat, 15-20 minutes total

BEEF

Steak, high/direct heat, turn once during cooking
2.5 cm/1 inch thick, rare 5 minutes, medium 8 minutes, well done 10 minutes
4 cm/1½ inches thick, rare 10 minutes, medium 14 minutes, well done 18 minutes
5 cm/2 inches thick, rare 14 minutes, medium 17 minutes, well done 20 minutes

Topside, Top Rump, Rolled Rump, Aitchbone, Rolled Rib, Low/indirect heat
Rare 15-18 minutes per lb, medium 18-22 minutes per lb, well done 20-22 minutes per lb
Rolled Brisket, well done only, 22-22 minutes per lb
Standing Rib on bone, rare, 18-20 minutes per lb, medium 20-25 minutes per lb, well done
25-30 minutes per lb
Thin Rib (Short Ribs), total time 1¼-1½ hours

Burgers, high/direct heat, turn once during cooking
2 cm/¾ inch thick, rare 6 minutes, medium 8 minutes, well done 10 minutes
2.5 cm/1 inch thick, rare 8-10 minutes, medium 10-12 minutes, well done 12-14 minutes

PORK

Chops, 2.5 cm/1 inch thick, high/direct heat, 12-15 minutes each side
Tenderloin, sear over high heat, 3 minutes each side, then low heat 45 minutes
Roasts: Leg, Shoulder, Loin, Blade, low/indirect heat, 18-20 minutes per lb
Liver, high/direct heat, 5-6 minutes each side
Kidneys, high/direct heat, 7-8 minutes each side

LAMB

Chops, high/direct heat, turn once during cooking
2.5 cm/1 inch thick, rare 10 minutes, medium 14 minutes, well done 16 minutes
4 cm/1½ inches thick, rare 14 minutes, medium 16 minutes, well done 20 minutes

Roasts: Leg, Shoulder on bone, Loin (rib), low/indirect heat
Leg, rare 18 minutes per lb, medium 22-25 minutes per lb, well done 28-30 minutes per lb
Shoulder, on bone, medium 33-35 minutes per lb, well done 35-40 minutes per lb
Loin (rib), rare 25-30 minutes per lb, medium, 30-35 minutes per lb, well done 35-40
minutes per lb
Liver, high/direct heat, 5 minutes each side
Kidney, cored and split, high/direct heat, 10 minutes each side
Kidney, in fat, low/indirect heat, 45 minutes total time

CHICKEN

900 g/1.35 kg/2-3 lb, low/indirect heat, 1-1¼ hours
1.35 kg-1.8 kg/3-4 lb, low/indirect heat, 1¼-1¾ hours
Jointed, low/indirect, 20-30 minutes each side
Poussin, low/indirect heat, 50 minutes-1¼ hours

CAPON

2.25 kg-3.2 kg/5-8 lb, low/indirect, 2-2½ hours

DUCK

Low/indirect heat, 2-2½ hours

GOOSE

Low/indirect heat, 20-30 minutes per lb

TURKEY

2.7-3.2 kg/6-8 lb, low/indirect heat, 2-2¾ hours
3.2-5.4 kg/8-12 lb, low/indirect heat, 2½-3¾ hours
5.4-7.2 kg/12-15 lb, low/indirect heat, 3½-4 hours
7.2-9 kg/15-20 lb, low/indirect heat, 5 hours

To help you to judge whether meat is cooked, it is best to use a meat thermometer for whole
birds and roasts. Insert in the thickest part of the meat, not touching any bone.

Temperatures of meat

	Rare	Medium	Well done
Beef	65°C/150°F	70°C/160°F	75°C/170°F
Pork	—	—	75°C/170°F
Lamb	60°C/140°F	65°C/150°F	75°C/170°F
Poultry	—	—	85°C/185°F

Electric Barbecues

Electric barbecues create no fumes and so can be used indoors or out. There are compact, table-top models which are superb used in the kitchen and larger ones which are really more suited to patio use. Others are built into a stand and can be used anywhere, provided you have an extension lead long enough to reach a power point. Most are designed to be used like a brazier-type barbecue without a cover.

Basically, all electric barbecues consist of a metal box, about 10 cm/4 inches deep. A large electric element is fitted about 4 cm/1½ inches above the bottom of the box. Under and around this is placed a bed of volcanic rocks which must be touching the element. The barbecue grill is fitted about 5 cm/2 inches above the rocks. Heat is produced simply by turning a switch, exactly the same as on a conventional electric stove. High, medium and low settings are usually available. Once the element has been switched on, wait 10 minutes for the rocks to heat up before using.

Cooking on an electric barbecue is exactly the same as cooking on an open charcoal barbecue and the cooking times are the same. Heat control is obviously easier and small drips of fat falling on the rocks will produce the barbecue flavour.

Should the fat flare, move the meat to another part of the barbecue. If the flaring persists, remove the meat completely and turn the heat to high to burn the fat away.

Clean the rocks by heating them on a high setting for 10 minutes after you have finished cooking.